TRANSFORMATIVE ADVENTURES VACATIONS & RETREATS

An International Directory of 300+ Host Organizations

John Benson

NEW MILLENNIUM PUBLISHING

TRANSFORMATIVE ADVENTURES, VACATIONS & RETREATS
An International Directory of 300+ Host Organizations

NEW MILLENNIUM PUBLISHING
P.O. Box 3065
Portland, OR 97208, USA
TEL: 503/297-7321   FAX: 503/297-0436

Copyright 1994 by John Benson

This book describes programs and their host organizations based on information publicly available in late 1993. But rates, programs and organizations change, evolve or disappear over time. So the author and publisher of this book cannot be held liable for any problems arising from decisions made solely on the basis of information contained in this book.

Library of Congress Catalog Card No. 93-74591

Cataloging in Publication Data:

Benson, John, 1947–
    Transformative adventures, vacations & retreats: an international
    directory of 300+ host organizations / by John Benson.—Portland, OR:
    New Millennium Publishing, c 1994.
    p.: maps; cm.
    ISBN 0-9639211-0-X: $14.95 Softcover
    Includes bibliographic references and indexes.
    1. Retreats—Directories.
    2. Health Resorts, watering-places, etc.—Directories.
    3. Package Tours—United States—Directories.
    4. Travel—Directories.
    5. Alternative Medicine—Directories.
    6. New Age—Directories.
    7. Self-help groups—Directories.
    8. Vision quests—Directories.
    I. Title.
    II. Title: Transformative adventures, vacations and retreats:
    an international directory of 300+ organizations.

BL628.B [RA794] [G153.4]
158.06'025 [269.66'06'025] [910.91'06'025] dc20

First edition & first printing, March 1993.
Printed in the USA on recycled paper.

10 9 8 7 6 5 4 3 2 1

Contents

Acknowledgments

The author has never had a more interesting and enjoyable job then researching and writing this book. The subject was fascinating. And virtually everyone who contributed to this project was friendly, helpful and sincerely interested in the final product.

Initial assistance came from reference librarians at the Library of Congress and the Arlington County, VA public library system.

Further along, it was a pleasure to work with the people who staff the organizations profiled in this book. Most of these people were quick to send information, answer questions, and review for accuracy the first draft profiles of their organizations.

Jean Adams (Southern Dharma Retreat Center), Arlene Devries (Spirit Rock Center), Shivam O'Brien (Spirit Horse Nomadic Circle) and Martin Roehrs (Zenith Institute) were particularly helpful in volunteering assistance or making suggestions leading to improvements in the book's format.

Pam Holt was of great service in co-creating the book's title. Robert Beatty and Kathleen McLaughlin reviewed and offered encouraging comments on the book's introductory and index material.

As the book's publisher, the author is also grateful for the helpful tips and services freely given by fellow members of the Northwest Book Publishers Association. Those people include Al Grossman, Bob Keene and Cheryl Long.

Thanks to Laird Schaub of the Communities Publication Cooperative for his advice on directory marketing. Thanks to Adam Ladd, N.D., L.Ac. for suggesting an order form in the back of the book.

And finally, thanks to the service providers who responded so well to the many tasks and challenges (such as working with a first time publisher) of getting this book into print. Those people and organizations are listed on the following page.

Printer: BookCrafters (Chelsea, MI)

Typesetter: Cambridge Desktop Publishing (Portland, OR)

Color House: Toucan Scan (Portland, OR)

Portrait Artist: Chi Shao (Portland, OR)

CIP: Linda Ellison (Asotin, WA)

Photo Credits:

        top left contributed by Sivananda Ashram Yoga Camp
        top right contributed by The Option Institute
        bottom left taken at Dharma Rain Zendo in Portland, OR
        bottom right taken at Trillium Lake near Mt. Hood, OR

Happiness is not a destination.
It is the attitude with which you choose to travel.
YOGI AMRIT DESAI

The journey to God is merely the reawakening of the knowledge
of where you are always, and what you are forever.
A COURSE IN MIRACLES

Man does not weave the web of life.
He is merely a strand in it.
Whatever he does to the web,
He does to himself.
CHIEF SEATTLE

Be a lamp unto yourself.
SHAKYAMUNI BUDDHA

1 Who This Book Is For

If you have just picked up this book and are wondering if its contents might enhance your life, you might consider the following statements. And if you can easily identify with any one of them, you may find this book to be a valuable guide to adventures, vacations and retreats that can serve as gateways to positive, personal change.

- You feel alienated and alone, cut off from meaningful relationships or any sense of community.

- You are having difficulties in important relationships with family, friends or co-workers.

- You are at a major life transition point such as getting married, losing a spouse, or changing careers.

- You have recently experienced severe physical or emotional trauma.

- You would like to go deeper into the psychological or recovery work to which you are already committed.

- You are yearning for a sense of meaning in your life that is greater than (without necessarily ignoring) material concerns.

- You wish to explore the spiritual dimensions of your gender or sexual preference group.

- You have some degree of proficiency in a particular healing or spiritual practice and would like to improve your skills.

By now you may have decided to explore this book. If so, welcome to the world of self-transformative adventures, vacations and retreats!

A few of the people who embark on these inner journeys experience sharp shifts in consciousness that may seem like instant, total healings. But most experience self-transformation as a process of gradual, gentle healing at one or several levels — spiritual, mental, emotional or physical.

So make yourself comfortable and read on with an open mind, sensitive to whatever new or familiar paths may work best for you.

2 Profiled Organizations

<u>Transformative Adventures, Vacations & Retreats</u> profiles 305 host organizations — based around the world and each year offering more than 3,000 adventure, vacation, and retreat opportunities ranging in length anywhere from weekend getaways to multi-month community sojourns. All provide lodging, meals (or meal preparation facilities), plus program activities presented on an ad hoc or ongoing basis. And all programs are conducted in English.

Profiled organizations include prayer and meditation retreats; personal growth centers; holistic health vacation spas and family camps; emotional and physical recovery centers; healing journeys and pilgrimages; and wilderness programs such as vision quests.

A few organizations address virtually all levels of mind/body well being. Many have a predominantly centering, psychotherapeutic or spiritual orientation. And some focus primarily on physical health concerns — special diet, recuperation, or general fitness. But all place significant emphasis on healing within a context broader than the physical body alone.

All profiles are contained in the book's four major chapters. Those chapters (and the number of profiles in each) are as follows:

- Chapter 6: SINGLE SITE VACATIONS & RETREATS ..... (237)
- Chapter 7: MULTIPLE SITE VACATIONS & RETREATS .... (25)
- Chapter 8: JOURNEYS .... (22)
- Chapter 9: WILDERNESS PROGRAMS .... (21)

The geographical split of the 237 SINGLE SITE VACATIONS & RETREATS organizations:

- 168 in the United States
- 30 in the British Isles
- 14 in Canada
- 9 in Continental Europe
- 9 in the Caribbean, Mexico and Brazil
- 7 in India, Australia and New Zealand

The geographical split of the 25 MULTIPLE SITE VACATIONS & RETREATS organizations:

    13 in North America
     7 under Two or More Continents
     5 in Europe

The geographical split of the 22 JOURNEYS organizations:

    11 under Two or More Continents
     6 in Asia
     2 in Europe
     2 in North America
     1 in South America

And the geographical split of the 21 WILDERNESS PROGRAMS organizations:

    18 in North America
     3 under Two or More Continents

At the end of the book, the LISTING CRITERIA section explains how organizations were selected to be profiled.

3 Exploring This Book

This directory is organized and indexed to allow the reader to identify adventures, vacations or retreats of particular interest in several ways — by geographical location, program type, participant's special needs and interests, spiritual/religious orientation, and name of organization. The locations of the 237 single site organizations are also pinpointed on 13 regional maps.

Geographical Layout

All profiles are arranged in alphabetical order within the smallest geographical area of each profile chapter. For example, single site vacations and retreats located in California are listed in alphabetical order under California within the South Pacific subsection of the United States in Chapter 6.

The four profile chapters, and their geographical contents, are listed below.

Chapter 6 —SINGLE SITE VACATIONS & RETREATS:

- United States
    South Pacific (California, Hawaii)
    Northwest (Montana, Oregon, Washington, Wyoming)
    Southwest (Arizona, Colorado, New Mexico, Utah)
    North Central (Illinois, Michigan, Minnesota, South Dakota, Wisconsin)
    South Central (Missouri, Oklahoma, Texas)
    Northeast (Maine, Massachusetts, New Hampshire, New York, Rhode Island, Vermont)
    Mideast (Indiana, Maryland, New Jersey, Ohio, Pennsylvania, Virginia, West Virginia)
    Southeast (Alabama, Florida, Georgia, North Carolina)
- Caribbean, Mexico & Brazil
    Bahamas, Barbados, Brazil, Jamaica, Mexico, Puerto Rico, U.S. Virgin Islands.
- Canada
    British Columbia, Alberta, Ontario, Quebec, Nova Scotia.

- British Isles
  England, Ireland, Scotland, Wales.

- Continental Europe
  France, Greece, Italy, Spain, Switzerland.

- India, Australia & New Zealand

Chapter 7 —MULTIPLE SITE VACATIONS & RETREATS:

- Two or More Continents, Europe, North America.

Chapter 8 —JOURNEYS:

- Two or More Continents, Asia, Europe, North America, South America.

Chapter 9 —WILDERNESS PROGRAMS:

- Two or More Continents, North America.

Profile Format

Each profile includes a description followed by line item entries. The description covers the nature of the host organization's programs and services, physical facilities and leisure activities, and staff or visiting teachers. Line item entries are for details such as address, phone number and fax number (if there is one), season of operation, summary of program types, and program rates.

Profiles in chapters 7,8 and 9 contain a line item entry noting the regions in which programs are conducted. Profiles in chapter 6 contain line item entries noting the nature of lodging, meals, and (in many cases) services available (unless identified as "free" or "courtesy") at additional cost.

Quoted rates usually cover the entire program cost — lodging, meals, board, tuition and airfare (in the case of trips). Otherwise, separate rates are given for tuition, lodging and meals. Some profiles in chapter 8 specify separate airfare rates or note that such rates are not included in the package.

"#" is used to abbreviate "pounds" (the monetary unit in the British Isles). "#" indicates Irish pounds if the profiled organization is based in Ireland. In all other cases, "#" indicates British pounds. Similarly, "$" indicates U.S. dollars in all cases except profiled organizations based in Australia, Canada or New Zealand (each of which has its own $ currency).

Other entry abbreviations: "BYO" for "bring your own"; "B&B" for "bed & breakfast" (a level of service or a type of inn); and "RV" for "recreational vehicle."

Indexes & Maps

Indexes and maps are placed at the front of the book to be easily accessible by librarians and research oriented readers. Other readers, particularly those with interests in specific geographical areas, may skip this material and go directly to the profiles.

Chapter 4 contains four indexes — the Program Type Index, the Special Needs & Interests Index, the Spiritual/Religious Orientation Index, and the Alphabetical Master Index.

Program Type Index: 20 general categories of transformative processes or experiences taught or enabled by host organizations.

Special Needs & Interests Index: 14 types of people, need or interest that is addressed by host organizations.

Spiritual/Religious Orientation Index: 14 types of spiritual or religious orientation embraced by a number of host organizations.

Alphabetical Master Index: offers a coded profile for each organization (numbered and listed in alphabetical order) by numbers and letters keyed to the other three indexes.

Chapter 5 contains 13 maps of 8 U.S. regions plus 5 other geographical areas, each using Alphabetical Master Index numbers to pinpoint the locations of single site host organizations.

Making Plans

Readers interested in a particular program are advised to call or write the host organization at least several weeks before the beginning of that program. Most programs have a limit on the number of participants, so reservations are a good idea.

Calling or writing in advance is required in the case of prayer and meditation centers, where unannounced visitors might disrupt the serene environment of a retreat-in-progress. Advance notice is also generally required by small centers where the staff cannot simultaneously tend to the needs of drop-in visitors and workshop participants. So please respect the note "No visits without prior arrangements" when it appears after a phone number in any entry.

Calling or writing in advance also allows you to verify the information in this book. All profiles were written or updated on the basis of information obtained from brochures (1993 and, in some cases, 1994) followed up by written and telephone inquiries. And every profiled organization was given the chance in late 1993 to review its profile and to submit any necessary amendments and corrections. However, organizations and their programs change over time.

4 Indexes

This chapter contains four indexes. The first three allow the reader to identify profiled organizations that address specific interests, needs and orientations. Because of the brevity of expression allowed by codes, the fourth index often gives a more complete picture of an organization's programs, activities and services than is possible in a written profile.

Program Type Index

The Program Type Index lists and defines 20 general categories. Each definition is followed by numbers corresponding to the numbered listings in the Alphabetical Master Index. This allows identification of organizations using particular transformative methods (e.g. breathwork, natural cures or yoga) in their programs, activities or services.

In this index, the "Creative Ceremony" category does not refer to fixed-form religious rituals. Program environments that may include fixed-form rituals can be found through the Spiritual/Religious Orientation Index.

The "Vision Quest" category refers to a solo wilderness experience that is usually just one component of an overall program that integrates psychotherapeutic techniques with shamanic ritual.

1. **Bodywork** — includes acupuncture, acupressure, aromatherapy, bioenergetics, cranials, do-in (self massage), hakomi, massage, polarity, rolfing, shiatsu and spa treatments:

    1,2,8,9,12,13,16,17,18,21,22,31,36,37,38,39,40,47,48,50,52,53,59,64, 66,71,73,74,75,77,92,93,96,97,98,100,101,102,103,104,105,106,108,109, 112,113,114,116,122,124,127,132,133,134,135,136,140,141,142,144,146, 147,149,150,151,152,,153,154,156,159,160,164,165,168,171,173,174,176, 177,178,180,181,183,187,189,191,195,196,197,202,203,205,207,208,209, 210,214,216,218,226,227,230,231,232,233,236,241,247,248,256,269,273, 279,280,284,286,287,301

2. **Breathwork** — therapies such as Brethwork, diakath breathing, Holotropic Breathwork, Integrative Breathwork, rebirthing:

    8,29,44,47,51,66,67,72,76,78,97,101,104,109,114,122,133,135,157,178, 185,195,202,241,287

3. **Counseling** — intuitive (e.g. astrological), spiritual and psycho-therapeutic counseling for individuals or couples:

    2,8,12,17,22,26,27,31,37,38,40,41,44,47,49,50,66,78,80,87,91,94,103, 104,105,116,126,134,135,137,152,153,159,164,172,174,194,202,203,209, 213,222,227,232,240,242,244,257,273,282,295

4. **Creative Ceremony** — loosely structured or spontaneously created ceremonies (including sacred dance) allowing epression of a group's communal identity:

    3,11,14,19,23,30,31,36,42,43,46,47,49,54,58,66,67,68,69,70,74,76,78, 91,92,96,99,101,103,114,117,118,119,125,143,144,154,160,161,162,165, 171,178,182,183,187,188,192,201,208,211,216,220,222,223,224,227,235, 242,243,245,260,267,272,273,276,283,292,293,295,296

5. **Self-Expression** — includes crafts (e.g. mask & drum making), drawing, music making, painting, poetry, pottery, sand tray, singing, song writing, and storytelling:

    1,2,3,4,9,19,24,31,34,36,42,46,48,50,52,53,54,55,65,66,68,69,74,75,76, 81,82,88,90,91,92,95,97,101,103,109,110,114,118,125,129,134,142,144, 146,151,159,160,163,164,166,168,171,174,178,180,183,185,187,188,189, 192,195,196,197,198,199,200,201,202,205,208,209,216,221,223,224,225, 227,230,231,238,241,243,247,249,250,252,256,260,267,272,274,277,278, 285,288,297,298,303,304,305

6. **Diet Modification** — cooking classes; fasting; living foods, macrobiotics, and nutritional counseling:

    12,13,18,21,22,26,37,38,54,73,74,76,80,87,100,102,105,111,112,113,114, 116,139,140,141,142,145,147,151,152,153,156,159,177,180,187,209,214, 225,226,233,236,237,244,250,251,252,257,279,280,286,290,304

7. **Group Process Work** — includes cooperative endeavor and teamwork (e.g. encampments), dyads, group discussion and sharing, psychodrama, and trust building exercises:

    1,2,8,11,14,19,26,30,41,42,44,48,49,52,54,56,60,68,69,70,75,81,84,86, 94,103,104,108,110,115,117,119,125,131,133,134,135,143,149,157,161, 162,164,166,167,168,171,176,178,179,182,183,184,188,190,193,194,200, 201,202,208,213,219,220,222,223,224,228,230,235,237,238,243,245,260, 264,276,282,286,290,291,292,293,294,296,297

8. **Hatha Yoga** — asanas (postures) and pranayama (yogic breathing) in various styles such as Dru, Iyengar, Kundalini, Kripalu, Viniyoga and Vinyasa:

    1,2,6,8,9,10,12,13,15,16,17,18,20,21,31,33,35,37,38,39,40,46,47,48,
    52,53,57,59,64,71,74,75,76,77,78,79,87,93,97,102,105,108,109,111,112,
    113,114,116,117,118,124,126,127,132,136,137,141,142,143,144,145,146,
    147,148,149,151,153,156,163,164,165,168,173,174,175,177,179,180,181,
    183,187,189,191,195,200,205,208,210,214,218,225,226,230,233,234,235,
    236,240,241,244,245,247,248,249,250,251,253,254,255,256,259,263,266,
    274,277,278,284,287,289,298,299,300,301,302,303,305

9. **Inner Process Work** — includes biofeedback and brainwave training, sound therapy, dreamwork, emotional release work, Gestalt, hypnosis, journal writing, regression:

    1,3,4,8,19,23,24,34,37,38,41,42,44,46,48,50,52,53,54,58,60,66,68,74,
    75,76,78,81,85,91,94,95,97,98,101,104,106,107,108,109,111,114,117,118,
    125,131,133,134,136,137,142,146,148,149,150,156,158,161,163,166,168,
    170,171,172,173,174,178,180,182,183,184,185,186,187,189,190,191,193,
    194,196,200,202,213,216,223,224,225,227,230,232,241,242,243,245,256,
    260,272,273,276,278,285,292,296,298

10. **Medicine Wheel** — ancient and universal shamanic ritual and teachings usually presented in Native American form:

    23,34,36,46,50,69,85,94,97,99,103,149,183,187,208,211,227,241,242,272,
    294

11. **Meditation/Relaxation** — concentration, focusing, guided visualization, inner listening, interspecies communications, mindfulness, nature and devic attunement:

    1,2,3,5,6,8,9,10,12,13,15,16,17,18,20,22,24,25,26,28,29,31,32,34,40,
    45,47,48,50,51,52,54,56,57,60,61,62,11,67,68,69,72,74,75,76,77,81,82,
    87,88,89,93,95,96,97,99,101,105,107,109,110,111,112,113,114,116,117,
    118,119,120,121,122,123,124,125,126,127,128,129,133,134,135,136,137,
    138,140,141,142,144,145,154,155,156,157,159,163,165,166,167,168,170,
    173,174,176,177,178,179,180,181,184,185,186,187,189,191,194,195,196,
    198,201,202,206,207,209,210,211,212,214,215,216,218,220,221,223,224,
    226,228,230,231,232,235,236,238,239,240,242,244,245,246,247,248,249,
    250,251,252,253,254,255,256,257,258,259,260,261,264,265,267,269,272,
    274,275,277,278,280,281,283,285,287,288,289,297,303,304,305

12. **Movement** — primarily aikido, Alexander Technique, chi gung, Feldenkreis, and tai chi:

1,2,4,8,9,15,17,19,22,24,29,30,31,34,36,42,48,50,52,55,56,74,75,81, 85,87,91,93,96,97,108,109,113,114,116,118,122,127,129,135,136,138, 140,141,142,143,144,146,149,157,163,165,167,168,171,173,174,176,178, 183,187,188,189,192,195,196,199,205,208,209,210,212,216,221,223,225, 228,230,238,244,256,260,268,269,270,271,273,275,284,288,290,297,298, 303,304

13. **Nature Cures** — includes Bach flower and herbal remedies, hot mineral springs, gardening, permaculture and tracking:

1,4,12,14,18,22,23,31,36,39,52,56,59,68,75,78,80,81,91,92,94,95,96,98, 105,106,109,110,114,117,127,137,139,141,142,144,146,152,156,160,163, 177,184,186,187,195,200,204,207,209,211,212,216,218,225,232,233,236, 238,244,252,267,270,272,274,279,280,286,287,288,295,304

14. **Prayer** — petitionary, intercessionary, contemplative/centering, devotional/chanting, mantra words and phrases (e.g. the Jesus Prayer):

1,2,3,6,9,10,19,22,25,26,28,29,40,43,47,48,50,53,55,57,60,73,74,77,78, 87,100,109,114,126,134,140,143,144,150,152,158,170,174,178,179,193, 192,198,203,206,220,223,231,232,235,236,239,243,249,251,252,254,257, 258,259,262,264,279,288,298,303,305

15. **Psychic Healing** — includes aura cleansing, chakra balancing, color and crystal healing, grounding, and laying on of hands:

9,22,27,31,44,50,52,53,56,61,75,78,82,96,116,127,147,151,160,174,183, 204,207,208,209,216,232,240,285,297

16. **Selfless Service** — practicing love in action by donating work to the the host community:

4,9,15,24,29,32,42,45,47,57,78,88,118,120,128,129,137,143,144,157, 184,206,221,231,236,238,246,249,250,252,255,256,258,260,265,267,278, 295

17. **Spirit Guidance** — guidance from channeled spirits in the form of general advice or answers to specific questions:

27,189,204

18. **Power Places** — homes of living saints; ancient monoliths, pyramids and temples; sacred mountains, lakes and Earth vortex locations; sites of religious apparitions:

7,27,34,40,41,54,58,59,61,63,67,81,93,99,101,121,130,141,155,162,166, 169,179,183,204,207,228,229,255,262,264,267,283,287

19. **Vision Quest** — several days alone in the wilderness (usually with fasting and vigil) to receive guidance (in a dream or vision) on one's purpose or direction in life:

    11,14,23,30,49,58,68,69,70,84,86,94,115,119,125,143,182,186,188,201, 216,219,228,282,291,292,293,294

20. **Wisdom Literature** — reading, study and talks on scriptures (e.g. Bible, Vedas, Buddhist Sutras and "A Course in Miracles") widely regarded as Divine revelation:

    3,8,9,10,15,32,45,48,60,62,74,75,81,83,88,95,120,123,128,129,134,139, 141,143,150,154,158,159,170,198,200,203,206,215,216,221,224,231,246, 247,249,251,252,255,258,261,274,285,288,303,304

Special Needs & Interests Index

The "Special Needs & Interests Index" lists and defines 14 categories. Each definition is followed by numbers corresponding to the numbered listings in the "Alphabetical Master Index." This allows identification of organizations offering programs, services or activities for people with special needs or interests.

The "Adults" category identifies programs open to any adult of either gender. The "Men" and "Women" categories identify programs restricted, respectively, to men or women. The "Homosexuals" category identifies programming for homosexual men, homosexual women, or both together.

A. **Adults** — programs open to any individual adult:

   All entries except 19,35,69,117,119,132,161,190,194,201,220,295,296

B. **Community Sojourns** — host community programs that accommodate short term residents or work/study guests:

   3,9,10,15,20,23,45,46,47,57,74,75,77,81,89,91,92,97,111,114,118,127, 129,131,133,136,143,146,160,173,177,178,187,193,196,198,200,206,216, 230,232,236,238,246,247,248,250,252,253,258,272,274,298,303,304,305

C. **Couples** — programs designed specifically for couples or to enhance understanding, love and sexuality in relationships:

   24,31,36,41,48,61,75,77,80,81,83,91,96,97,98,104,109,114,122,125,127, 132,134,135,136,137,140,145,150,151,165,166,174,178,186,187,189,193, 195,196,204,209,213,222,224,237,240,242,243,245,256,260,278,285,289, 298

D. Families — programs with organized activities for adults and their children:

1,3,10,24,31,35,36,71,74,75,81,87,97,103,104,114,117,118,120,129,136, 140,141,143,153,160,163,171,183,187,191,193,198,208,209,221,225,247, 249,252,260,267,271,288,298,305

E. Homosexuals — programs of a generally spiritual nature for homosexual men and/or women:

57,134,187,200,202,224,243,304

F. Individual Retreats — solo rest, meditation and spiritual retreats, self-directed or with advisor input:

4,5,6,9,10,15,17,25,31,41,42,44,45,46,47,48,56,57,60,62,66,82,83,89, 91,102,107,109,110,120,126,127,128,134,136,137,143,144,146,147,150, 151,154,164,165,173,174,175,185,186,193,200,202,206,218,223,231,239, 240,241,258,259,272,273,275,277,288,289,297,305

G. Men — programs that initiate or re-initiate men into the deeper, spiritual and emotional dimensions of being a man:

11,15,30,31,41,42,43,48,69,75,84,88,96,97,103,109,125,127,132,134,136, 150,161,162,171,182,187,200,209,211,219,223,224,225,239,242,243,272, 276,278,292,298

H. Recovery — programs for people working on emotional issues such as dysfunctional family, abuse or addictive behavior (e.g. smoking and overeating):

8,26,31,37,38,41,48,54,57,73,75,76,85,100,103,105,109,111,126,131,133, 134,140,141,150,152,164,170,173,177,187,190,194,196,203,209,213,224, 226,230,272,279,288,290

I. Regeneration/Healing — programs suitable for people in post-operation recovery or with a life threatening illness:

2,18,26,37,38,54,73,100,107,177,203,257,280,285

J. Rental Facilities — centers that allow use of their facilities by outside groups for private or public workshops:

4,17,22,34,36,41,42,43,45,46,48,52,77,91,96,97,110,127,137,142,147, 151,154,165,173,175,180,186,191,200,202,230,241,272,275,285,297

K. Spiritual/Life Transition — for people at a life turning point or experiencing spiritual disorientation:

11,14,30,42,49,68,69,70,84,90,94,115,119,136,162,182,184,201,202,216, 219,220,227,228,282,291,292,293,294,296

L. Facilities for the Disabled — host organizations that offer wheelchair access or wheelchair-suitable quarters:

2,4,38,74,75,249,251

M. Teacher/Professional Trainings — programs that train teachers, healers or others in the helping professions:

11,18,34,48,56,75,76,81,83,92,97,109,111,122,129,136,141,182,186,187, 190,193,199,200,207,231,232,236,240,243,250,251,252,253,255,257,273, 275,280,285,289,296,298

N. Women — programs for women to explore and celebrate the spiritual and emotional dimensions of being a woman:

3,4,8,11,14,15,19,30,31,36,41,42,46,48,51,55,61,62,64,66,68,69,70,74, 75,78,84,88,89,96,97,103,109,111,114,117,119,120,125,127,132,133,134, 136,146,150,158,165,167,171,182,185,187,188,195,200,201,202,209,211, 216,220,221,223,224,227,239,242,243,252,272,275,277,280,288,291,292, 293,295,296,297

Spiritual/Religious Orientation Index

The "Spiritual/Religious Orientation Index" lists and defines 14 categories. Each definition is followed by numbers corresponding to the numbered listings in the "Alphabetical Master Index." This allows identification of organizations embracing a particular spiritual or religious tradition.

In some cases, an organization may embrace two or more spiritual/religious traditions. These cases account for some of the listings under the "Alphabetical Master Index" that have two or more small cap letter codes.

Under the "Alphabetical Master Index," listings with multiple small cap letter codes may also indicate sectarian Buddhist retreat centers (noted by all three Buddhist tradition codes) or communities with a primary tradition that also encourage multi-traditional worship (the "t" code).

m. Catholic — Roman Catholic faiths with a contemplative and/or broadly ecumenical outlook:

150,154,158,262,264

n. Christian Fundamentalist — non-Catholic, Christian faiths emphasizing Bible study and prayer:

26,80,152,203,257,279

o. **Goddess/Eco-Spirituality** — ancient and modern traditions (including Wicca and Deep Ecology) honoring the interdependence of Earth, its plants and creatures:

19,46,66,68,92,110,201,211,228,295

p. **Hindu/Yogic** — the Indian spiritual paths of bhakti yoga (devotion), jnana yoga (self-inquiry), karma yoga (selfless service), and raja yoga (meditation):

9,10,18,111,121,130,137,173,191,229,236,239,240,249,250,251,252,253, 255,298

q. **Judaic** — Judaic religious traditions that encourage joyous celebration, creative self-expression and/or mystical union with the Divine:

74,107,223

r. **Liberal Protestant** — non-Catholic, non-Metaphysical Christian faiths stressing social service and prayer:

24,50,60,134,198,285

s. **Metaphysical Christian** — new or non-churched faiths honoring Jesus as a teacher and exemplar of the divinity in all people:

10,47,77,83,232,239

t. **Multi-Traditional** — spiritual communities that accommodate the ritual practices of several (or even all) religions:

3,107,154,223

u. **Native American/Shamanic** — a largely American form of spirituality with rituals such as sweat lodge, pipe circle, medicine wheel and vision quest:

23,36,58,68,85,86,103,155,211,235,267,272

v. **Sufi** — a mystically oriented spiritual path that originated in the Muslim faith:

3,43,305

w. **Theosophical/Ascended Masters** — certain societies and new religions that believe angels and ascended spiritual masters are assisting mankind:

118,225

x. **Theravada Buddhist** — a form of Buddhism (dominant in Burma, Ceylon, India and Thailand) known for its Vipassana (insight) meditation:

5,15,25,51,62,88,120,215,261,281

y. Tibetan Buddhist — a form of Buddhism emphasizing compassion, ritual practices and visualization meditations:

15,45,51,88,89,128,129,130,221,231,267

z. Zen Buddhist — a form of Buddhism (dominant in China, Japan, Korea and Vietnam) known for its koans, rigorous sitting meditation, and its aesthetics:

15,32,51,57,88,95,121,144,206,246,258,274,303,304

Alphabetical Master Index

Each numbered entry in this index is followed by numbers, capital and small cap letters. Each number is the code number for a specific category in the "Program Type Index." Each capital letter is the code letter for a specific category in the "Special Needs & Interests Index." And each small cap letter is the code letter for a specific category in the "Spiritual/ Religious Orientation Index."

Each entry also notes the page on which the entry is profiled. This page number follows the number and letter codes at the far right side of the page.

#	Name / Index Codes	Page
1.	A.R.E. Camp 1,5,7,8,9,11,12,13,14,A,D	169
2.	A.R.E. Medical Clinic 1,3,5,7,8,11,12,14,A,I,L	95
3.	Aegis at the Abode 4,5,9,11,14,20,A,B,D,N,t,v	139
4.	Akala Point 5,9,12,13,16,A,F,J,L,N	207
5.	Amaravati 11,A,F,x	208
6.	Amrit Trust 8,11,14,A,F	208
7.	Ana Tours 18,A,o	277
8.	Anabasis 1,2,3,7,8,9,11,12,20,A,H,N	178
9.	Ananda Ashram 1,5,8,11,12,14,15,16,20,A,B,F,p	140
10.	Ananda Assisi 8,11,14,20,A,B,D,F,s,p	235
11.	Animas Valley Institute 4,7,19,A,G,K,M,N	283
12.	Ann Wigmore Foundation 1,3,6,8,11,13,A	128
13.	Ann Wigmore Institute 1,6,8,11,A	194
14.	Antelope Retreat Center 4,7,13,19,A,K,N	93
15.	Aryaloka Buddhist Center 8,11,12,16,20,A,B,F,G,N,x,y,z	137
16.	Ashram 1,8,11,A	49
17.	Astral Mountain Retreat 1,3,8,11,12,A,F,J	50

5 Maps

This chapter's 13 maps identify the locations of the 237 single-site host organizations by their Alphabetical Master Index numbers.

For a quick overview of this chapter, check the map index below:

U.S. South Pacific

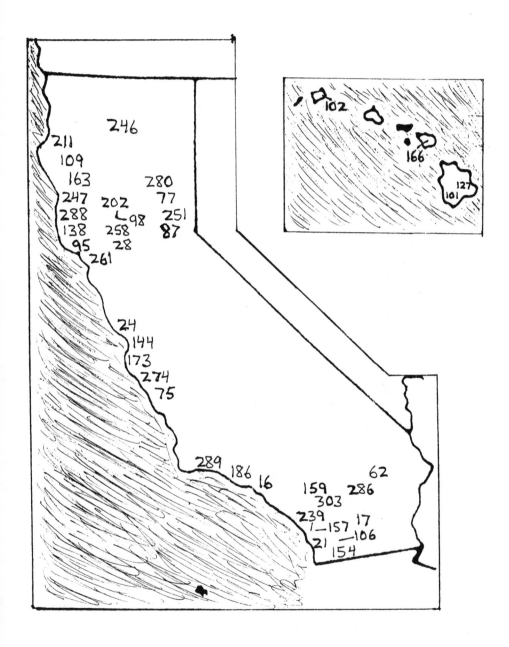

U.S. Northwest

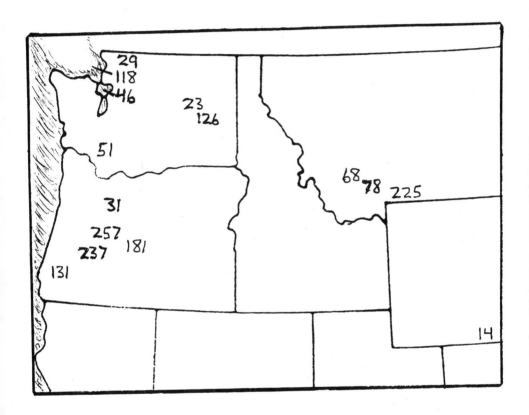

U.S. Southwest

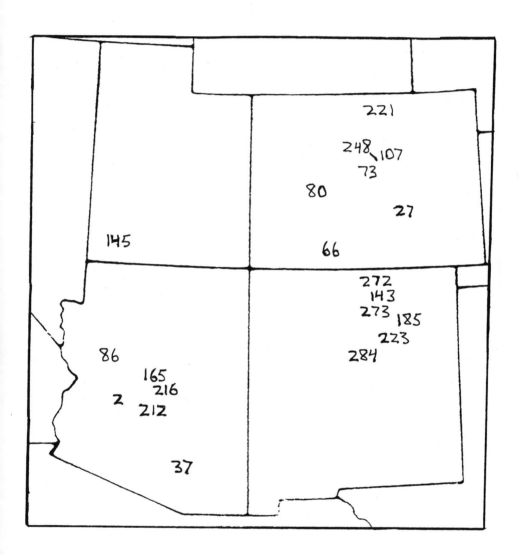

U.S. North Central

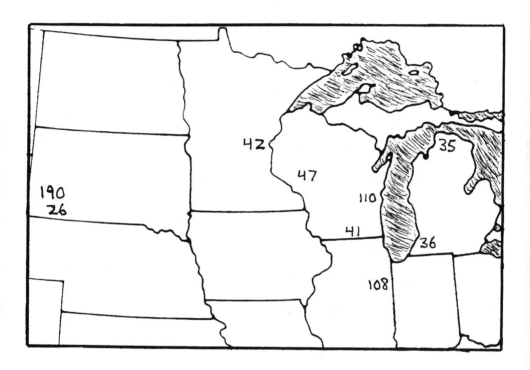

U.S. South Central

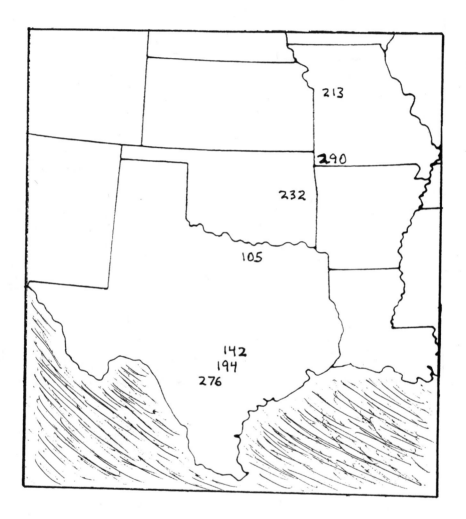

U.S. Northeast

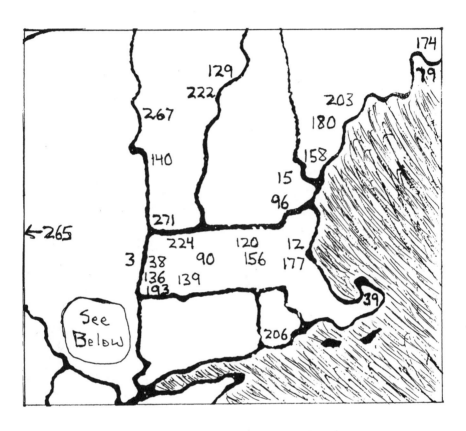

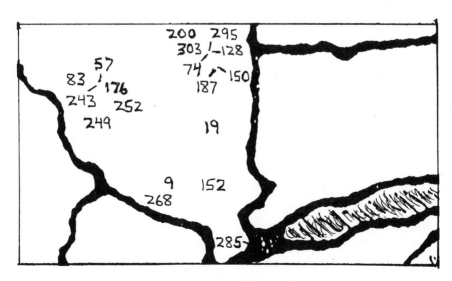

U.S. Mideast

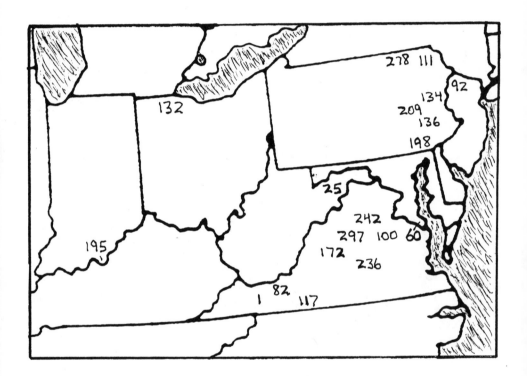

U.S. Southeast

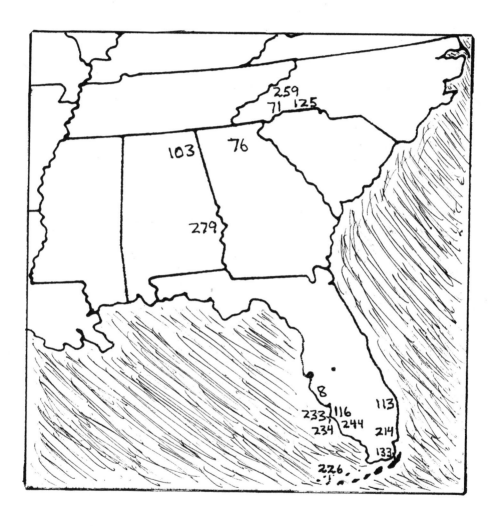

Caribbean, Mexico & Brazil

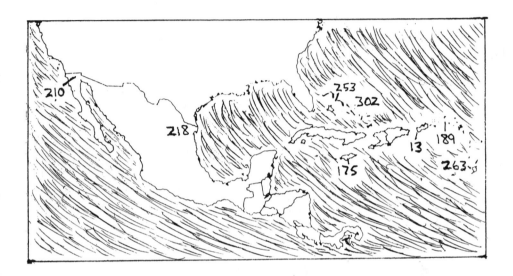

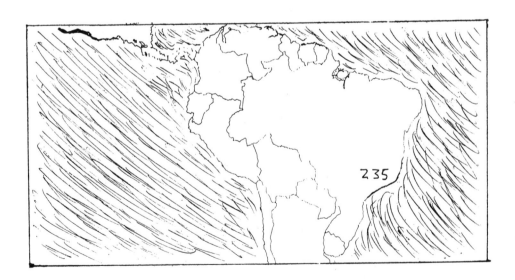

Canada

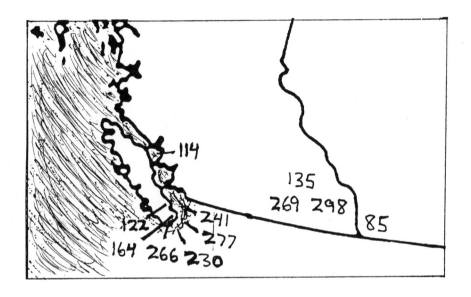

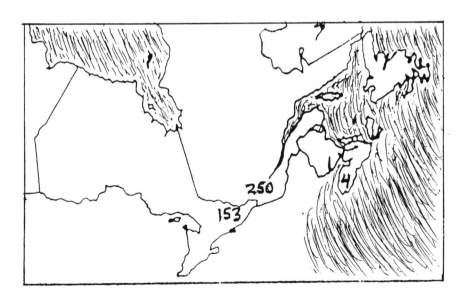

British Isles

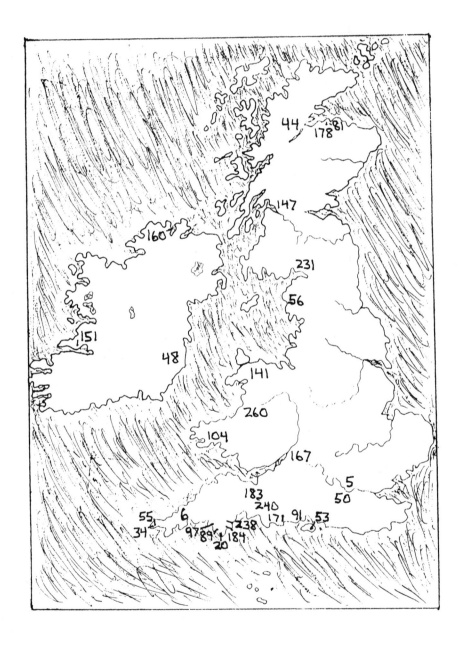

Continental Europe

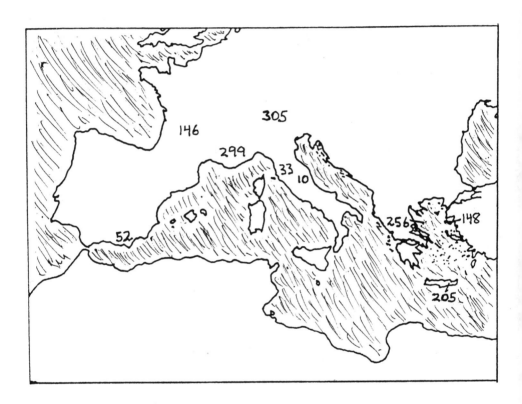

India, Australia & New Zealand

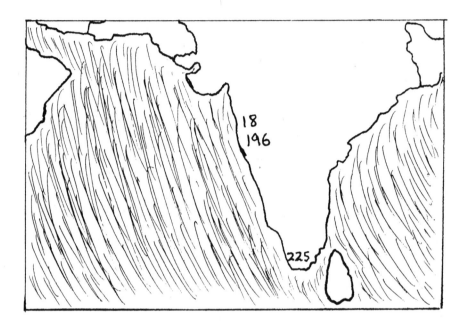

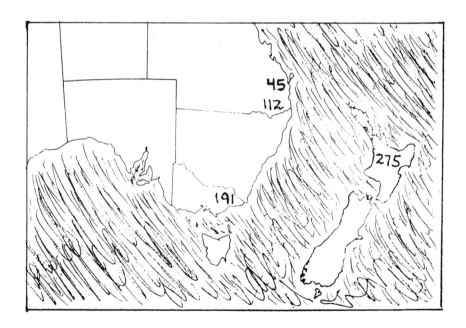

6 Single Site Vacations & Retreats

This chapter contains profiles of vacation and retreat providers organized by regional, national and state/province areas. And within these geographical categories, profiles are arranged in alphabetical order by organization name.

U.S. states are covered in alphabetical order under 8 regional state groupings. Canadian provinces are covered in alphabetical order under that nation. Ireland and the major parts of Britain are covered in alphabetical order under British Isles. Other nations are covered in alphabetical order under regions such as Continental Europe.

UNITED STATES   South Pacific Region

The Ashram   Calabasas, CA

The Ashram is a two-story stucco house 15 minutes north of Malibu Beach in the Santa Monica Mountains. Its grounds contain a garden, a small heated swimming pool and jacuzzi, a sunbathing solarium, and a redwood geodesic dome for yoga and meditation sessions. The house has spacious porches, a gymnasium, exercise area, and beds for 10 guests with two-to-a-room. Half of the guests are returnees, including many Hollywood celebrities.

The Ashram's success is based on a program of rigorous exercise, diet and inner centering. Up at 6:30 AM for yoga and meditation followed by a glass of grapefruit juice for breakfast, a guest can look forward to 5 hours of steep mountain hiking, an hour of calisthenics, an hour of weight training, and an hour of exercise in the pool — each day. For daily relaxation, there is also an hour of massage.

The Ashram's proprietor is Anne-Marie Bennstrom, a former Swedish cross-country ski champion and ex-owner of a popular pre-Fonda Hollywood gym.

Address   P.O. Box, 8009, Calabasas, CA 91372, USA

Phone   818/222-6900.

Season   Year-round.

Programs Standard, one-week program "to enhance your physical, mental and spiritual well-being."

Lodging   Guest capacity of 10 in 5 bedrooms, 2 in each room.

Rates $2,000 per week.

Meals   3 daily vegetarian meals, mostly raw food. Lunch can be a bowl of steamed vegetables and a wheatgrass-like potion. Dinner can be watercress, mushrooms, mung beans and alfalfa.

Services   Free van pick-up & drop-off at nearby locations.

Astral Mountain Retreat   Julian, CA

Secluded in a wilderness of pine, cedar and oak trees patched with alpine meadows bordering on the Cuyamaca Mountains, Astral Mountain Retreat is a haven of fresh air and serenity 50 miles northwest of San Diego. The living room in the house has a huge rock fireplace and 6 foot high windows. Outside are secluded porches, patios, a sun deck, swimming pool and sauna. There are hundreds of acres for hiking and hammocks for taking it easy.

Astral Mountain also offers unusual meals and movement sessions, both the creation of proprietor Joel Hirsch. Meals are based on a combination of macrobiotic and live food principles. Even more eclectic, Joel's "movement class" combines elements of hatha yoga, kundalini yoga, tai chi, chi gung, bioenergetics, mentastics and dance-like primal movements.

Guests are free to join Joel on his daily 7:30 AM hike to a nearby lake for a short session of breathwork and energizing movements. They may also join him for a before-dinner movement class. Monthly release/growth yoga weekends include several movement sessions, a trip to a nearby hot springs, and explanations of macrobiotic/live food philosophy and meal preparation.

Address   Joel Hirsch, P.O. Box 1881, Julian, CA 92036, USA

Phone   619/765-1225.

Season   Year-round.

Programs Daily yoga/movement sessions. Monthly yoga/movement weekends.

Lodging   Main house accommodates up to 20 overnight guests in rooms of varying sizes. Also a poolside cottage suitable for a couple.

Rates   Release/growth yoga weekend: individual $125, couple $200. Bed & breakfast: $50-70 per room, discounts for midweek & long stays. Lunch $6. Dinner $8. Groups of 10 or more: $25/person plus $5 for each meal.

Meals   3 daily gourmet meals — macrobiotic/live food & home baked bread.

Services   Trager, acupressure & deep tissue massage; intuitive astrological counseling with chart & cassette; musical personality portraits intuitively composed, played on piano & captured on cassette.

Beach Retreat   San Diego, CA

Beach Retreat is an ocean side yoga retreat in the Ocean Beach community of San Diego. Located between San Diego Bay and Ocean Bay Park, the community retains a small village atmosphere while being close to San Diego's main attractions — Sea World, the Zoo and Wild Animal Park. Ocean Beach's public recreation facilities include a large fishing pier, beach volleyball, park tennis courts and picnic areas.

The Retreat's twice daily yoga classes are led by Marguerite Tyrell, a Registered Dietician and certified yoga instructor whose style favors attention to detail, precision and use of props. The chef is Marguerite's husband Jachin, an experienced counselor with bodywork and bioenergetics expertise. A disciple of both B.K.S. Iyengar and the Himalayan Institute's Swami Rama, Jachin invites guest participation in evening meditations.

Address   5122 Longbranch Ave., San Diego, CA 92107, USA

Phone   619/225-1054 (day). 619/225-9661 (eve). No visits without prior arrangement.

Season   Year-round.

Programs 5-day & weekend yoga retreats.

Lodging   Two cottage units, each with private, fully equipped kitchen; private bath; plus sleeping area accommodating up to 4 people. Airy living space with skylights, stained glass & plants.

Rates   5-day: 1st person $500, each additional person $100. Weekend: 1st person $200, each additional person $50.

Meals   5-day: daily continental breakfast. Weekend: continental breakfasts plus dinners with choice of menu — macrobiotic, raw foods, oriental or nouvelle cuisine. For other meals, guests may use cottage kitchens or dine out at the many local restaurants.

Services   Healing massage, aromatherapy, herb baths, nutrition counseling.

Ben Lomond Quaker Center   Ben Lomond, CA

Ben Lomond Quaker Center is an 80 acre retreat and conference facility set among towering redwoods, fir trees and ferns 10 miles north of Santa Cruz in the Coastal Range. The property includes hiking and nature trails, two lodges, a private retreat cottage, and a Friends Meeting House with majestic vistas of the

San Lorenzo River Valley. All guests are welcome to attend the daily, early morning centering/meditation meeting.

The Center hosts both Quaker and general public retreats. Public retreats scheduled for 1994 address topics such as "Spirituality and Sexuality," "Couples Enrichment," and "Non-Defensive Communication." The public is also invited to three annual weeklong events: an early July "Art and the Spirit" retreat with daily morning and afternoon workshops led by skilled artists and teachers; a fall workcamp with time for meditation, community building, fun and fellowship; and a year-end reflection and renewal retreat guided by experienced life journey counselors and therapists.

Address   P.O. Box 686, Ben Lomond, CA 95005, USA

Phone   408/336-8333.

Season   Year-round.

Programs Weekend & weeklong retreats fostering self-exploration and centering, creative self-expression, and creative fellowship.

Lodging   First come, first served accommodations in semi-private rooms for 2-3 people, bunk bed rooms, and an open dorm. Shared bathrooms.

Rates   Workcamp volunteers pay only for food. Weekend retreat $95. Year-end retreat week $190. "Art and the Spirit" week $215.

Meals   3 daily vegetarian meals. Participants share in kitchen chores & final, pre-departure clean-up.

Blue Mountain Center of Meditation   San Rafael, CA

45 miles up the Pacific coast north of San Francisco, Blue Mountain Center of Meditation each year conducts several (4 in 1994) weekend meditation retreats in a former Catholic convent adjacent to Dominican College. In their free time, retreatants can enjoy a walk in the hills, volleyball or a swim. The pool is open from May through October.

All retreats are based on the teachings of Eknath Easwaran on meditation and the other points of his Eight Point Program — mantram repetition, one-pointed attention, slowing down, training the senses, putting others first, satsang (devotional worship), and spiritual reading. Sri Easwaran is a prolific author and former U of C Berkeley professor of English literature.

Each retreat includes basic instruction in meditation; morning, noon and evening meditations; Friday and Saturday evening video (or in person) talks by Sri Easwaran; small group sessions after breakfast and after lunch on Saturday; plus panel sessions on mysticism after breakfast on Sunday. All retreats are conducted by Sri Easwaran's closest students, many of whom are involved in establishing a nearby residential community devoted to Sri Easwaran's vision of aging as an opportunity for inner growth of wisdom.

Address   Box 256, Tomales, CA 94971, USA

Phone   707/878-2369. No visits without prior arrangements.

Season   From time-to-time throughout the year.

Programs Weekend meditation retreats.

Lodging   Double occupancy rooms. A few single rooms. Shared bathrooms.

Rates   Tuition, room & board $250.

Meals   Three daily vegetarian meals on Saturday & on Sunday.

Dhamma Dena Desert Retreat   Joshua Tree, CA

Dhamma Dena is a silent meditation retreat center on 12 acres a few miles north of Joshua Tree National Monument. The center's purpose is "to serve those engaged in the conscious process of seeing into the conditioned mind." The high desert site is encircled by distant mountains and illumined by ever changing desert hues. Water is trucked in and reused.

Center owner Ruth Denison each year leads at least three Vipassana programs — a 4-week retreat in late December/early January, plus 2-week women's retreats in the spring and fall. Dhamma Dena also hosts public, guided meditation retreats conducted by other organizations.

Self-led retreatants are welcome to join early morning stretching and meditation sessions plus evening meditations on days when guided retreats are not in progress. All retreatants, teacher-guided and self-led, are expected to help out with center chores.

Address   HC-1, Box 250, Joshua Tree, CA 92252, USA

Phone   619/362-4815. No visits without prior arrangements.

Season   Year-round.

Programs Teacher-led meditation retreats ranging from 3 days to 4 weeks in length. Also self-led meditation & meditation/work retreats.

Lodging   Simple accommodations for over 50 retreatants in the main house, cabins and bunkhouses. Separate housing for men & women. Japanese style outhouses. BYO sleeping bag.

Rates   Facility fee $25 per day. Guided retreatants customarily make an additional donation for the meditation teachings.

Meals   3 light vegetarian meals eaten each day in communal peace.

Esalen Institute   Big Sur, CA

High above the Pacific 45 minutes south of Monterey, Esalen Institute is well known for its panoramic coastal vistas and its residential workshops. But the Institute's greatest achievements have been in the realm of human potential research and development. For example, it was during his years as an Esalen Scholar in Residence that Stanislav Grof (founder of the International Transpersonal Association) invented Holotropic Breathwork.

The Institute's hand-in-glove approach to research and education is exemplified in the "The Future of the Body," written by Esalen co-founder Michael Murphy. The book's theories are based on insights from 30+ years of public Esalen workshops taught by a faculty of visiting and resident artists, psychologists, psychiatrists, healing arts practitioners, spiritual teachers, and educators from many fields.

Weekend and 5-day workshops are offered continuously throughout the year. The Esalen campus includes a heated swimming pool and ocean view, hot spring baths where clothing is generally discarded. Casually furnished guest quarters are bathed in ocean air and the sound of the surf.

Participants in Esalen's "Work Study Program" work 32 hours each week for periods of one, two or three months. The study portion of the program has two monthly sections that are different each month. Each participant selects one section, which focuses on one type of growth practice — gestalt, meditation, massage, etc.

Longer stays are possible through the "Ongoing Residential Program," offered from mid-September through mid-June for minimum stays of one month. Participants may attend any of the 5-day workshops during their stay. They may also attend weekend workshops at reduced rates.

Address   Big Sur, CA 93920, USA

Phone   408/667-3000 (general info.) or 408/667-3005 (reservations).

Season   Year-round.

Programs Weekend and 5-day workshops on topics in one or more of 16 general fields: the arts, biofeedback/hypnosis, business/social responsibility, contemplative/shamanic, dreams, health/healing, integral practices, intuitive development, martial arts/sports, mythology/anthropology, philosophical inquiry/intellectual play, psychological process, relationships, somatics, wilderness/ ecology, women's/men's studies. Also work study programs.

Lodging   Capacity for over 100 overnight guests in shared (2 or 3/room) & bunk bed (4-6/room) accommodations. Also indoor sleeping bag space. Limited wheelchair access.

Rates　Weekend workshop: shared $380, bunk $300, sleeping bag $200. 5-day workshop: shared $740, bunk $550, sleeping bag $375. "Work Study Program" $750. "Ongoing Residence Program" 26-day rates: shared $3,195, bunk $2,520.

Meals　3 daily buffets with vegetarian option. Vegetables and greens from Esalen gardens.

Services　Cranial-sacral work, Feldenkrais, rolfing, Esalen and deep-tissue massage. Also pre-school children's program.

The Expanding Light at Ananda　　　Nevada City, CA

The Expanding Light is a meditation and yoga retreat center 90 minutes northwest of Sacramento in the foothills of the Sierra Nevada Mountains. Located in the heart of 800 acres of woods and meadows that are the home of Ananda Village (some 275 adults and 100 children), the center is operated by Ananda members under the spiritual guidance of Swami Kriyananda (J. Donald Walters) — an American disciple of the late Paramhansa Yogananda.

The center's Personal Retreat program, for stays of any length, offers classes and spiritual counseling from Ananda ministers. Expanding Light programs include "Rest & Recharge" weekends, with guided meditations and hatha yoga classes, plus theme weekends such as "Healing by God's Unlimited Power" or "The Spiritual Power of Music." 5-day programs are conducted on subjects such as "Life/Work Planning" and "Superconscious Living."

A typical day's schedule begins at 6:30 with sadhana (spiritual practices) — energization exercises, yoga postures, chanting and meditation. There is group affirmation at 9:45, meditation at noon, and sadhana again at 4:30. Mornings and afternoons from 10 to noon and 2 to 4:30 are set aside for classes, group activities or free time. The day ends with evening chanting, singing and meditation, or a sunset walk.

Address　14618 Tyler Foote Road, Nevada City, CA 95959, USA

Phone　800/346-5350 or 916/292-3496 from outside US & Canada.

Season　Year-round.

Programs　Weekend, 5-day, 7-day, 12-day, and 4-week courses focusing on meditation & hatha yoga. All courses taught by resident s t a f f . Also work/study & work exchange programs plus retreats tailor made for groups of at least 10 people.

Lodging　Indoors capacity for about 50 guests in two large buildings plus single room cabins with nearby shower houses. Tent/RV sites.

Rates　2 & 3-day weekends at multiples of personal retreat daily rate: tent/RV $38, shared room $57, private room $75. 5-day programs: tent/

RV $225-315, shared $325-410, private $415-500. 7-day programs: tent/RV $392, shared $539, private $665. 12-day programs: tent/RV $526, shared $764, private $980. 4-week programs: tent/RV $1,049, shared $1,527, private $1,962.

Meals   3 daily vegetarian meals.

Services   Available in Ananda Village: massage & yoga therapy, chiropractic & medical care, jacuzzi.

French Meadows Summer Camp   Tahoe National Forest, CA

The French Meadows Summer Camp is a quarter century old camp for families committed to learning and living a macrobiotic way of life. The event's annual National Forest site is 80 miles northeast of Sacramento at a 6,000 foot altitude on the western slope of the Sierra Nevadas. The campground is bordered by a stream and a reservoir is a quarter mile away. The camp is sponsored by the George Oshawa Macrobiotic Foundation (G.O.M.F.), which also operates the Vega Institute.

Each day begins with activities such as meditation, yoga, tai chi, walks and cooking. A chanting session is led by Vega Institute founders Herman and Cornellia Aihara. Mid-morning lectures by Herman and guest teachers touch on subjects such as "Controlling Food Addictions," "The Tao of Laughter," and "Essence of Macrobiotic Psychology." Early afternoon is free for swimming, hiking or just taking it easy. Afternoon workshops include macrobiotic cooking, Do-In self-massage, yoga and tai chi. The day ends around a campfire with singing, storytelling and variety shows.

Address   GOMF Summer Camp, 1511 Robinson Street, Oroville, CA 95965, USA

Phone   916/533-7702.   Fax 916/533-7908.

Season   10 days in mid July.

Programs Family summer camp celebrating a macrobiotic lifestyle.

Lodging   Tent sites for up to 125 people near outhouses, the campsite's only permanent structures. BYO tent & sleeping bag.

Rates   Early registration rates: $550 for non-G.O.M.F. member; $500 for G.O.M.F. member; (G.M.O.F. membership is $20/year, including subscription to the bi-monthly magazine "Macrobiotics Today"); youth (8-16) $350; child (up to 7) $200.

Meals   3 daily macrobiotic meals prepared over open wood fires.

Services   Program includes children's & youth's activities offered during lectures. Also massage & dietary consultations.

Green Gulch Farm   Muir Beach, CA

A 25 minute drive north of San Francisco, Green Gulch Farm is a 115 acre property adjoining Golden Gate National Recreation Area and a 1/2 mile ocean beach. The property contains a tea house, meditation hall, guest house, and 15 acres of vegetable, herb and flower gardens. The resident community tends the gardens and offers classes, workshops and retreats.

A sister community to the San Francisco Zen Center (SFZC) and Tassajara, Green Gulch was opened in 1972 as a place where a large spiritual community (mostly non-resident) can study Buddhist teachings, practice meditation, experiment with organic gardening, and serve as a learning center for the general public. Programs are led primarily by Bay area SFZC members.

Those new to meditation may take a one-day "Beginner's Sitting" class and/ or participate for as briefly as several days in the 7 and 8-week, spring, winter and summer "Practice Periods." "Practice Period" participants join the resident community in work, lectures, classes, meals, morning and evening meditation. During the "Summer Ecology Practice Period," residents and guests pay equal attention to meditation and horticulture.

Address   1601 Shoreline Drive, Muir Beach, CA 94965, USA

Phone   415/383-3134. Fax 415/383-3128.

Season   Year-round.

Programs Residential retreats & workshops on Zen meditation, social & psychological challenges from a Buddhist perspective, writing & the expressive arts. Non-residential Zen sittings, Buddhist studies classes, gardening workshops, tea classes & ceremonies.

Lodging   Artistically handcrafted wooden guesthouse with 12 rooms surrounding an atrium plus 3 rooms elsewhere. All rooms have 2 beds. A family suite elsewhere on the property.

Rates   7 & 8-week meditation & meditation/gardening "Practice Periods" $15/day; 5-day intensive meditation retreat $125; weekend workshops — private $230-240, shared $205-215.

Meals   3 daily, vegetarian buffets with produce from the gardens.

Harbin Hot Springs   Middletown, CA

Harbin Hot Springs is a retreat and workshop center encompassing 1,160 acres in a rugged foothill canyon 2 1/2 hours north of San Francisco. The property's natural mineral water supplies two warm pools, a hot pool, a cold plunge and a large chlorine-free swimming pool. Clothing is optional at the pools and adjacent dry sauna and redwood deck areas, open 24 hours daily every day of the year as a quiet meditation area.

Workshop participants and guests with a current membership ($15 annual, $5 one-month trial) may use the pools and participate in community activities - daily meditations, yoga classes, nightly videos, an "unconditional dance" most Tuesday evenings, full and new moon gatherings, plus other non-sectarian spiritual gatherings. Harbin members also receive workshop schedules in a quarterly literary publication.

Harbin is operated by a New Age community of some 150 adults and children. Work opportunities are often available (especially during harvest and construction months) for those experienced in organic gardening, construction trades, landscaping, cooking, bookkeeping, office management, and auto mechanics. Through its School of Shiatsu & Massage, Harbin also offers certification programs in various bodywork therapies including its own Watsu (water Shiatsu) massage.

Address   P.O. Box 82, Harbin Hot Springs, CA 95461, USA

Phone   707/987-2477.

Season   Year-round.

Programs   Roughly 100 2-day to 11-day workshops each year on bodywork, personal growth & relationship topics. Day visits allowed for participation in community events & use of pools. BYO towels.

Lodging   Creekside camping (some wooden platforms); male & female dorms; single, double & family rooms with shared, half or full bath. Children permitted at campsites & limited family rentals.

Rates   Weekend workshop $150-350. Camping: adult $14-23/night, $105/week; child $10-14/night, $70/week. Dorm $23-35/night, $154/week. Double room $60-125/night, $336-434/week. Single $40-80/night, $231-280/week. Day visit: adult $12-17, child $10-12.

Meals   A restaurant, poolside cafe, and vegetarian kitchen available for use by all guests including campers & day visitors.

Services   Massage: Esalen, deep tissue, rebalancing, Zen shiatsu & Watsu. Also energy work, rebirthing, chiropractic & cranial therapy.

Health Institute of San Diego   Lemon Grove, CA

On four quiet acres of verdant lawns and gardens in the hills of suburban San Diego, the Health Institute of San Diego offers a residential self-improvement learning experience within the philosophy and context of a living foods diet. The Institute's revitalizing curriculum is designed as a 3-week program, but 1 or 2-week stays are also beneficial and permitted.

Classes are conducted Monday through Friday on topics such as mental and emotional detoxification, self esteem, relaxation/pain control, the body, personal care, elimination and digestion, menu planning, food combining and preparation, organic gardening and wheat grass planting. There are daily exercise sessions. In their spare time, guests may enjoy the jacuzzi.

Address   6970 Central Avenue, Lemon Grove, CA 91945, USA

Phone   619/464-3346.

Season   Year-round.

Programs   Ongoing weekly optimum health program focusing on improving nutritional, physical, mental and emotional balance.

Lodging   Private & double accommodations in standard rooms, large rooms, suites and townhouses in comfortable one & two-story buildings.

Rates   Per week: standard room — double $295, single $425; large room — double $350, single $475; suite or townhouse — double $425, single $575.

Meals   3 daily "living foods" meals — sprouts, greens, fruits, vegetables, fruit juices, rejuvelac & wheatgrass juice.

Services   Colonics, massage & chiropractic.

Heartwood Institute   Garberville, CA

Heartwood is a rustic 240 acre healing community set amidst rolling forests and meadows on the eastern slope of a mountain 200 miles north of San Francisco. Facilities include a picturesque log lodge with a spacious deck; a large converted barn for crafts and classes; outdoor hot tub, wood fired sauna and large pool; gardens and campsites tucked in the trees. It is a serene and beautiful place, rich with wildlife and sweeping vistas.

Operating on a four quarter school year schedule, the Institute runs 11-week vocational training programs in transformational therapy, massage therapy, and addiction counseling. Heartwood encourages students to avail themselves of its many body-mind therapies and to participate in daily hatha yoga practice, including meditation and breath awareness. Dances, talent shows and rituals further unite the community.

Heartwood also offers 2-day to 3-week intensives and retreats on bodywork and massage, oriental healing arts, hypnotherapy, personal growth and recovery. All programs are facilitated by well qualified resident and visiting faculty. 1993 special event weekends included "Healing Your Life" with Heartwood founders Bruce and Chela Burger plus the annual "Women's Gathering" hosted by Chela and the Heartwood women.

Address   220 Harmony Lane, Garberville, CA 95542, USA

Phone   707/923-2021.   Fax 707/923-4906.

Season   Year-round.

Programs 2-day to 22-day personal growth retreats & intensives; personalized wellness retreats; 11, 22 & 33-week alternative healthcare training courses; 11-week personalized "Life Exploration Program"; 3-month work exchange program.

Lodging   Small & simple "preferred private," "preferred shared" & "standard shared" rooms. "Preferred" rooms have sheets, pillows, comforters and bath towels. Campsites also available.

Rates   Sample retreat & intensive tuitions: 2-day $100-135; 7-day $395-545; 14-day $840-1,500. 11-week Life Exploration Program tuition $1,950. Retreat room & board per day: private $55, preferred shared $45, standard shared $32.50, camping $27.50. 11-week room & board: private $2,618; shared $1,694; camping $1,475.

Meals   3 daily, mostly vegetarian meals with herbs, fruits & vegetables from the gardens. When "sensitive" ingredients (e.g. dairy, eggs, wheat or fish) are used, that food is labeled & an alternative is served. Guests are free to use the snack kitchen.

Services Bodywork & massage, breathwork, transformational therapy, hypnotherapy, and nutritional assessment.

Kumar Frantzis Summer Retreats   Sonoma County, CA

Kumar Frantzis was the first Westerner certified by the People's Republic of China to teach the complete system of tai chi. Kumar holds an advanced degree in acupuncture and has practiced chi gung and Tuina bodywork therapy in Chinese hospitals and clinics. As a young man, Kumar trained in kung fu while earning black belts in judo, ju-jitsu, karate and aikido.

Each summer, Kumar and his staff lead two 6-day intensive workshop retreats at Ranch Retreat — 45 minutes north of San Francisco. The first retreat allows students to choose one of two tai chi courses — "Wu Long Form" and "Wu Short Form Energy Mechanics." The second retreat allows a choice of two chi gung courses — "Spiraling Energy Body" and (for beginners) "Opening the Energy Gates."

During the retreats, Taoist meditation is practiced every other day from 7 to 8 AM. During the tai chi retreat, push hands is offered at 7 on alternate mornings. Each day there is 5 hours of tai chi or chi gung class instruction. Between classes, students can hot tub, swim, and hike in the hills of the 12,000 acre ranch. Ranch Retreat lies in Sonoma County wine country less than 20 miles from scenic Point Reyes National Seashore.

Address   1 Cascade Drive, Fairfax, CA 94930, USA

Phone   415/454-5243.

Season   First 2 weeks of August.

Programs   Two 6-day intensive retreats — the first on tai chi and the second on chi gung. The tai chi retreat requires knowledge of the Wu short form. Health aspects are emphasized, but self-defense also is taught. The chi gung retreat, open to beginners, teaches the use of Water and Earth energies.

Lodging   Large rooms for 3 to 8 people, a few 2-bed rooms for couples, plus tent sites. Those attending both retreats can stay at the ranch on the intervening Sunday night for a small fee.

Rates $725 for each retreat.

Meals   Food is provided but participants are requested to help prepare and clean up after meals.

Services   Free at each retreat: a 1 PM shuttle from Santa Rosa to Ranch Retreat on the 1st day and a 1 PM shuttle back on the final day.

Land of Medicine Buddha   Soquel, CA

Land of Medicine Buddha is one of the many FPMT (Foundation for the Preservation of the Mahayana Tradition) centers founded around the world by the late Lama Thubten Yeshe and Lama Zopa Rinpoche. Located 75 miles south of San Francisco and a few miles inland from the Pacific coast, the center occupies 55 acres of forest and meadow land bordering a state park. The property includes trails, a sauna and a swimming pool.

All center programs are designed to help people release their potential to live healthy, happy lives. Programs include "Chi Gung," "Wu Je Chi" and "Jin Shin Jyutsu" life energy workshops; "Insight Meditation," "Nyung Ne Purification" and "Medicine Buddha" retreats; plus residentials on dreamwork, initiation, "Awakening to Spirit" through shamanic traditions, astrology and tarot as intuitive tools, plus organic gardening and cooking.

The center generally offers 3 to 6 residential programs each month. The faculty is composed mostly of visiting teachers. The center's small staff invites workshop participants to contribute one or two hours of work — usually in the kitchen or on the grounds. There are weekly, public chi gung classes, Dharma talks and meditations. When residential programs are not in session, individuals may stay at the center on a getaway basis.

Address   5800 Prescott Road, Soquel, CA 95073, USA

Phone   408/462-8383. No visits without prior arrangement.

Season   Year-round.

Programs   2 to 7-day programs with teachings from different spiritual traditions. Focus on experiential healing of mind & body.

Lodging   Most guests share a room with 1 or more others. Attached bathroom. A few private rooms.

Rates   Program tuition: weekend $75-200 (most $115); 3-day dreamwork $275; 11-day (one 3 & two 4-day sessions) Wu Je Chi $450; "Medicine Buddha" — 3-day $75, 7-day $175; other retreats — donations only. Room & meals: generally $46/day, though as low as $33/day during Buddhist retreats.

Meals   3 bountiful & varied vegetarian buffets served each day.

Services   Massage, acupuncture, personal counseling therapies.

Madre Grande Monastery   Dulzura, CA

Madre Grande is a 264 acre wildlife sanctuary and retreat center set in a valley on the slope of Mother Grundy Mountain, 15 miles southwest of San Diego and a few miles north of the Mexico border. On the grounds is a combination sanctuary/library/meeting facility, a meditation dome, a medicine wheel, a campfire circle, a sweat lodge, hiking trails and several lakes — often the site of unsupervised, suit optional swimming.

Madre Grande is also headquarters of the Paracelsian Order and the home of a small community of male and female Johannine Catholic monks, who raise bees. The Order and center welcome monks and guests of all ages, religious and cultural backgrounds. The center hosts solstice and equinox weekend gatherings with ceremonies and workshops on various holistic healing practices. Each October, it also hosts a 4-day Peace & Unity Prayer-Dance created from traditions of the indigenous American peoples.

Each weekday morning there is group meditation on mindfulness and loving kindness. Regular weekend activities include an early Friday evening reading/discussion on comparative philosophy, a late Friday evening video (usually on some general aspect of spiritual practice), Saturday evening hot tub, early Sunday morning Bible class, and mid-Sunday morning Johannine Catholic Eucharist. Gnostic Mass is held on the last Sunday of each month.

Address   18372 Highway 94, Dulzura, CA 91917, USA

Phone   619/468-3810 (voice mail system).

Season   Year-round.

Programs   Equinox & solstice weekend celebrations. Also regular broadly ecumenical spiritual practice activities — mostly on weekends.

Lodging   Single & double rooms, dorms, caves "in early neolithic decor (no utilities)," vehicle & tentsite camping. Solar heated showers.

Rates   Nightly rates: single room $30; double room $40; dorm bed $20; cave, tent & vehicle campsites — adult $10, child over 12 yrs. $5, child under 12 yrs. free. Dinner $5. Breakfast $3.

Meals   Family style vegetarian breakfast & dinner — mostly organic.

Services   Healing massage.

Manzanita Village   Warner Springs, CA

Manzanita Village is a new, 18 acre meditation center backing on the canyons of Cleveland National Forest at a 3300 foot altitude 45 minutes west of Escondido. In 1993, the center hosted four weekend retreats including one with deep ecology ritual, meditation and inter-active exercises "to hear within ourselves the sound of the Earth crying." Two weekend retreats combined meditation with the practice of aikido. There were also 4 and 8-day meditation retreats, each with a 4-day option.

All 1993 retreats were led by Christopher Reed and Michele Benzamin-Masuda, both students of Thich Nhat Hanh and deep ecology teacher/activist Joanna Macy. Chris is a clinical hypnotherapist with many years of Vipassana meditation experience. Michele is an artist and performer with black-belts in both Aikido and Iaido. Beyond 1993, the center will also host public guided meditation retreats led by other teachers (such as Lama Surya Das).

Address   Ordinary Dharma, 246 Horizon, Venice, CA 90291, USA

Phone   310/396-5054. No visits without prior arrangement.

Season   Year-round.

Programs Teacher-led meditation retreats ranging from a weekend to 10 days in length. Also individual retreats & long stays by arrangement.

Lodging   Men's & women's dorms in 4-room bunkhouse with kitchen & shower. Toilets in nearby outhouse. BYO sleeping bag.

Rates   Teacher-led retreats: weekend $185, 3 & 4-day $185, 8-day $245, 10-day $275. Partial scholarships available. Individual retreat $25 per day.

Meals   3 daily vegetarian meals.

Meadowlark Village   Hemet, CA

In the foothills of the San Jacinto Mountains, 40 miles from the ocean and roughly equidistant from metropolitan Los Angeles and San Diego, Meadowlark Village is a 35 year old, nonsectarian holistic health center. The pastoral 20 acre setting contains a crafts and pottery shop, holistic health library, orchard, vegetable garden, putting green, swimming pool, sun deck and hot tub, bio-feedback and exercise equipment.

The weekly "Guests & Craft" Program runs from Monday evening to Sunday morning. Each week covers two or three themes such as "Spiritual Wisdom,"

"Mind/Body Healing," "Psychoneuroimmunology," "Sacred Music," and "Career/ Life Design." The Program includes an M.D.-guided fitness regimen; yoga and aerobics; crafts such as pottery, jewelry, weaving, painting and flower arranging; classes relating to the week's themes; and chapel quiet times.

Address   26126 Fairview Avenue, Hemet, CA 92544, USA

Phone   909/927-7000.   Fax 714/927-0268.

Season   Year-round.

Programs Weekly 6-night/5-day holistic health program.

Lodging   Capacity for up to 50 overnight guests in single & double occupancy rooms, each with private bath.

Rates   Daily rates: double occupancy $146, single occupancy $295.

Meals   3 gourmet vegetarian meals/day.

Services   Spiritual & psychological counseling, therapeutic body treatments.

Mendocino Summer Retreat   Mendocino, CA

Mendocino Summer Retreat is an annual holistic health family camp three hours north of San Francisco. The major camp activities are morning presentations on the retreat's theme ("Awakening to Community" in 1993) and afternoon workshops on topics such as cooking, drawing and painting, journal writing, organic gardening and home remedies. There are pre-breakfast meditation, yoga and tai chi sessions; late afternoon group projects and discussions; evening meditations and campfire gatherings.

The event's sponsors are Joel Huckins and Donna Wilson. Joel is a San Francisco Bay area owner/operator of a macrobiotic grocery, restaurant and learning center. Donna is a Los Angeles area owner/operator of a bookstore and natural foods cooking school. Joel and Donna usually hold the event at a riverside, redwood forest campground with trails and meadow areas plus dining and classroom areas furnished with fireplaces and electricity.

Address   The Ginko Leaf, 21109 Costanso St., Woodland Hills, CA 91364, USA

Phone   818/716-6332 or 800/700-4499.

Season   8-10 days in late June &/or early July.

Programs Annual family retreat focusing on the elements of holistic living — nutrition, inner development and environmental awareness.

Lodging   Cabins with 2 & 4 beds. BYO bedding. Hot & cold running spring water showers & flushing toilets in 4 group areas.

Rates   Adult $425. Child 2-12 years $150. Child under 2 $75.

Meals   3 daily vegetarian meals made by experienced macrobiotic cooks. Snacks, desserts & beverages available for purchase in cafe.

Services Cost includes full day children's program staffed by experienced Waldorf teacher & assistants. (Parents may be asked to assist 1 morning &/or afternoon.) Other services: bodywork, nutritional counseling, psychological type profiles.

Mount Madonna Center   Watsonville, CA

Mount Madonna Center is a spiritual education and retreat center operated by a non sectarian, international community of about 75 adults and 30 children. The center's 355 acres contain 30 buildings in redwood forest and grasslands overlooking Monterey Bay from a mountain top east of Santa Cruz. On the grounds are hiking trails; a hot tub and a small lake suitable for swimming; a gym; volleyball, tennis and basketball courts.

Mount Madonna's programs are led by well known teachers from throughout North America. Recent program topics included sacred ecology, shamanism, creative self-expression, inner child work, Zen meditation, Ayurveda, Sanskrit training, a meditative Shuva/Yom Kippur retreat, and many hatha yoga offerings. Program participants are invited to join in ongoing center celebration, work and play activities. Those interested in a longer stay may apply for work/study, half or full-time staff status.

The center is sponsored by the 400 member Hanuman Fellowship, a diverse group unified in practice of yoga as a spiritual path. A number of these people were among the center's founders — all followers of Baba Hari Dass. Present at center yoga retreats and at services several times each week, Baba Dass has maintained continuous silence (communicating by writing on a slate) for over 40 years.

Address   445 Summit Road, Watsonville, CA 95076, USA

Phone   408/847-0406.   Fax 408/847-2683.

Season   Year-round.

Programs Weekend and longer workshops & retreats designed to nurture the creative arts & health sciences in a spiritual growth context.

Lodging   Accommodations for up to 300 overnight guests in single, double, triple & dorm (4-7 person) rooms; center tents; own tent or van. Most rooms share bathrooms. Campsites have running water.

Rates   Programs: multi-day workshops $60/day, 4-day yoga retreats $60. Lodging: Rooms — single $65, double $49, triple $43, dorm $38; center tent $27; own tent or van $22.

Meals　Cafeteria style breakfast, dinner & snack — vegetarian, with dairy options & produce from own gardens.

Services　Oil massage & herbal steam bath.

Ojai Foundation　　　　　　　　　　　　Ojai, CA

Less than a 2 hour drive northwest of Los Angeles, the Ojai Foundation is a rustic camp in a semi-wilderness setting bordering Los Padres National Forest. The camp is run by four resident caretakers assisted by work exchange students, each contributing up to 25 hours of work each week.

Ojai's group retreats and workshops emphasize personal reflection, self-renewal, creation of sacred space, and deep connection with the natural world. Program topics include vision fast training, spiritual ecology, bioregionalism, and permaculture. 1993 program titles included "Singing the World Alive," "Earth as Home," and "Meeting the Shadow." Ojai also supports 1 to 5-day vision fasts and individual retreats of up to 30 days.

All group programs are facilitated by counselors, educators, writers and artists, mostly from southern California. Some programs are restricted to Ojai's Council of Friends, educators, environmentalists or therapists. The Foundation was founded in 1980 by Joan Halifax — author, anthropologist and teacher/practitioner of shamanistic and Buddhist wisdom.

Address　P.O. Box 1620, Ojai, CA 93024, USA

Phone　805/646-8434. No visits without prior arrangement.

Season　Late February through June and October through December.

Programs　2 to 5-day group retreats & workshops encouraging spiritual healing through a deeper connection to soul and nature. Also individual retreats & vision fasts plus work exchange program.

Lodging　Campsites & hermitages: domes, yurts & tipis. Flush toilets, hot shower, sinks. BYO sleeping bag.

Rates　Group programs: 1 1/2 to 3-day weekend $160-285, 5-day $600. Individual retreat: own tent $18/night, hermitage rental $30/night, personalized vision fast approximately $100. Work exchange $100/month (food not included).

Meals　"Camp-style" food preparation & eating area. BYO food.

Pocket Ranch　　　　　　　　　　　　Geyersville, CA

Pocket Ranch is a rolling 2600 acre property in the Alexander Valley wine country, two hours north of San Francisco. Nestled in the shadows of Geyser and Pocket Peaks, the Ranch is a peaceful grazing ground for cattle, horses and deer. It is also a sanctuary-like setting for workshops and retreats run by a staff of clinical psychologists, psychiatric nurses, counselors and interns under the direction of Ranch founder Barbara Findeisen, a leader in the field of pre and peri-natal psychology.

The Ranch's STAR program is a 17 or 21-day individualized intensive process conducted in a group context within a safe and nurturing environment. Healing modalities include individual processing sessions, daily writing assignments, breathwork, emotional release work, guided imagery, sand-tray therapy, and integrative bodywork. STAR is designed to help adults recover their natural condition of emotional vibrancy, openness and love.

The "Woodlands Program" offers short-term residential treatment for adults experiencing acute distress from burnout, grief, childhood and sexual abuse issues, and spiritual emergency. The program provides round-the-clock clinical care using both traditional and alternative healing methods to assist people return as quickly as possible to well functioning lives. The average length of stay is two to three weeks.

The Ranch also offers various workshops including a year-end "Holiday Spiritual Renewal Workshop," "Healing Pre & Peri-Natal Wounds," "Women and Spirituality," and "Gay Men and Spirituality." Participants have access to hiking trails, an outdoor swimming pool, jacuzzi, and volleyball court.

Address   P.O. Box 516, Geyersville, CA 95441, USA

Phone   707/857-3359.   Fax 707/857-3764.

Season   Year-round.

Programs STAR programs — 21 & 17-day intensive inner journeys; "Woodlands" treatment program for people in emotional or spiritual crisis; individual self-directed retreats; 2 to 6-day workshops.

Lodging   Double occupancy accommodations for 40 in rustic cabins. "Woodlands" guests separately housed in a comfortable building with open air decks & a whirlpool bath.

Rates   STAR: 21-day $5,100-5,200, 17-day $4,280-4,360. "Woodlands": $600 per day plus cost of off-site psychiatric consultations (if necessary). Self-directed retreat: double $80, single $95. Workshops: 2 to 4-day $230-370, 6-day $590-655.

Meals   3 tasty, daily meals. Selections for meat-eaters & vegetarians.

Services   Individual counseling, sand-tray therapy, emotional release work, hypnosis, birth work, breathwork, and bodywork/massage (Swedish, Esalen, shiatsu & deep tissue).

Redwood River Lodge   South of Eureka, CA

Dr. Rosalind "Skyhawk" Ojala and the Thunderbird Clan each summer conduct a 7-day "Visions of the Goddess" women's gathering in two parts — a 3-day session introducing beginners to a rich heritage of the American Goddess tradition and teachings; and a 4-day session for advanced students and teachers in the Crone Dancing Women Come Thundering Lodge. This camp accommodates up to 50 tenters in an old grove Redwood park.

Skyhawk also conducts two annual, 7-day "Sacred Tree Teachings" apprentice camps — one for beginners and one for graduates. Each is limited to 10 men and women, who camp on the four acre property of Skyhawk's home (with hot tub and organic garden) on the Van Dusen River. Apprentices receive thorough training, a ritual guide gook, a tape and a class/circle format.

Skyhawk, of Blackfoot and Ojibway descent, learned the medicine ways from her grandmother and elders. After 25 years of teaching these ways, Skyhawk believes that "the essence of humanness can only be found within service to others." Her emphasis on teacher apprenticeship reflects that belief.

Address   Dr. Rosalind Ojala, 111 Orchard Lane, Carlotta, CA 95528, USA

Phone   707/768-3226. No visits without prior arrangement.

Season   Summer.

Programs 7-day "Visions of the Goddess" women's gathering & 6-day "Sacred Tree Teachings" apprentice camps for men & women.

Lodging   BYO tent & sleeping bag.

Rates   Goddess Gathering — Session I $200, Session II $300, both with a pit barbecue. Apprentice camp $300, no meals provided.

Meals   BYO food, camp stove & cooking gear. Access to refrigerator, coffee & tea for apprentices only.

Self-Realization Fellowship Retreats   Metro San Diego, CA

Self-Realization Fellowship (SRF) operates two southern California retreat centers, both 25-30 miles north of San Diego. The Encinitas center hosts co-ed and women-only retreats in a beautifully landscaped 17 acre property overlooking the Pacific from a bluff above a beach. 30 miles east in Escondido, the Hidden Valley center hosts men-only retreats on 100+ acres of peaceful hill country.

Both centers offer general and conducted weekend retreats. General retreats include devotional services, evening classes, daily meditation sessions (15 minutes of energization exercises and 45 minutes of sitting), plus personal counseling. Conducted weekend retreats have more classes, less free time, and are restricted to SRF members and students.

SRF was founded by the late India-born yogi Paramahansa Yogananda (author of the widely read "Autobiography of a Yogi") to teach the spiritual practice of Kriya Yoga.

Address   3880 San Rafael Avenue, Los Angeles, CA 90065, USA

Phone   213/225-2471. No visits without prior arrangement.

Season   Year-round.

Programs   1 to 14-day general retreats open to all. Conducted weekend retreats for SRF members & lesson students.

Lodging   Private single rooms, all with shared baths at Encinitas and half with private baths at Escondido.

Rates   Suggested donation: general retreat $50/day, conducted weekend retreat $60/day.

Meals   3 daily vegetarian meals.

Shasta Abbey   Mount Shasta, CA

Set on 16 acres of evergreen forested land near majestic Mount Shasta, Shasta Abbey is a monastery in the Buddhist tradition of Serene Reflection Meditation (a hybrid of Japanese Soto Zen and Chinese Tsao-Tung). The abbey is home for 35 male and female monks under the spiritual guidance of Rev. P.T.N.H. Jiyu-Kennett, a British native certified in Japan as a Meditation Master. Rev. Jiyu-Kennett's formal music education is reflected in the 4-part harmony of morning and evening offices sung in English.

Shasta Abbey also serves as a retreat center for lay peole who are interested in Buddhist training. Nearly every month, the abbey hosts introductory weekends with meditation instruction and basic Buddhist teachings. Other programs open to all are weeklong "Basic Teaching and Practice" retreats conducted during the summer.

A typical introductory weekend begins with a Friday afternoon orientation followed by dinner, meditation instruction and meditation. Saturday wake-up and lights out times are 5:55 AM and 10 PM. During the day there are sitting meditation periods, classes, services, working meditation periods, and times for rest and spiritual reading. After a similar Sunday morning schedule, guests depart after lunch. Social conversation is limited to tea times, and all guests must follow the schedule.

People who have attended an introductory retreat or a "Basic Teaching & Practice" retreat may apply for non-introductory weekend and week retreats that emphasize formal meditation. They may also apply for resident lay training, which focuses on applying meditation in daily life. An important part of the practice is bringing to all activities the compassionate awareness of meditation.

Address   P.O. Box 199, Mount Shasta, CA 96067, USA

Phone   916/926-4208. Contact 1+ month before preferred visit period.

Season   Open to guests year-round except 3-4 weeks in late Dec/early Jan.

Programs   Weekend & weeklong retreats on meditation & Buddhist teachings. Also short or long-term resident lay & monastic training.

Lodging   20 guest house rooms — all private except during large retreats.

Rates   Weekend retreats: introductory $70, other $60. Weeklong retreats $130-150.   Resident training: 1-week $90, 2 weeks $160, 3 weeks $230, per month $300.

Meals   3 daily vegetarian meals (including eggs & dairy products). Meals are usually held formally & eaten in silence.

Services   Spiritual counseling; Buddhist weddings, child namings, funeral & memorial services; quarterly "Journal"; and Buddhist supplies.

Shenoa Retreat and Learning Center   Philo, CA

About 2 /12 hours north of San Francisco, Shenoa is a 160 acre retreat and learning center adjoining Hendy Woods State Park and bounded on three sides by the Navarro River. The grounds include an open air sanctuary, a large meadow, hiking trails, a swimming hole and a swimming pool. Guests can also enjoy tennis, volleyball, ping pong and badminton.

Founded by former members of Scotland's Findhorn community, Shenoa hosts programs focusing on positive personal and planetary transformation. The annual schedule of 20 or so events includes holiday weekend family gatherings, yoga retreats and vacations, and a "Course in Miracles Camp."

1993 offerings also included a one-week spiritual fasting retreat, a one-week "Living with Focusing" workshop, and a two-week "Deep Ecology School." Shenoa also offers personal retreats, work exchange visits up to two weeks long, a 6-month garden intern program, and a learning environment (two hours of weekly classroom study plus optional classes) for employees.

Address   P.O. Box 43, Philo, CA 95466, USA

Phone   707/895-3156.   Fax 707/895-3236.

Season   May through November (plus Dec. & Jan. on a limited basis).

Programs   2 to 14-day workshops, retreats & family gatherings focusing on holistic health, community building and environmental harmony. Guests make reservations directly with the visiting teachers.

Lodging   2 to 5-person cabins with comfortable beds, handmade quilts, hot showers & electricity. Couples & families guaranteed private spaces. Campsites with lighted trail to bathrooms & showers.

Rates Program rates range: 3-day family gathering — cabin $143, tent $88; 2-week deep ecology school — cabin $1,400, tent $1,140. Personal retreat: cabin — weekday $53, weekend $58; tent — $29.

Meals 3 daily gourmet vegetarian meals with produce from 1-acre organic garden. Non-dairy entrees available on request.

Sivananda Ashram Yoga Farm   Grass Valley, CA

The 80 acre Sivananda Ashram Yoga Farm lies in a valley in the northern Sierra Nevada foothills about 90 minutes from both Sacramento and Lake Tahoe. The simple farmhouse serves as an all purpose lodge, dining hall, practice and meeting facility. Meals are at 10 AM and 6 PM. Daily hatha yoga sessions are at 8 AM and 4 PM. The day begins and ends with satsang -meditation, chanting, readings and discussion.

Each weekend has a theme such as "Fasting, Diet & Health," a juice fasting weekend that explores the role of food in health and spiritual practice. Another popular theme is "Five Points for a Healthy, Balanced Life" — exercise, proper breathing, proper diet, proper relaxation, positive thinking/meditation. Theme topics are often discussed or demonstrated in mid-day lectures or workshops. Otherwise, 11 AM to 4 PM is free time.

Address 14651 Ballantree Lane, Grass Valley, CA 95949, USA

Phone 916/272-9322.   Fax 914/434-1032.

Season Year-round.

Programs Regular daily program, with mandatory attendance of hatha yoga and meditation sessions. Classes taught by ashram staff. Also work-study program and 4-week May Teachers' Training Camp.

Lodging 8 guest rooms with 3 beds each plus shared showers & toilets. Tent space on the grounds. Limited access for the disabled.

Rates Adult nightly rates: tent site $25, dorm $35, double $40, private $50. Rates $5/night higher on holiday weekends. Teachers' Training Camp: outdoors camping $1,295, dorm $1,545.

Meals 2 daily buffet style, vegetarian meals.

Services Massage.

Sonoma Mountain Zen Center   Santa Rosa, CA

Sonoma Mountain Zen Center is a cluster of spare wooden buildings set on 80 hilltop acres 11 miles southeast of Santa Rosa. The 20 year old center is run by a small residential community under the spiritual direction of Jakusho Kwong-roshi, the Chinese-American born Dharma successor to the late Soto Zen master Shunryu Suzuki-roshi.

Those new to meditation and/or Zen may come on designated Saturdays to an "Introduction Zen Workshop" (9 AM to 4 PM) or a "One Day Sitting" (4:45 AM to 5 PM). A first time attendee may stay for free at the center on the preceding Friday night. During the July "Ango Practice" period, more ambitious guests may participate in one week to one month of regular daily practice — including six daily meditation periods.

The center's formal Guest Practice Program allows visitors to experience "everyday Zen" by living and practicing in the community for anywhere from a few days to three months. Daily practice includes morning and evening meditation (sitting and walking), chanting, 3 1/2 hours of work-practice, informal communal meals, study groups and private interviews. Each day begins at 5:15 AM and ends at nine.

Serious Zen students may apply for resident training, which requires full participation in all center activities including intensive three to five-day retreats (each with 10 daily meditation periods).

Address   Genjo-ji, 6367 Sonoma Mountain Road, Santa Rosa, CA 95404, USA

Phone   707/545-8105 mornings. No visits without prior arrangement.

Season   Year-round except last 2 weeks in December.

Programs   Introductory 1-day workshops and sittings, 3 to 5-day intensive retreats, guest residency opportunities ranging from a few days to 3 months, and residency training program.

Lodging   3 bedroom house with bath & kitchen plus 5 rustic cabins heated by wood stoves & electric heaters. BYO sleeping bag.

Rates   "Introduction Zen Workshop" $35. "One Day Sitting" $25. Intensive retreat $30/day. Guest residency $20/day. Residency training $390/month.

Meals   3 daily vegetarian meals.

Spirit Rock Center   San Francisco Bay Area, CA

Spirit Rock is a non-residential retreat center consisting of a meditation hall and kitchen/dining hall on 400 acres of rolling hills and meadows 30 miles north of San Francisco. Residential facilities are planned for 1996. Until then, residential programs are being conducted at rented facilities.

Residential retreats are led by Spirit Rock teachers such as Jack Kornfield, James Baraz and Sylvia Boorstein. Most retreats have a 5 AM to 10 PM daily schedule with sitting and walking meditation, group and individual interviews with instructors, plus talks on Buddhist teachings.

Current Spirit Rock on-site activities include evening classes and one-day (9 AM to 5 PM) weekend retreats for people new to meditation. One-day retreatants bring their own sitting cushions.

Address   P.O. Box 909, Woodacre, CA 94973, USA

Phone   415/488-0164. Fax 415/488-0170. Call before visiting.

Season   Year-round.

Programs Non-sectarian courses & retreats (1-20 days long) usually on Vipassana (insight) & Metta (loving kindness) meditation.

Lodging   Generally men's & women's dorms.

Rates   Non-residential program — 1-day $20, 2-day $40, plus teacher donation. Residential program — 2 or 3-day $75-180, 7-day $280-325, 10-day $390, 20-day $780 ($10/day discount for those unable to pay full cost). Teacher donations made at end of retreat.

Meals   Residential retreat — vegetarian breakfast, large lunch and late afternoon tea. One-day retreatants bring their own lunch.

Tassajara   Carmel Valley, CA

Tassajara is a remote, year-round Zen monastery open to guests during the summer months. Overlooking the Pacific Ocean from deep in the heavily forested and mountainous Ventana Wilderness, the community is located 2 hours southeast of Carmel at the end of a 14-mile dirt road that climbs 5,000 feet in 6 miles, levels off for 3 miles, then descends steeply.

Originally constructed as a hot springs resort, Tassajara features a bath house with showers, steam rooms, creekside sun decks, large plunges and small tubs fed by hot sulphur springs. Men and women bathe in separate areas. Guests can also enjoy a swimming pool and hiking trails that wind out into the wilderness, once the native soil of the Esalen Indians.

Each year, the center hosts about a dozen Zen retreats and workshops. In 1993, these included two "Zen/Yoga" workshops, a "Zen-Vipassana" retreat, and a "LamRim/Zen Way" retreat. Other workshops explored Zen pain therapy, sensory awareness, Zen and nature, organic gardening/vegetarian cooking, and spiritual poetry. Many program leaders are associated with Tassajara and its sister organizations San Francisco Zen Center and Green Gulch Farm.

There are also "Guest Practice" and "Work-Practice" programs. For a minimum of three days, a "Guest Practice" participant joins in the morning monastic schedule — Zen meditation at 6 AM followed by 3 1/2 hours of work. Participants may also meet with program teachers plus attend classes and lectures. For anywhere from five days to the entire summer season, Work-

Practice participants follow the monastic schedule of meditation and work. Season-long participants may enrol free in some workshops and retreats.

Address   Zen Center, 300 Page Street, San Francisco, CA 94102, USA

Phone   415/431-3771. No visits without prior arrangement.

Season   May through early September.

Programs 5-day Zen retreats. 4 & 5-day workshops. Guest Practice & Work-Practice programs. Resort vacation stays.

Lodging   Rustic dorms, cabins, yurts & suites with no phone & no electricity. Linens, blankets & towels provided. Rooms & pathways lighted by kerosene lamps. Shared & private bathrooms.

Rates   Zen retreats: shared $500-690, single $690-930. Workshops: shared $480-790; single $635-1,030. "Guest Practice" $45/night. "Work Practice" $10/night for 7 nights, then free. Resort vacation stays: dorm $65-75; cabins & rooms — shared $75-129; single $110-180; child 3-11 $40-50; child under 3 free.

Meals   3 tasty, buffet style vegetarian meals each day. Options of non-dairy dinner & oil-free salad at lunch.

Services   Jamesburg pick-up & delivery by 4-wheel-drive "Stage."

Vega Institute   Oroville, CA

1 1/2 hours north of Sacramento on Highway 70, Vega Institute is located in the residential heart of Oroville. A few blocks away is the peaceful Feather River. The surrounding countryside is rich with organic farms and orchards — a suitable environment for a 20 year old residential study center dedicated to teaching macrobiotics as a way of life.

The Institute hosts two to five programs each month. The most frequent offering is the 12-day "Macrobiotic Lifestyle & Essentials" — a course on the elements (including cooking) of a macrobiotic lifestyle. Workshops focusing on psychospiritual healing include "12 Steps and Macrobiotics," and "Personal Journeys through Ancient Pathways." Other residential programs include "Cancer and Healing," cooking and counselor trainings.

All programs are conducted by Institute program directors David and Cindy Briscoe with assistance from Institute founders Herman and Cornellia Aihara. David specializes in macrobiotic counseling and education. Cindy is a chef and cooking class instructor. The Aiharas have over 40 years of experience as teachers of macrobiotics throughout the world.

Address   1511 Robinson Street, Oroville, CA 95965, USA

Phone   916/533-7702.   Fax 916/533-7908.

Season   Year-round.

Programs   Weekend, 5-day, 2-week to 4-week programs on macrobiotic cooking, healing, lifestyle and counseling.

Lodging   Cottage, private rooms, double rooms for couples, and 8 shared occupancy rooms. All rooms near private saunas, tubs & showers. Most have sink & toilet. Natural cotton futon beds. BYO linens.

Rates   Tuition, shared room & board: per day $150, 1 week $595, 2 weeks $1,095. Add $100/week for private room or $200/week for cottage. Discounts for 1 month advance registration or if registering with a companion: per day $25, 1 week $50, 2 weeks $100.

Meals   2 daily macrobiotic meals with plenty of locally grown organic grains & produce.

Services   Macrobiotic counseling.

We Care Health Center   Desert Hot Springs, CA

Guests at We Care Health Center can enjoy the swimming pool, nearby hot mineral springs, and early morning walks in the desert — usually with vistas of the jagged San Jacinto Mountains etched against an azure sky. Along with this natural beauty, clean air and exercise, guests also enjoy the friendly atmosphere fostered by Center director Susana Lombardi — a certified lymphologist, massage and colon therapist.

We Care offers a rejuvenation program through an all natural liquid diet. Both Private and Retreat types of accommodation are offered with 8-day, 6-day and weekend programs. 8 and 6-day program elements include yoga classes (meditative light stretching), nutrition classes, cooking demonstrations, lymphatic massages, and colon hygiene.

Address   18000 Long Canyon Road, Desert Hot Springs, CA 92241, USA

Phone   619/251-2261 or 800/888-2523.

Season   Year-round.

Programs   8-day Deluxe Revitalization (Plan A), 6-day Vegetarian Cleanse (Plan B), weekend Mini Cleanse (Plan C).

Lodging   Private: large private room (in main building) with TV, telephone, maid service & private bath. Retreat: small private room sharing a bath & with no TV, phone or maid service.

Rates   Plan A: Private $1,299, Retreat $999. Plan B: Private $1,050, Retreat $850. Plan C: Private $399, Retreat $299.

Meals   Hourly drinks — raw vegetable juices, herbal teas, water with lemon, and detox drinks (with psyllium, bentonite, chlorophyll).

Services Massage (shiatsu, deep tissue & lymphatic), foot reflexology, aromatherapy, iridology, scalp revitalization, ear cleaning, colon hygiene, salt rubs, herbal glows, facials.

Wellspring Renewal Center   Philo, CA

Wellspring Renewal Center is a 45 acre retreat site 20 miles inland from the Mendocino coast. The farmhouse and cabins open onto rolling meadows cut through by the beautiful Navarro River, suitable for summer rafting and swimming. The property includes volleyball and basketball courts, a sweat lodge, campground, campfire pit, plus trails into the redwood forests of an adjacent state park. Private retreatants are welcome when programs are not in progress. All guests are asked to contribute one hour of work each day.

Some Wellspring programs are loosely structured family weekends hosted by the resident staff. But most programs are led by visiting teachers on topics such as "Storytelling," "Reclaiming Scripture," "Art & Imagery," and "Healing as a Spiritual Gift." Annual programs include "Twelve Steps in Spiritual Living," "Arts & Crafts Week," "Five Day Silent Retreat," "Women's Fall Renewal Weekend," and "Winter Solstice Celebration."

Address P.O. Box 332, Philo, CA 95466, USA

Phone 707/895-3893. No visits without prior arrangement.

Season Year-round.

Programs Weekend, 5 & 7-day programs focusing on healing, creativity and spirituality that are in harmony with nature.

Lodging Accommodations for over 80 guests in 2 lodges with double bedrooms & small kitchens, 3 modernized & 4 rustic cabins.

Rates Programs: weekend — adult $75-170, child $45-65; 5 to 7-day — adult $200-975, child $110-160. Room & board: lodges & modern cabins — adult $25, child $10; rustic cabins — adult $18, child $8; 15% week night winter season discounts.

Meals 3 daily meals — mostly vegetarian with fruit & vegetables from organic garden & neighboring farms. Bake own breads & deserts.

White Lotus Foundation   Santa Barbara, CA

With a main building snug against a canyon wall on the San Marcos Pass, White Lotus is a 40 acre yoga training and retreat center overlooking Santa Barbara, the Pacific Ocean and the Channel Islands. Guests can hike to the nearby Chumash Medicine Caves and swim in the Red Rock sandstone pools or at the Santa Barbara beaches.

During most residential programs, the day begins with optional silent meditation followed by asana practice and instruction. Early afternoons are free for hikes, massage or relaxation. At 4 there is a second hatha yoga session. Supper is followed by program discussions, guest speakers or special activites such as music, dance, meditation and fire ceremony.

The most frequent programs are weekend workshops, holiday retreats, and 16-day "In-Depth Yoga & Teacher Trainings" (open to all levels). Between scheduled programs, White Lotus can accommodate individual retreatants — welcome to use the kitchen for vegetarian meals, read in the airy living room/ library, and participate in the twice weekly hatha yoga classes.

A pioneer of modern yoga, White Lotus founder Ganga White invented Double Yoga (practiced by 2 people). He and co-director Tracey Rich favor the Vinyasa approach, "linking the poses into a flow that becomes an exhilarating union of asana, pranayama, and meditation."

Address   2500 San Marco Pass, Santa Barbara, CA 93105, USA

Phone   805\964-1944.

Season   Year-round.

Programs   Hatha yoga. Unstructured personal retreat; weekend workshops & retreats; 5-day programs; and 16-day "Yoga Training" programs open to beginners but designed primarily to certify teachers.

Lodging   Capacity for 28 overnight guests. Indoors futon bedding in the loft; 5 heated yurts each sleeping up to 4; campsites along the creek, in the bay forest, or on the plateau overlooking the city.

Rates   Personal retreat $35/night with no meals or $125/night with massage, continental breakfast & dinner; weekend workshops & retreats $250-285; 5-day programs $595-650; Yoga Training $1,650.

Meals   2 daily gourmet vegetarian meals — a large brunch & supper. Hot tea, juices and fresh fruit in the morning.

Services   Massage, shiatsu, acupuncture & chiropractic.

Zen Mountain Center   Mountain Center, CA

Zen Mountain Center (ZMC) is a rustic meditation retreat set on 160 acres in a steep mountain canyon at an altitude of 5,500 feet and a distance of 120 miles southeast of Los Angeles. The cabins and meditation hall are of unfinished wood. Solar energy provides electricity and bathhouse water heating. The Pacific Coast trail through the San Jacinto Mountains cuts across a corner of the property, from which point the Pacific Ocean is visible over the mountains 60 miles to the west.

A small community lives at ZMC throughout the year, supporting private meditation retreats and occasional weekend theme retreats. Typical theme retreats are "Tai Chi and Zen," "Beginners Mind" (an introductory meditation retreat), and "Life As Art" (with classes in tea ceremony, bamboo flute and one stroke brush painting). All ZMC programs are led by abbots and other members of Zen Center of Los Angeles (ZCLA).

Each summer there is a 90-day practice period including three intensive one-week retreats. Each day of this "Ango" period begins at 4:30 AM and includes seven hours of sitting meditation, teacher/student interviews, work periods, and study of a discipline such as tai chi, Alexander Technique, yoga, tea ceremony, sutra chanting or calligraphy. Each week there is a 1 1/2 day break from scheduled activities. Guests may join in Ango for anywhere from a few days to the entire three month period.

Address   P.O. Box 43, Mountain Center, CA 92561, USA

Phone   909/659-5272. No visits without prior arrangement.

Season   Year-round.

Programs 2 & 3-day weekend theme retreats, intensive one-week meditation retreats, summer meditation practice, plus private retreats.

Lodging   Dormitory housing for up to 30 in small cabins & trailers. Also 20 summer campsites. Bathhouses & outhouses. BYO sleeping bag.

Rates   Daily rates: ZCLA member $30, non-member $50. Monthly rates: ZCLA member $450, non-member $550, with own tent $500. Those who help with Ango set-up get 6 weeks of Ango practice at 2/3rds off.

Meals   3 daily vegetarian meals, generally eaten together oryoki-style. Oryoki sets can be purchased at the center for $22.

Services   Car pooling between ZMC and ZCLA can generally be arranged.

Hawaiian Healing Arts and Massage   Wood Valley, HI

Each year since 1982, Ken Kimmel and Shawn LaSalla-Kimmel have conducted weeklong residential workshops at the Wood Valley Retreat Center on the Big Island of Hawaii. Ken is a Jungian-oriented therapist. Shawn is a licensed massage therapist and long-time healing arts apprentice to Hawaiian elders. They are assisted by teachers of the Hawaiian culture.

All workshops include breathwork, sacred Hawaiian rituals, and exploration of sacred sites. Rituals include ceremonial lei making, hula basics and the vision walk. Sacred sites include Kilauea Volcano, ancient temples, and the City of Refuge. Other common workshop elements are Hawaiian massage, visualization/imagery centering techniques, Gestalt dreamwork, drumming and sacred dance. Workshop participants have time each day to explore Hawaii's black sand beaches, hidden coves and high deserts.

Address   Pacific Northwest Center for Hawaiian Healing Arts & Massage, 219 1st Ave. S., Suite 405, Seattle, WA 98104, USA

Phone   206/447-1895.

Season   February & March.

Programs   2 weeklong healing arts workshops ("Living and Breathing Hawaii" and "Ke Alana, The Awakening" in 1994) plus a weeklong healing & transformative dream workshop ("Ke Ano Akua, The Divine Seed").

Lodging   Shared rooms.

Rates   Early payment $895. Payment after December 30 $995.

Meals   3 daily meals with vegetarian options.

Hawaiian Wellness Holiday   Koloa, Kauai, HI

Hawaiian Wellness Holiday focuses on rejuvenation, detoxification, exercise, and developing positive health habits. Daily activities include yoga, stretching and breathing exercises, meditation, aquacise, group hikes and van excursions to scenic places, nutritional counseling, and cooking demonstrations. Each guest receives three free weekly massages and/or chiropractic sessions. Guests can also enjoy tennis, snorkeling, swimming and sunning on a white sand beach or at a palm shaded pool.

The program is limited to ten guests per week to ensure adequate personal attention from program directors Grady and Roberleigh Deal. Dr. Grady Deal is a chiropractor, psychological counselor, gourmet cook, and author of "Dr. Deal's Delicious Detox Diet & Wellness Lifestyle" (each guest receives a copy). Roberleigh Deal is a hike leader, massage therapist, yoga and aquacize teacher, and author of "Letters in Action" (numerology) and Hawaiian Astrology."

Address   P.O. Box 279, Koloa, Kauai, HI 96756, USA

Phone   808/332-9244 or 800/338-6977.

Season   Year-round.

Programs   1 to 4 week vacations with full daily schedules of holistic health activities. Participation in all activities is optional.

Lodging   Garden view rooms at the Sheraton Kauai Beach Resort or Waikomo Streams Condominiums. Also ocean view rooms at Nihi Kai Villas Condominiums. All accommodations in the Poipu Beach area.

Rates   1 week rates: Garden view — 1 guest $1,795, 2 guests $2,895; Ocean view — 1 guest $2,095, 2 guests $3,295. Discounts on longer stays.

Meals   3 daily meals selected from several options — vegetarian, Fit for Life, macrobiotic, raw foods, juice fasting, and Dr. Deal's Delicious Detox Diet. Fish & eggs available.

Services   Courtesy airport pick-up & drop-off service. Self-administered colonics (guests purchase equipment), plus additional massage & chiropractic sessions (beyond those included in the program).

Kalani Honua   Kalapana, HI

Kalani Honua ("harmony of Heaven and Earth") is a 20 acre conference and retreat center 45 minutes by car from Hilo Airport and one hour from Hawaii Volcanoes National Park on Hawaii island. Bordered by tropical forest and cliffs overlooking the ocean, the property includes a large outdoor pool, tennis court, dry sauna and jacuzzi. Clothing is optional after 7 PM at the center's pool/spa area and at the natural steam baths, warm springs and black sand beach a few minutes away.

There are many ways of visiting Kalani Honua as an overnight guest — on private vacation, as a participant in a private group program, or as a participant in one of the 50 or so public group workshops and retreats offered each year. Organized by both the center and outside groups, public residential programs tend to focus on physical, energetic, creative and celebratory forms of well being. Anyone may also participate in inexpensive, ongoing classes in tai chi, hula and contemporary dance.

The center's purpose is to support the arts, physical and emotional healing, and traditional Hawaiian culture. It gives 50% lodging rate discounts to resident professional artists and sponsors free weekly talks on Hawaiian history, mythology and crafts. The center also offers a work study program requiring a 3 month commitment to 30 hours of work each week in exchange for room, board and opportunities for personal growth.

Address   R.R. 2, Box 4500, Pahoa, HI 96778, USA

Phone   808/965-7828 or 800/800-6886 (reservations). Fax 808/965-9613.

Season   Year-round.

Programs   2 to 14-day workshops & retreats encouraging personal growth, holistic health, spiritual realization, and creative expression.

Lodging   Accommodations for 75-85 overnight guests in private cottages and three two-story cedar lodges (each with kitchen, dorm space, private rooms & suites). Also 25 campsites.

Rates   Program tuition fees range $20-50/day. Nightly lodging fees: campsite $15/person, dorm $28/person, single/double with shared bath $52/62, single/double with private bath $65/75, private cottage — single/double $85, each additional person $15.

Meals   3 mostly vegetarian meals/day with produce from organic garden.

Services   Massage. Airport transfers. Summer children's programs.

META Institute   Maui, HI

The META Institute hosts two annual vacations combining self-discovery, life-enhancement and spiritual renewal. The vacation site is Akahi Farm — a private 55 acre estate with hot tub, tropical gardens and secluded meadows in the north shore countryside of Maui, HI. Leisure activities include bodysurfing, snorkeling, hiking in the bamboo forests, and camping at the waterfalls of the Seven Sacred Pools.

There are also daily sessions with Institute directors Paul and Niyaso Carter. Paul is a professional psychotherapist and hypnotherapist who uses Gestalt process, sacred arts and expressive arts (e.g. drawing, movement and chanting) in his healing work. Niyaso teaches and facilitates meditation, yoga, breathwork, movement awareness and voice dialogue.

Each vacation offers the option of a one-week workshop created by the Institute in partnership with Alan Lowen, British born founder of Belgium-based The Art of Being. This "Body, Heart & Soul" workshop focuses on the tantric path to higher consciousness through the awakening of sexual energy. Paul, Niyaso and Alan also conduct this workshop in Europe, Australia and elsewhere in the USA.

Address   P.O. Box 38, Paia, HI 96779, USA

Phone   808/572-2234.   Fax 808/572-1435.

Season   Vacations generally in February & July.

Programs 1 & 2-week Hawaii holistic healing vacations, each with option of extra 1-week workshop on transforming sexual energy into love.

Lodging   A variety of accommodations — single, double and shared rooms.

Rates   1993 vacation rates (with or without optional 1-week workshop): 1-week $975-980, 2-week $1,765-1,850, 3-week $2,580. Standalone 1-week workshop $975-980.

Meals   3 daily gourmet vegetarian meals.

Services   Massage.

UNITED STATES   Northwest Region

Eagle Song Camps   Ovando, MT

Each summer, author/teacher/Earthkeeper Brooke Medicine Eagle hosts five camps at Blacktail Ranch, set in a cottonwood-lined valley a few miles east of the Continental Divide. The ranch bunkhouse contains a kitchen, dining hall, lounge, bathrooms, hot tub and sauna. Meetings are held in tipis and a large yurt. Campers pitch their tents in a wildflower-filled meadow below mountains cloaked with pine and aspen groves. This 8,000 acre property also contains ancient ceremonial medicine wheels, a huge cave once used by Native shamans, and a sweatlodge by a beaver-dammed creek.

Since the camps began in 1989, the two most popular annual events have been the 14 and 10-day, women-only "Deepening of Spirit" and "Healing Vision" camps. These "vision camps" include 2-day solo vision quests, ritual, drumming, dance, chanting and meditation. Another annual vision camp is a 10-day offering for returning women vision quest campers. In 1994, a vision camp will be offered that is open to men as well.

In 1993, there were also two weeklong gatherings — one on ceremonial arts and the other on shamanic empowerment. Most camps offer opportunities for horseback riding, swimming and hiking. Some camps are facilitated with the assistance of guest teachers, such as naturopathy experts.

Address   Sky Lodge, P.O. Box 121, Ovando, MT 59854, USA

Phone   406/793-5730. No visits without prior arrangement.

Season   June through August.

Programs   7, 10 & 14-day Earth Wisdom healing camps, some for women-only. 10 & 14-day camps include 2-day solo vision quests.

Lodging   Camping. BYO tent, sleeping bag & pad. Bathrooms at bunkhouse.

Rates   Rates: 7-day $995, 10-day $1,025, 14-day $1,475.

Meals   3 nutritious daily meals prepared by the ranch staff under Brook's guidance.

Feathered Pipe Ranch   Helena, MT

A 15 minute drive from downtown Helena, Feathered Pipe Ranch is a 110 acre frontier outpost of log and stone buildings close to the Continental Divide. As in the days when Native Americans lived at this place, visitors can enjoy a swim in the lake or hike up into the surrounding Rockies. A recent addition to the land is a cedar bathhouse holding huge hot tubs, a sauna, and massage rooms staffed by professional massage therapists.

The ranch is named after the feathered pipe, which Native Americans have used for many centuries to receive direction from the Great Spirit and to connect all beings in the circle of life. In this same spirit, Feathered Pipe Ranch has been offering programs for over 18 years to help people remember their wholeness and interconnectedness to all life.

Most programs are six or seven days long. And of the 13 programs in the 1993 season, six focused on hatha yoga, two on shamanism and two on astrology. All are led by well known teachers in their respective fields. Vacationers have the option before heading home of the one-day "Flowing with Nature," a river rafting trip with storyteller/naturalist Tom McBride.

Address   Box 1682, Helena, MT 59624, USA

Phone   406/442-8196.   Fax 406/442-8110.

Season   April through August.

Programs Weekend, 6-day, 7-day and 10-day programs in natural health, sacred ecology, astrology, shamanism and hatha yoga.

Lodging   Main lodge has guest 10 rooms, most with bunk beds for 4 to 6 people. Those wishing privacy may camp out in one of the ranch's tipis, tents or yurts — all near bathroom facilities.

Rates   Program rates for shared & camp out accommodations: weekend $225; 6-day $899; 7-day $999; 10-day $1,199. $150/person extra for double room with shared bath. $250/person extra for double room with private bath. 1-day river rafting adventure $100.

Meals   3 gourmet natural food meals, vegetarian except for occasional fish and chicken.

Services   Massage.

Royal Teton Ranch Summer Conference   Livingston, MT

Royal Teton Ranch is a 600 member spiritual community spread across 28,000 acres of alpine forests and meadows at an altitude of 6,400 feet. It is also the international headquarters of Church Universal and Triumphant, Summit University, Summit University Press, and Montessori International.

The Church was founded in 1974 by Elizabeth Clare Prophet to spread the teachings of the Ascended Masters dictated through Mrs. Prophet.

Each summer, the Ranch hosts a 10-day, family-oriented camp/conference attended primarily by Church members but open to all. Each day contains morning and early evening workshops on Ascended Master teachings, early afternoon dictations by Mrs. Prophet, plus Church rituals and sacraments including baptisms and weddings. In the evenings, there are talks of interest to all on the conference theme ("Healing the Earth" in 1993).

Primarily for non-Church members, there is also a full daily schedule of morning activities and courses. Activities include hatha yoga, tai chi, Ranch tours and guided hikes. Classes include Brain Gym movements, blended sight-sound learning program, macrobiotic cooking, basic astrology, and inner child workshop. On the day after the conference ends, there are guided tours of Yellowstone National Park — a 45 minute drive to the south.

Address   Summit University, Box 5000, Livingston, MT 59047, USA

Phone   800/245-5445.

Season   10 days in late June and early July.

Programs Conference with holistic health courses & activities, plus workshops & dictations on Ascended Master teachings.

Lodging   Camping in large, tree lined meadows. Campers may use own tents or same-sex dorm "tent houses" — each holding 12 people & with foam pads. BYO sleeping bags. RV parking for 40 trailers. Also rooms for rent in private Glastonbury homes — 25 miles away.

Rates   Pre-registration rates: 5 to 10-day stay — adult $195, children 3-18 yrs. $65, morning activities only $75; 1 to 4-day stay — adult $99, children 3-18 yrs. $35, morning activities only $40. The "morning activities only" option usually available only for family members that are not Church members. Families with more than 2 children pay only for the 2 oldest children.

Meals   Cafeteria offers macrobiotic cuisine (whole grains, vegetables & fish) plus poultry & meat. Average meal costs — breakfast $2-4, lunch or dinner $5-7. Also campsite cooking.

Services   Parent co-op children's programs supervised by Montessori staff.

Breitenbush Hot Springs   Detroit, OR

Breitenbush Hot Springs is a natural hot springs, holistic health retreat, and intentional community set on 86 acres straddling the Breitenbush River 2 hours southeast of Portland. Guest facilities include a large lodge built in the 1930s plus cabins with hydro-electric and geothermal heating. There is a sauna, hot and cold tubs, and hot springs pools where swimsuits are optional at all times. Hiking trails snake out from Breitenbush into the surrounding National Forest and Mt. Jefferson Wilderness.

Breitenbush programs focus on the expressive arts, body/mind disciplines, and relationship (past and present) healings. Most programs are led by healing arts practitioners from the Pacific Northwest, including the Breitenbush community. One popular workshop teaches the invented-at-Breitenbush EDGU system — spinal maintenance through a series of free-flowing upper body rotations made while grounded in a fixed stance.

Guests can also enjoy Breitenbush on a personal retreat basis. Daily events include pre-breakfast meditations and post-breakfast sharing circles in the Sanctuary, where all spiritual traditions are respected. Weekly activities may include Breitenbush tours; sessions in tai chi, yoga and EDGU; evening concerts, storytelling and drumming circles. There are also monthly sweat lodge ceremonies and seasonal celebrations.

Address   P.O. Box 578, Detroit, OR 97342, USA

Phone   503/854-3314.

Season   Year-round.

Programs 2 to 13-day programs on body/mind disciplines; relationship healings; and expressive arts. Also personal retreats.

Lodging   Forty 1 and 2-bedroom cabins — all with heat & electricity, some with toilet & sink, each with 2-5 person capacity. 10 large tents, with mattresses, on platforms. Also campsites. Shower houses & rest rooms nearby. BYO towels & warm bedding.

Rates   2 to 4-day workshop $115-500. Personal retreat: adult — weekend $45-75/day, weekday $45-70/day; child — ages 13-16 $20/day, ages 7-12 $15/day, ages 4-6 $10/day, under 3 free. 10% personal retreat discount for seniors & stays over 1 week. Mid-week personal retreat discounts up to 20% during winter months.

Meals   3 daily vegetarian meals for overnight guests. Can accommodate dairy, egg & wheat-free diets. Provide herb teas & hot water.

Services Massage, hydrotherapy, herbal sheet wraps, aromatherapy, Reiki.

Ken Keyes Center   Coos Bay, OR

Ken Keyes Center was founded in 1982 by Living Love Church to teach the life enhancement techniques formulated by Ken Keyes in books such as "Handbook to Higher Consciousness" and "The Power of Unconditional Love." Defining an "addiction" as "any desire that makes you upset or unhappy if it is not satisfied," Ken invented a "Science of Happiness" to free people from negative emotional patterns.

Now operated by the Vision Foundation, the Center conducts two 5-day workshops — one on Living Love techniques and the other on inner child work. Both of these 5-day workshops are incorporated into "The Life Changing" (TLC) program — a 7-week residential course conducted five times each year. There are also residential weekend workshops on subjects such as self-esteem, self-empowerment, and community building.

The Center's 5-day and TLC programs are led by a team of about 20 permanent staff and volunteers. Weekend workshops are facilitated by both Center staff and visiting teachers. All programs are conducted in a campus-like environment 150 miles north of California in the coastal town of Coos Bay. Nearby are tennis courts and a quiet duck pond. A few miles away is the scenic Oregon Dunes National Recreation Area.

As of late 1993, the Center was also creating a "Residential Community" program for people wishing to live and participate in shared community.

Address   790 Commercial Avenue, Coos Bay, OR 97420, USA

Phone   503/267-6412 or 800/545-7810. Fax 503/269-5712.

Season   March through November.

Programs 7-week, 5-day and weekend programs teaching methods for enhancing the experience and expression of peace, love and happiness. Also 3-month volunteer programs that include a 1-week "Living Love" workshop, weekly classes and discounts on scheduled programs.

Lodging   Shared rooms in a handsome, 4-story, former hospital building.

Rates   7-week program — sliding scale tuition $1,755-2,745, room & board $685. 5-day programs — sliding scale tuition $395-615, room & board $90. Weekends — tuition $195, room & board $37-42.

Meals   3 daily meals — mostly vegetarian.

Northwest Yoga Vacation   Western OR

Each year for over a decade, Portland, OR-based Julie Lawrence has hosted a one week yoga vacation at a scenic location on a bend in the wild Rogue River in southwestern Oregon's Siskyou National Forest. In 1994, this annual summer vacation will be held at an equally scenic western Oregon spot in or near the snow capped Cascade Mountains.

Julie is a certified Iyengar yoga instructor and long time student of B.K.S. Iyengar and his daughter Geeta. During the summer retreat, Julie leads two daily classes in yoga, breathing and meditation. Massage is available from a licensed massage therapist. There is also plenty of time for recreational activities such as fishing, hiking and swimming.

Address   600 SW 10th Avenue, Suite 406, Portland, OR 97205, USA

Phone   503/227-5524.

Season   One week in August.

Programs Iyengar style, hatha yoga camp.

Lodging   Comfortable, shared accommodations.

Rates   1993 rates: 2 nights $290; 4 nights $510; 6 nights $750. Fees include lodging, meals and yoga instruction.

Meals   3 daily vegetarian meals.

Services   Massage.

School of Experimental Ecology   Fall Creek, OR

The School of Experimental Ecology (SEE) is located in a riverside country retreat house set amidst lawns, gardens and forest a few miles southeast of Eugene. Roughly once each month, SEE hosts a five-day program for four men and four women to "optimize personal creativity by modifying the ecology or total environment — physical, biological and social — of each person."

Each program begins on Monday with a six hour audiovisual presentation of the "Creative Transformation" process. The following days include workshops on applying the process to overcome fear and solve practical life problems. Each day includes 20 minutes of pre-breakfast breathing, isometric and isotonic exercises. Participants depart on Saturday morning.

SEE's founder is John David Garcia — inventor of numerous patented technologies, founder of several successful engineering firms, and author of books such as "Creative Transformation." The "Creative Transformation" process rests on the premise that enduring happiness cannot be attained unless one's primary goal is to maximize creativity in others and oneself.

Address   P.O. Box 10851, Eugene, OR 97440, USA

Phone   503/937-3437. Fax 503/937-2314. Call before visiting.

Season   Year-round.

Programs 5-day program to encourage creative transformation. Course graduates eligible for 100% paid apprenticeships & permanent staff positions (described in detail in free brochures).

Lodging   Private bedrooms for couples. Semiprivate rooms for singles. Everyone contributes 1/2 hour of housekeeping work each day.

Rates   Lodging & food $200. Program free. Donations not accepted.

Meals   3 daily meals — mostly vegetarian (1 fish dinner). Only beverage is unchlorinated well water & herbal tea made from this water.

Son-Lit Acres   Sweet Home, OR

Resting on 40 peaceful acres in west central Oregon, Son-Lit acres is a homey lifestyle modification center dedicated to reducing the risk and severity of certain illnesses. The program has proven helpful for people recovering from cardiac surgery and for people suffering from pulmonary and cardio-vascular diseases, stroke, cancer, obesity, diabetes, hypoglycemia, allergies, and arthritis. The center accepts only ambulatory guests.

Guests merge into the daily schedule at their own pace. The schedule is as follows: 6 AM soft music wake-up; 6:30 calisthenics followed by a walk; 7:45 morning prayer & meditations; 8 breakfast; 9:15 stress control through the power of prayer; 10 exercise and treatments; 12:30 PM rest period; 2 dinner; 3:30 lectures and demonstrations; 4:30 exercise and treatments or free time; 6:30 community sharing and worship; 9 "rest in God's love."

The grounds of Son-Lit Acres contain a garden, an orchard, views of mountain peaks, and walking trails leading out into the surrounding woods. The center is guided by Elder Bob and Gladys Skinner, a devout Seventh Day Adventist couple who have been married for over 50 years. Center staff includes a nutritionist, a social worker, a physician and nurses. Guests may join the resident staff for a Saturday morning church service.

Address   1112 Turbyne Road, Sweet Home, OR 97386, USA

Phone   503/367-5430.

Season   Year-round.

Programs   2-week & 23-day lifestyle modification programs attended by healthy people, people diagnosed as "high risk," and people diagnosed as ill.

Lodging   Comfortable single rooms.

Rates   2-week program: $1,550. 23-day program: guest patient $2,500, companion guest patient, non-patient companion $1,250. Patients receive M.D.• supervised exams & attention.

Meals   2 vegan (non-dairy vegetarian) meals prepared each day by cooks who occasionally run cooking school instructor seminars.

Bear Tribe Programs   Eastern WA

Most Bear Tribe programs are conducted 35 miles from Spokane, WA on the side of Vision Mountain — looking out across the Spokane Indian reservation. Each summer, the Mountain has a few work/study openings. Regional weekend Medicine Wheel Gatherings plus some Mountain programs are also conducted at camp grounds elsewhere in America and in Europe.

The Tribe's "Introductory Program" is a 10-day course on its work, beliefs and lifestyle offered several times each year. 1993 advanced programs included a five-day pipe ceremony workshop and a 10-day earth awareness workshop. Tribe vision quests are nine-day programs, each including four days of time alone in the wilderness.

The Tribe also conducts "Self-Reliance" and "Permaculture" workshops. "Self-Reliance" programs, five to seven days long, teach how to live with the land. This includes gardening, hunting/fishing, livestock, shelter and daily ceremony.

Two-week "Permaculture" programs teach permaculture theory and practice through lectures, demonstrations and field trips.

The Bear Tribe Medicine Society was founded by the late Sun Bear to share the wisdom of Native American healing and spiritual practices with all peoples. Tribe activities are now being focalized by Wabun Wind, an author and co-author with Sun Bear of nine books. The Tribe continues to publish "Wildfire," a quarterly network magazine.

Address   P.O. Box 199, Devon, PA 19333, USA

Phone   215/993-3344.   Fax 215/993-3345.

Season   Mostly May through September.

Programs Native American & Earth medicine gatherings & trainings.

Lodging   Campsites & limited dormitory space. Outhouses & solar showers.

Rates   4 to 14-day programs $350-1,350 with fees based on income. Weekend Medicine Wheel Gatherings $180-220 + $15-30 for campsite or bunkbed dorm. Vision Mountain visits $30/day, $175/week.

Meals   3 daily vegetarian meals. Medicine Wheel Gatherings — BYO eating utensils, cup, bowl, plate & napkins.

Bodhi Creek Farm   Sumas, WA

Organic gardens, friendly farm animals and a spring-fed pond add to the safe and supportive ambiance of Bodhi Creek Farm, 25 acres of forest and meadow in the foothills of Mt. Baker. Guests can enjoy hiking, swimming, a cedar sauna and a wood-fired hot tub. Only one hour from Vancouver, B.C. and two hours from Seattle, the six year old center has created a community that meets each month for a potluck supper and a Sacred Circle Dance.

The farm's retreat center is a 1000+ square foot building with carpeting, vaulted ceiling, skylights and sound system. The center's directors are Djuna and Rollin Harper. Djuna is a transpersonal psychotherapist with training in Therapeutic Touch and Holotropic Breathwork. Rollin is a singer, storyteller and meditation teacher. Together, Djuna and Rollin lead Therapeutic Touch, breathwork, meditation and sacred dance programs.

Address   7601 Kendall Road, Sumas, WA 98295, USA

Phone   206/599-2106. No visits without prior arrangement.

Season   Year-round.

Programs 2 to 5-day workshops focusing on inner healing & self discovery. Also individual retreats.

Lodging   Dormitory & campsites (RVs OK). Hot showers. BYO sleeping bag.

Rates   Sample program rates (including meals, lodging & tuition): meditation weekend $125, breathwork weekend $225, 5-day breathwork intensive $395.

Meals   3 daily vegetarian meals in indoor & outdoor dining areas during scheduled programs. Individual retreatants do own cooking.

Chinook Learning Center   Clinton, WA

1 1/2 hours (by car and ferry) north of Seattle, Chinook is a converted farm on 72 acres of Whidby Island forest and meadowland with Olympic Mountains vistas and beaches a few miles away. The grounds contain a sweat lodge; marked trails; herb, flower and vegetable gardens; two retreat houses and two rustic cabins. Honoring its environment, the center is committed to exploring the interconnectedness of all life through experiential education, community building and ritual time on the land.

Chinook sponsors and hosts one-time and series workshops. Major 1993 one-time workshops included "The Sacred Female" with Vicki Noble and Demetra George, plus two "Change Agent Training" intensives — one on making inner change happen, the other on creating a sustainable world. Other one-time workshops included seasonal celebration, creative writing and wildlife art weekends. 1993 series workshops included "Green Retreat" and medicine wheel weekends, plus "Journey Into Fire" weekends with David Spangler.

The learning center is operated by two resident caretakers assisted by interns and work/exchange guests. Interns work up to 30 hours per week over usually one to three months. Two miles away in the town of Clinton, Chinook's administrative center runs a gift shop, book store and evening talks popular with the center's large, Seattle area membership community.

Address   Box 57, Clinton, WA 98236, USA

Phone   206/321-1884.

Season   Year-round.

Programs Weekend & occasional 5-day workshops, celebrations and retreats emphasizing creative expression, self-affirmation and connection with nature. Also private retreats and evening talks.

Lodging   Shared & dorm accommodations for up to 22 people in 2 lodges & 2 cabins. Cabins have electricity but no running water. Bathhouse & outhouses nearby. Also campsites for up to 150.

Rates   Sample rates for workshops with all meals: 5-day "Sacred Female" retreat $675-750/person, "Change Agent Training" weekend $125-150/person. Nightly rates for breakfasts-only workshops $25/room & $10/campsite. Private retreat nightly lodging: room — $30-35/

individual, $45-50/couple; campsite — $10/person, $15/couple. Work/exchange $15/night. Intern — lodging free, food $40/month.

Meals   For private retreats & most workshops, breakfast is provided on a make-it-yourself basis and kitchen space is available for other meals. For some programs, the center provides vegetarian meals.

Cloud Mountain   Castle Rock, WA

Cloud Mountain is a rustic retreat center on 5 acres of wooded land containing several buildings, a sauna, a small lake, an organic garden and green house, a fish pond, cats, chickens and peacocks. A short walk up the road leads to views of snow capped Mt. Rainier and Mt. St. Helens. Seattle is a 2 1/4 hours to the north, and Portland, OR is 1 1/4 hour to the south.

The Center supports the work of the Northwest Dharma Association (NWDA), sponsor of workshops and retreats led by monks and lay teachers representing Zen, Tibetan, and Theravada/Vipassana traditions. Internationally known teachers come from as far away as Asia and England.

The center also hosts workshops for groups other than NWDA — typically combining meditation with other centering and spiritual disciplines.

A schedule of Cloud Mountain programs and other Northwest Dharma activities is published in NWDA's bi-monthly, 24-page newsletter. Subscriptions are available from NWDA at 311 West McGraw, Seattle, WA 98119 (206/286-9060).

Address   P.O. Box 807, Castle Rock, WA 98611, USA

Phone   206/274-4859. No visits without prior arrangement.

Season   Year-round.

Programs Frequent meditation and Buddhist teaching retreats of 2 to 9, 16 & 27 days in length.

Lodging   Accommodations for up to 35 overnight guests in a dorm with 2-5 beds/room plus a building with some private rooms. Hot water shower house separated for men & women. There are outhouses & indoor flush toilets. BYO bedding, towels & meditation cushion.

Rates   Typical food & lodging rates for meditation & Buddhist teachings retreats: weekend $70, long weekend $105, 6-day $210, 16-day $560 or $35/day, 27-day $700 or $280 for first 8 days. Teacher contributions ("dana") made at end of each retreat.

Meals   3 daily vegetarian meals with alternatives (on request) to wheat or dairy dishes. Tea, fruit & snacks available throughout the day. Retreatants help with meal preparations and cleanup.

Indralaya   Eastsound, WA

Indralaya is a remote Orcas Island retreat founded in 1927 to investigate the potential for human self transformation through community and in cooperation with nature. The 75 acre property includes pebbled shoreline beaches, a boat dock in a sheltered cove, forest trails, a spacious community center, an ancient apple orchard, and a large organic vegetable garden. By car and ferry, the camp is 3 hours northwest of Seattle.

Camp programs include silent meditation, yoga and tai chi retreats; personal growth intensives such as "Jungian Inner Work," "Personal Mythology," and "Facing the Inner Self"; light hearted offerings such as "Creativity Week," "Celebrating Families," and "Therapeutic Touch"; plus lectures and seminars such as "Subtle Human Anatomy," and "Perspectives in Spiritual Traditions." In the summer, regular activities include early morning group meditation and evening campfires.

Though open to all, Indralaya retains a strong orientation toward the theosophical interests of its founding members. For example, the 1993 schedule included a long weekend "Angelic Forces" workshop led by author Dora Kunz, past president of the Theosophical Society in America and a co-founder of Indralaya. And current members of the Theosophical Society receive 10% individual rate discounts on all Indralaya programs.

Address   Route 1, Box 86, Eastsound, WA 98245, USA

Phone   206/376-4526. No visits without prior arrangement.

Season   Mid-March through October.

Programs 1 to 4-day residential programs on Theosophical topics, psychospiritual self-discovery, plus various centering practices. Work/study involves 3-4 hours of daily chores.

Lodging   Capacity for up to 100 overnight guests in the Round House plus 30 rustic cabins, some with plumbing. BYO bedding.

Rates   Nightly double occupancy adult (ages 18 & over) rates: RVs, tents, trailers & cabin without plumbing $35; Round House $45; cabin with plumbing $50. Single occupancy adult rates are 50% higher. Other nightly rates: teen $25, child 6-12 $7.50, child under 6 free. $5/day discount for any adult bringing a child under age 6. Work/study $20/day.

Meals   3 daily buffet style vegetarian meals in the community center.

Services Courtesy pick-up & drop-off of guests at the Orcas ferry landing.

Kairos House of Prayer   Spokane, WA

Several miles north of downtown Spokane, Kairos House of Prayer is a contemplative retreat center with fine views from its hilltop altitude of 2,300 feet. The 27 acres of wooded grounds contain a large brown barn, a large brick house, and several rustic hermitages nestled among the pines.

The founder and director of this small contemplative community is Sister Florence Leone, who has created a type of meditative prayer by applying Buddhist meditation and hatha yoga techniques to Benedictine contemplative prayer. Four days a week, Sister Leone teaches the yoga postures, deep relaxation and breathing methods that are the main elements of this meditative prayer — practiced by the community three times each day.

Two or three times each month, the Kairos community welcomes retreatants for weeklong periods. Sometimes weeklong retreats may be combined into a single month long retreat. All retreats are silent, with retreatants free to participate (or not participate) in prayer instruction, community meditations, scriptural reflections and short services. Once in a while there is a special one-week program such as the midyear 1993 "Twelve Step Program of Christian Transformation through Centering Prayer."

Address   W. 1714 Stearns Road, Spokane, WA 99208, USA

Phone   509/466-2187. No visits without prior arrangement.

Season   Year-round.

Programs Month long and weeklong silent, contemplative prayer retreats. Also occasional 1-week special programs co-facilitated by visiting teachers (such as experts in 12 Step counseling).

Lodging   9 private rooms in main house & barn. Also 7 hermitages with electricity & either porta-potty or short walk to shared baths.

Rates   Contemplative retreats: 1-week $190, 1-month $700. 1-week special topic retreat $300.

Meals   Silent, communal vegetarian meals served three times daily in main house kitchen. Food furnished to hermitage retreatants that opt to prepare their own meals.

Antelope Retreat Center   Savery, WY

The 2 hour drive from Steamboat Springs, CO to southern Wyoming's Antelope Retreat Center passes along the edges of Medicine Bow National Forest and the Continental Divide. Guests enjoy a family atmosphere of working together on ranch chores, camping trips in the summer to the Rockies and the Red Desert, cross-country skiing in the winter.

Summer programs include a Native American teachings week, a women's healing week with a 2-day desert solo fast, and three one-week vision quests (each with a 3-day solo fast). The ranch can also arrange weekend vision quests (with a 1-day solo fast) plus weekend or weeklong nature awareness programs (including survival skills teachings and Earth spirituality explorations).

The retreat center is run by John and Liz Boyer, Tom Barnes and Gina Lyman. John grew up on the ranch and founded the center in 1986. He and Tom facilitate the Wyoming vision quests plus two weekend vision quests each spring in western Massachusetts. Gina facilitates the women's week.

Address   P.O. Box 166, Savery, WY 82332, USA

Phone   307/383-2625.

Season   Primarily summer.

Programs Vision quests, Native American teachings, and women's week.

Lodging   Capacity for 16 in 1890s ranch house and two 4-bed yurts.

Rates   Weeklong program $500-650. Weekend program $225-275. Non-program vacations: week $235-375, day $36-58.

Meals   3 daily family style meals. Special diets accommodated.

Services Courtesy transportation provided to & from Steamboat Springs, CO airport & Rawlins, WY train station.

UNITED STATES   Southwest Region

A.R.E. Medical Clinic   Pheonix, AZ

Arizona's A.R.E. Medical Clinic offers an 11-day "Temple Beautiful Program" based on the physical regeneration and spiritual growth concepts expounded in Edgar Cayce readings. The program is designed and administered by a physician and a registered nurse for individuals seeking education on a healthier lifestyle and an adventure in consciousness.

Each "Temple Beautiful Program" begins with a physician evaluation of the participant's medical records and laboratory tests. There is individual and group counseling; daily morning exercise designed to fit each individual's needs; plus formal lectures and informal sessions on topics such as meditation and prayer, guided imagery, dream interpretation, music and movement in dance, psychic insights, journal keeping and group work.

"Temple Beautiful" includes massage, acupressure, reflexology, steam cabinet, whirlpool and colon therapy; biofeedback instruction and monitored autogenic exercises to teach relaxation skills; plus pain and/or stress reducing energy therapies such as Myopulse, Electro-Acuscope, and electromagnetic balancing with the ETA machine. The staff also works with each participant to design an ongoing program to be followed at home.

Address 4018 North 40th Street, Phoenix, AZ 85018, USA

Phone 602/955-0551.

Season Year-round.

Programs Monthly, 11-day holistic health lifestyle programs not limited to people with serious or chronic health problems.

Lodging Accommodations for up to 17 people in the clinic's spacious Oak House. Private rooms may be available. Wheelchair accessible, but non ambulatory guests must come with an attendant.

Rates 11-day residential program $4,100.

Meals 3 daily meals with emphasis on fruits & vegetables. Some guests may be placed on a special diet by the clinic physician.

Services Complementary transportation from and to airport.

Canyon Ranch   Tucson, AZ

Canyon Ranch is an ultramodern holistic health spa complex built around a spacious hacienda on 60 acres of desert oasis in the foothills of the Santa Catalina Mountains. The complex contains eight outdoor tennis courts, three outdoor and one indoor pools, sunlit gyms, whirlpools, saunas and steamrooms.

The scent of sagebrush, the ever changing light and shadow of the surrounding mountains, and saguaro cactus pointing at the dry desert skies all create an inspiring landscape for hiking and mountain biking.

The Ranch's premier offering is its "Life Enhancement Program," designed to address health objectives such as smoking cessation, weight loss, stress reduction, prevention and reversal of heart disease. The program includes medical evaluation and supervision, a program of daily indoor and outdoor exercise, daily meetings with behavioral health counselors, access to a broad array of professional health and personal/sports services, nutritional counseling and full use of Ranch recreational facilities.

Like its sister resort in Massachusetts, Canyon Ranch has been voted the world's best health spa by the readers of Conde Naste "Traveler" magazine. The magazine notes that Canyon Ranch offers "a rounded, holistic approach" with individual counseling, group workshops, plus techniques such as biofeedback and hypnotherapy. Ranch staff includes physicians, psychologists, registered dieticians, exercise physiologists, and certified health educators — a nearly three-to-one ratio of staff to guests.

Address   8600 East Rockcliff Road, Tucson, AZ 85715, USA

Phone   602/749-9000 or 800/742-9000.

Season   Year-round.

Programs 5-day "Getaway Plan;" 8 & 11-day "Total Lifestyle Plans;" 1 & 2 week "Life Enhancement Programs."

Lodging   140 rooms in suites & private condominium cottages with modern, southwestern furnishings & decor. The Life Enhancement Center has special quarters for 25. Limited wheelchair access.

Rates   "Life Enhancement Program" 7-night rates: single $2,230-3,110, double $2,2040. 15% discount on 2nd, consecutive week. Prices do not include 18% service charge or applicable sales tax.

Meals   3 daily gourmet meals with alternative vegetarian menu.

Services   Packages include a selection of professional health services (nutrition, movement therapy, exercise physiology, medical & behavioral health services) plus a selection of personal/sports services (private sports lessons, massage, herbal & aroma wraps, hydromassage, haircut, shampoo & hair styling, manicure & pedicure, makeup consultation & application).

Four-Fold Way Trainings   Paulden, AZ

Author/teacher Angeles Arrien each year conducts "Four-Fold Way Trainings" at Wildflower Lodge, a high desert site surrounded by national forest 130 miles northwest of Phoenix and 110 miles south of the Grand Canyon. Guests are free to enjoy the swimming pool and jacuzzi.

In the six-day "Foundational Training," participants are taught to use multicultural healing practices from different cultures to access their inner teacher, healer, visionary and warrior. Healing is experienced through singing, storytelling, dancing and silence.

Open to graduates of "Foundational Trainings," 12-day "In-Depth Training" encourage development of personal resourcefulness and creativity plus leadership skills. Each "Foundational Training" explores a different theme, but all include a two-night solo wilderness experience plus a trip to the Grand Canyon.

Address   Angeles Arrien, P.O. Box 2077, Sausalito, CA 94966, USA

Phone   415/331-5050. Fax 415/331-5069.

Season   January through October.

Programs   6 & 12-day group trainings designed to empower participants to connect to their own authenticity, to let go of limiting behavior patterns, and to envision new goals.

Lodging   Comfortable shared (2 per room) accommodations.

Rates   6-day program $1,200. 12-day program $2,400.

Meals   3 daily, mostly vegetarian meals.

Merritt Center   Payson, AZ

Nestled in the Tonto National Forest at a 5,000 foot altitude 90 miles north of Phoenix, the Merritt Center is a place for personal renewal. On the grounds is a meditation garden, an organic garden, and a spa/jacuzzi. Nearby are quiet forest hiking trails near the base of the Mogollon Rim.

Most programs are facilitated by Center owner Betty Merritt. Frequent weekend offerings are meditation retreats, wellness retreats (with massage, yoga or tai chi), women's empowerment gatherings, and workshops drawing on Native American medicine traditions (including sweat lodge ceremony). Betty's husband Al joins her to host couples weekends. The Center also hosts Elderhostel weeks, usually focusing on wellness and self-renewal.

Address   P.O. Box 2087, Payson, AZ 85547, USA

Phone   602/474-4268 or 602/948-8550 (Scottsdale). Fax 602/474-8588. No visits without prior arrangement.

Season   Year-round.

Programs   Weekend workshops & retreats on self-renewal & empowerment.

Lodging   Capacity for 30 overnight guests in double occupancy rooms.

Rates   Weekend retreats & workshops — $95 (double occupancy) to $250/ person. Mid-week Elderhostel programs $315/person. Mid-week getaway — double occupancy $20/person, single $30/person. Special rates for private groups, with or without meals.

Meals   3 daily, family style meals with no red meat & no alcohol.

Services Massage & flotation tank.

Reevis Mountain School   Roosevelt, AZ

Reevis Mountain School, a wilderness learning center for self-discovery and self-reliance, resides next to Pinto Creek in Tonto National Forest. Self-discovery is encouraged through tai chi chuan, meditation and Personal Health retreats. Self-reliance is taught through courses on land navigation, herbal pharmacology and Oriental touch healing.

The School's resident directors are Peter Bigfoot Busnack and Angelique Zelle. Peter once tested his self-reliance skills by walking 85 miles in 15 days through the Sonoran Desert — with no food or water (foraging for his needs) and in temperatures up to 135 degrees F. Angelique too has pushed the limits of human survival — completing five 40-day fasts.

Address   HCO2 Box 1534, Roosevelt, AZ 85545, USA

Phone   602/467-2536. No visits without prior arrangement.

Season   Year-round.

Programs 2 to 7-day courses focusing on self-discovery & self-reliance.

Lodging   BYO tent or rent a "yurpi" — a combination tent/yurt. BYO sleeping bag.

Rates   Program rates (including meals & yurpi space): 2-day $60-100, 3-day $110-160, 4-day "Fasting Meditation Retreat" $175, 7-day "Personal Health Adventure" $500. Daily personal retreat rates: campsite & meals $20; yurpi & meals — individual $30, couple $50; children 7-12 years 1/2 price, 4-6 years 1/4 price, under 4 free.

Meals   Two meals, primarily vegetarian, are served each day at 9 AM and 4:30 PM. Tea and snacks are available at midday. Much of the School's fruits & vegetables are grown in its organic gardens.

Services Free shuttle to & from the School over a primitive 8 mile road. Reevis Mountain herbal & tincture remedies on sale at store.

Rim Institute   Christopher Creek, AZ

Located in east-central Arizona's Tonto National Forest at an altitude of 6,300 feet, the Rim Institute is an interdisciplinary healing, educational and research center dedicated to exploring the spiritual, psychological, physical and planetary dimensions of being human. Facilities include a main cabin, a large yurt with an adjoining redwood deck, and a hot tub overlooking the creek that flows by the organic garden. Regular daily activities include two short meditations open to all.

Institute offerings include open house retreat weekends, vision quests and several women-only events. These and other programs draw on healing techniques from a rich variety of spiritual traditions such as Taoist, Tibetan Buddhist, African and Native American. Reflecting its partial research orientation, the Institute also has conducted programs such as "Time Travel and the Alien Presence" and "Oracles, Intuition and the New Millennium" charting the borders of science and spirituality.

Address   Summer — HCR Box 162-D, Payson, AZ 85541, USA
Winter — 4302 N. 32nd Street, Phoenix, AZ 85018, USA

Phone   602/262-0551 (summer), 602/478-4727 (winter). No visits without prior arrangement.

Season   May through September.

Programs   Weekend & midweek programs designed to expand inner consciousness and its relationship to outer realities. The work study program requires a minimum one-month commitment.

Lodging   2 to 3-person yurts with skylight, windows, futons & carpeted floors. Also campsites. Two nearby bathhouses. BYO bedding.

Rates   Program tuition: weekend $150-195; 5-day $425-495. Lodging & meals: yurt $45-50/night; campsite $35/night. Food & lodging costs included in tuition of open house & vision quest programs.

Meals   3 daily gourmet meals with vegetarian options.

Services   Massage.

Blue Mountain Center   Colorado Springs, CO

Located at a 7,400 foot altitude high above Colorado Springs, the Blue Mountain Center is a 44 acre summer workshop site dedicated to facilitating personal transformation. The center's seasonal kitchen, dining and shower house structures are surrounded by 12,000 acres of national forest. The views are spectacular from this high energy spot, where UFO sightings and powerful healings are not uncommon.

All workshops are led by Dr. Verna Yater, a psychic healer and trance medium whose work has been researched by the A.R.E. Each workshop is different, but all include elements such as discussions with spirit, meditations, chanting, and healing sounds projected through Dr. Yater or created from crystal bowls. Participants' unspoken individual concerns are often addressed with specific advice from spirit. As needed, Dr. Yater eases participants past fears and other blockages to self realization.

From time to time, Dr. Yater conducts residential workshops in Santa Barbara, CA and Sedona, AZ — both on a standalone basis and as part of the Year Long Transformation Program that also meets at Blue Mountain.

Address   Dr. Verna Yater, 2281 Las Canoas Rd, Santa Barbara, CO 93105, USA

Phone   805/564-4956. Fax 805/682-8627. Call before visiting.

Season   June through August.

Programs   5 and 10-day experiential, spiritual expansion workshops.

Lodging   Campsites for up to 30 people. Center provides 4-person, zip-up tents for 1 or 2 people in each tent. BYO sleeping bag.

Rates   5-day workshop $550-600. 10-day workshop $1,065-1,165.

Meals   3 tasty vegetarian meals each day.

Services   Transportation to & from Colorado Springs airport or base camp — 4 1/2 miles below the center. Some workshops offer massage.

Dragonback Ranch   Pagosa Springs, CO

Dragonback Ranch is a 100 acre property in the San Juan National Forest. The property is crisscrossed by elk, eagles and coyotes, and the Continental Divide lies both 32 miles due north and 32 miles due east. Nearby are the rock spires of Chimney Rock, where Anasazi ruins mark the northernmost border and only known mountain home of the Chacoan Empire. Also nearby are Colorado's largest and hottest mineral pools, free to soakers and named by Native Americans "Pagosah" — land of healing water.

Dragonback's 1993 workshops included "Stories as Seeds," "Triple Goddess Journey," "Touching the Earth," "Loving Yourself" women's gatherings, dreamwork weekends, and a 5-day "Brethwork Retreat." Most programs are led by southwestern healing arts practitioners. Some are led by Ranch owner/ host Donna Lee Graham, a licensed clinical social worker with 30+ years of spirit-centered psychotherapy experience. Donna also offers individualized workshops on dreamwork, painting, writing, music, and/or bodywork.

Address   Summer: HC 60 Box 58A 864, Pagosa Springs, CO 81147, USA
Winter: Route 4, Box 292, Hedgesville, WV 25427, USA

Phone   Summer: 303/731-4534. Winter: 304/754-8629. No visits without prior arrangement.

Season   April to November.

Programs   Weekend, 5 & 7-day workshops & gatherings with ritual, deep ecology & personal transformation focus. Also self-guided retreat & individualized workshops.

Lodging   Dragonback Ranch is a solar heated, red cedar home with futons. Sleeping bag floor space for up to 20. Also campsites.

Rates   Weekend group workshops & gatherings (tuition, food & sleeping space): $150-300. Daily camping: self catered $15, with meals $30. Daily lodging: self catered $35, with meals $50. Individualized workshops about $50/day.

Meals   3 wholesome meals served on program weekends. Self catering is allowed for individual visits.

Services   Psychotherapeutic counseling. Sometimes also bodywork & massage.

Eden Valley Lifestyle Center   Loveland, CO

Founded in 1987, Eden Valley is a homey wellness center set on 550 acres of woods and fields in the eastern foothills of the Rocky Mountains. Center facilities include a sun deck, exercise equipment, a sauna and a jacuzzi. On the grounds are walking trails, a garden, a senior citizens' home plus small agriculture and medical missionary schools. The center shares a dedicated Seventh Day Adventist staff with its neighbor institutions.

Each standard Eden Valley program includes a complete physical examination by an M.D., pre and post-program blood chemistry analyses, stretching exercises, hydrotherapy and massage sessions, health lectures, cooking demonstrations, walks and outings in the fresh (and usually sunny) mountain air. Those who wish may attend daily morning and evening worship services — community prayer, singing and scripture readings.

The center's standard programs usually succeed in inspiring its guests to adopt a more positive and cheerful state of mind. The programs have also proven successful in curing or ameliorating smoking addiction, obesity, heart problems, adult-onset diabetes and hypoglycemia, high blood pressure, stress, stroke damage and stroke risk, allergies and arthritis. From time to time, Eden Valley also conducts weekend lay counseling programs.

Address   6263 North County Road 29, Loveland, CO 80538, USA

Phone   800/637-9355.

Season   Year-round.

Programs   1, 2 & 3-week "New Start" lifestyle programs to combat & prevent diseases brought on by unhealthy lifestyles. All programs include optional Christian prayer & worship services.

Lodging   5 rooms with twin beds in lifestyle center ranch house. Can accommodate additional guests at other campus facilities.

Rates   Shared room program rates: 1-week $745, 2-week $1,395, 3-week $1,995. $30/night additional fee for private room.

Meals   3 daily, buffet style vegan meals with fruits & vegetables from the center's own organic gardens.

Filoha Meadows   Redstone, CO

Filoha Meadows is a Christian family vacation and lifestyle counseling center set amidst fir and aspen covered mountains at a 7,000 foot altitude. An indoor pool and outdoor hot tubs are fed by a natural hot mineral waters spring. Also on the grounds is a par course; beaver pond and observation blind; plus trails for hiking, mountain biking and cross country skiing. Filoha is 45 miles from Aspen's cultural arts and skiing. Other local activities include horseback riding, river rafting and trout fishing.

Center hosts Robert and Melody Durham offer holistic lifestyle counseling suitable for Christian couples. Robert is a clinical psychologist who specializes in conflict-resolution and communications skills. Melody is a registered nurse who specializes in exercise and nutrition. Robert and Melody together tailor make programs for people at high risk of stroke, heart attack or other lifestyle diseases. Most guests stay for four to seven days, taking two hours of counseling each day.

Address   14628 Highway 133, Redstone, CO 81623, USA

Phone   800/227-8906.

Season   Year-round.

Programs   Individually-tailored, health education & Christian counseling in a vacation environment. Occasional weekend parenting seminars.

Lodging   Main lodge has 4 private bedrooms. River House has 2 bedrooms that sleep up to 8. Shared bathrooms.

Rates   Health education & counseling $35/hour. Nightly lodging: adult couple (or individual) $70, each child under 12 years old $5, each additional person $15.

Meals   Guests make their own meals in main lodge & River House kitchens.

Services   Christian lifestyle counseling. Also psychiatric, pediatric & orthopedic medical services available from resident physicians.

Heart of Stillness Retreats   Jamestown, CO

At an 8,600 foot altitude 35 minutes from Boulder, Heart of Stillness is located on 25 quiet, wooded acres surrounded by national forest. There are panoramic vistas of the plains to the east and the Continental Divide to the west. The main house has a Japanese style shower and deep soaking tub. Hiking and cross country skiing trails start at the back door.

Annual programs include a weeklong New Year's retreat, a weeklong Yom Kippur retreat, and a 40-day Vipassana meditation retreat. The New Year's retreat includes contemplative sitting and walking, Japanese Tea Ceremony, exercises with waking dreams and journaling, plus a New Year's eve Japanese dinner followed by a midnight meditation. The Yom Kippur retreat focuses on Kabbalistic prayers and insight as a path for returning to the Divine.

All retreats are led by Rabbi David Cooper and his wife Shoshana. David is a Sufi initiate; a student of Kabbalah, Zen and Theravada Buddhism; a long-time Lama Foundation retreat facilitator; and author of books on spiritual retreat and practice. Shoshana is an oncology nurse; teacher of Japanese Tea Ceremony; astrological counsellor; and committed caretaker of the visible and not so visible creatures of the land.

Address   P.O. Box 106, Jamestown, CO 80455, USA

Phone   303/459-3431. No visits without prior arrangement.

Season   Year-round.

Programs   Guided weeklong group retreats plus 40-day meditation retreat. Also individual retreats, retreats for people/families in health crisis, plus spiritual bed & breakfast stays.

Lodging   Accommodations for up to 10 overnight guests in centrally heated double occupancy rooms plus a cabin with a wood stove.

Rates   40-day retreat $1,150. 7-day retreat $375-435. Individual retreat — 1st 4 days $45/day, thereafter $35/day. Health crisis retreat — individual $35/day, family rates negotiable. Spiritual B&B — individual $45/day, couple $75/day.

Meals   3 daily vegetarian meals, taken in communal silence. Cater to some special diets (e.g. kosher). Independent retreatants prepare own meals from food provided by the retreat caretakers.

Rocky Mountain Dharma Center   Red Feather Lakes, CO

Rocky Mountain Dharma Center (RMDC) occupies over 500 acres of property surrounded by National Forest at an altitude of 8,000 feet. A sister organization to Boulder's Naropa Institute, the center is primarily a non-sectarian Buddhist teaching and meditation retreat with a strong foundation in Tibetan Buddhism. In addition to its own programs, the center hosts an annual tai chi summer camp that includes sitting meditation.

In the spring and fall, RMDC offers two types of introductory meditation weekends — one with a distinctly Buddhist flavor, and the other (Shambala Level I) of a non religious nature. Other 1993 general public programs included a family summer camp and Thanksgiving retreat, a wilderness retreat with a one day solo quest, plus 2 to 3-day workshops on Ikebana and Native American spirituality. Most programs include meditation practice.

Most other RMDC programs are advanced Buddhist teachings and intensive meditation retreats. Of these programs, the one best suited for beginner to intermediate meditators is "Shambala Dathun" — a one month retreat that can be attended for one week periods. This retreat contains nine hours of daily sitting and walking meditation, talks on meditation practice, instructor interviews, and daily tasks performed as meditation in action.

Address   4921 County Road 68C, Red Feather Lakes, CO 80545, USA

Phone   303/881-2184. Fax: 303/881-2186. Call before visiting.

Season   Programs year-round except during September.

Programs Meditation, contemplative arts & wilderness retreats.

Lodging   May through Aug: windowed tents mounted on wooden platforms, each with 2 single beds, bookshelves, garment rack & front porch. Oct. through April: well heated dormitories. BYO sleeping bag.

Rates   2 & 3-day programs $75-130. 5-day wilderness retreat $200. 9-day family camp — adult $200, child $100. One month meditation retreat $600 or $180/week. Childcare $12/day. 1-week tai chi camp $300 (contact Rocky Mountain Tai Chi at 303/447-2556).

Meals   3 daily meals with vegetarian & special options. One month retreat meals eaten oryoki style (BYO oryoki set).

Services   Childcare from May through August, laundry (for stays over 2 weeks), Ft. Collins pick-up & drop-off.

Shoshoni Yoga Retreat   Rollinsville, CO

A 35 minute car climb from Boulder at an 8,500 foot elevation, Shoshoni Yoga Retreat is a 210 acre valley refuge surrounded by national forest and Rocky Mountain peaks. Hand-hewn wooden cabins connect by dirt pathways to the yoga/meditation hall and the main lodge, with an outdoors hot tub and sauna. Deer, elk and red-tailed hawks floating on mountain breezes are a common sight in this wilderness area, where a 45-minute hike through pine and aspen forests leads to a view of the Continental Divide.

Shoshoni is a spiritual retreat/holistic health spa where guests design their own day. Elements of the day can include group meditation before breakfast and dinner, morning and late afternoon hatha yoga sessions, and a mid afternoon hike. Late evening is a time for music on the lodge's antique piano, or a relaxing massage. Weekend rejuvenation retreats include therapeutic massage, meditation flushing techniques, plus training in self-nurturing and stress release.

Originally built as a children's summer camp, Shoshoni is now owned and operated by a small spiritual community blending the Indian and Tibetan traditions practiced by its founder, Swami Shambhavananda. Bright prayer flags adorn many of the buildings, large Buddhas are painted on rock walls, and a Medicine Buddha healing ritual is conducted once each week at dawn.

Address   P.O. Box 410, Rollinsville, CO 80474, USA

Phone   303/642-0116.

Season   Year-round.

Programs   Daily meditation and hatha yoga sessions led by resident staff and instructors from the Yoga Institute of Colorado. Weekend rejuvenation retreats. Work study positions available.

Lodging   Accommodations for up to 35 in furnished cabins, each with 2 to 4 beds, carpeting, shower and bathroom. Towels & linens provided. Also tent sites & retreat cabin with no plumbing.

Rates   Daily rates for classes, meals & lodging: private furnished cabin $100, shared furnished cabin $65, dorm cabin $50, remote retreat cabin $45, tent site $35. Rejuvenation weekend $100 extra.

Meals   3 tasty vegetarian meals prepared each day with organically grown ingredients and in various styles: Japanese, Mexican, Indian, Italian, Chinese, French plus Shoshoni's own creative dishes.

Services   Herbal body scrubs, aromatherapy facials, and massage.

Lama Foundation   San Cristobal, NM

Nineteen miles north of Taos at 8,600 feet on the side of Lama Mountain high above the Rio Grande Gorge, the Lama Foundation (founded in 1967) is a colorful collection of domed and adobe buildings. It is also a community of people tolerantly and conscientiously practicing different spiritual traditions side by side on a daily basis.

Each year the community offers 6-10 summer retreats to allow guests to experience the harmonious diversity of Lama's major spiritual practices — Buddhist, Christian, Hindu, Islam, Jewish, and Sufi. In 1993, Ram Dass led "Tuning to the Wisdom Heart." There were also three one-week retreats, each exploring a different Western mystical tradition. Retreatants offer one hour of service each day and participate in community meditations.

This rustic community of 20-25 hard working souls doubles in size during the summer months. People who join as summer staff may apply for residency in the fall. Community leadership rotates among the members, who make all major decisions by consensus. Lama supports itself through the summer retreats and Flag Mountain Cottage Industries, which sells prayer flags, banners and t-shirts silkscreened by hand on muslin in bright colors.

Address   Box 240, San Cristobal, NM 87564, USA

Phone   505/586-1269 (10 to noon). No visits without prior arrangement.

Season   Public programs May through September. Year-round community.

Programs   1 to 2-week group retreats, some with long weekend options. All group retreats emphasize spiritual practice. Some focus on one tradition, but most explore many traditions. Also opportunities for private retreats & community visits.

Lodging   Campsites — BYO tent. Limited space in 2 dorms — BYO sleeping bag. 2 hermitages. Clean outhouses & solar showers.

Rates   Weekly retreat fees (tuition meals & campsites): Ram Dass retreat $650; "Western Wisdom Traditions" $375; other group retreats $150 (or $75 for 3 days). Dorm fee $7/night. Childcare $18/day. Community visit $18/day. Hermitage retreat (food & lodging) $18/day. Summer staff & residents $240/month up to $1,500.

Meals   3 daily vegetarian meals. Food mostly from own organic gardens.

Services   Childcare for children 3 years & older at most major retreats.

Ocamora Foundation   Ocate, NM

Ocamora is northeast of Santa Fe in the foothills of the Sangre de Cristo Mountains at an elevation of 7,500 feet. 300 acres of serene northern New Mexico landscape buttress Ocamora's purpose to support solitude, deep relaxation and inner work. There is an apple orchard, garden, greenhouse, hot tub, and a pond suitable for swimming. The Cloisters guest residence complex includes a library, meditation hall and small kitchen.

Though primarily a personal retreat center, Ocamora also hosts residential summer workshops. The 1993 schedule contained 3 workshops on holotropic breathwork, a workshop on storytelling and singing, a workshop on dreamwork and writing, a women's gathering, and a Vipassana meditation retreat.

Address   P.O. Box 43, Ocate, NM 87734, USA

Phone   505/666-2389. No visits without prior arrangement.

Season   Workshops from late May through mid-September. Open most of the year for personal retreats.

Programs   Site of 4 to 8-day workshops & retreats conducted & promoted by southwestern teachers & healers.

Lodging   Wood stove heated private rooms & bathrooms clustered around a courtyard. BYO sleeping bag for yurt & tipis, with sleeping platforms & foam pads, nearby outhouses & a hot solar shower.

Rates   8-day meditation retreat $300 in 1993. Daily personal retreat rates: single $30, couple (double occupancy) $45.

Meals   3 daily meals, generally vegetarian, at workshops. Personal retreatants BYO food but may use kitchen — fully stocked with kitchenware, basic supplies & condiments.

Rose Mountain   Las Vegas, NM

Surrounded on three sides by national forest and looking out over the Pecos Wilderness, Rose Mountain is an intertraditional retreat center at an 8,000 foot elevation in New Mexico's Sangre de Cristo Mountains. The center generates all of its electricity through solar photovoltaics. The grounds contain organic gardens, greenhouse, ceremonial tipi, and sweatlodge.

In 1993, the center hosted men-only and women-only retreats (with sweat lodge and solo quests), tai chi retreats, yoga retreats, retreats with a meditation and spiritual song orientation, the annual "Deep Listening Retreat," workshops on Jewish renewal, plus a retreat on "The Path of Devotion" in Christianity, Judaism and Islam.

The center's director is Andy Gold — a Sufi initiate, rabbinic pastor, and a former Lama Foundation coordinator. 1993 guest teachers included Pauline Oliveros and Rabbi David Zeller. Pauline is a composer, performer and creator of deep listening as a meditative art. Rabbi Zeller is a singer, composer, and director of the Network of Conscious Judaism.

Address   P.O. Box 355, Las Vegas, NM 87701, USA

Phone   505/425-5728. No visits without prior arrangement.

Season   June through October.

Programs   Guided thematic retreats, most 6 days long and all devoted to some form of inner healing in a spiritual context. Also individual private & guided retreats at a remote hermitage.

Lodging   Private rooms and camping.

Rates   6-day group retreat $350-450. 3-day group retreat $220. Individual private retreat $35/day.

Meals   3 daily gourmet vegetarian meals.

Takoja Retreats   Questa, NM

Takoja Retreats are conducted on forty acre Ranchos Mesclados, 28 miles north of Taos. Located in the Rio Grande Valley under the peaks of the Sangre de Cristo Mountains, the ranch is at about the same altitude as Machu Pichu — the ancient Peruvian city that inspired Judith Sauceda to found and direct Takoja Retreats. Judith is an artist, teacher and follower of Taoist and Lakota (Native American) spiritual traditions.

Takoja retreats include offerings for men, for women, and for all. Virtually all retreats employ creative ritual, and many also include spirit led, self-expressive painting. The also accommodates private, individual group retreats. Nearby are the free hot springs at Arroy Hondo, the 1000 year old Taos Pueblo, and the village of Taos — a folk arts mecca.

Address   Summer — 656 North Star Route, Questa, NM 87556, USA
Winter — 4495 Lakeridge Road, Denver, CO 80219, USA

Phone   505/586-1086 (summer), 303/934-3607 (winter). No visits without prior arrangement.

Season   May through October.

Programs Workshops centered around Native American healing ceremonies, creative ritual, and creative self-expression.

Lodging   2 large domed structures sleeping up to 16 people in single or group quarters.

Rates   3 & 4-day scheduled workshops — $125-395 (lodging & meals included). Private retreat — bed & breakfast $40/day, workshop with private teacher $75/day.

Meals   Gourmet meals made to order by London trained chef.

Taos Wellness Center   Taos, NM

The Taos Wellness Center conducts natural healing retreats in and around the picturesque, high desert village of Taos, NM. A "Health Rejuvenation" retreat includes counseling, polarity therapy and massage sessions, Synergy dance, lectures and discussion, nutritional and lifestyle evaluation, homeopathic interview, physical exam, and personalized treatment plan. A special "Chronic Fatigue" retreat includes all of the elements of the standard "Health Rejuvenation" retreat plus bio-magnetic treatments.

The Center's tailor-made, five-day minimum "Personal Transformation Retreats" can include bodywork, energy balancing, counseling, emotional release, and creation of personal rituals. Four-day guided "Wilderness Retreats" focus on trekking skills and environmental sensitivity. The Center also offers non-residential polarity therapy certification programs.

The Center's staff is Roger Gilchrist and Joanie Kirk. Roger is a psychotherapist, certified chemical dependency counselor, and registered polarity therapist. Joanie is a licensed naturopathic physician.

Address   P.O. Box 2843, Taos, NM 87571, USA

Phone   505/758-8900.

Season   Late January through mid-November.

Programs 7-day group "Health Rejuvenation" and "Chronic Fatigue" retreats. Also "Personal Transformation" and "Wilderness" retreats, plus non-residential polarity therapy training programs.

Lodging Single & double occupancy accommodations with kitchenettes, private patios & communal hot tub at Sonterra Condominiums — walking distance from the Center & the historic town plaza.

Rates 7-day group retreat $1,000. Individualized "Personal Transformation Retreat" $750.

Meals Make your own at the condo &/or dine out. Nearby markets & restaurants to suit all budgets.

Vista Clara   Galisteo, NM

At a 6,100 foot altitude 17 miles south of Santa Fe, Vista Clara is a combination health spa and retreat housed in authentic pueblo-style adobe buildings. Facilities include a gym, treatment center, sauna, enclosed outdoor pool, outdoor jacuzzi, sweat lodge, and aerobics studio designed as a replica of a Native American ceremonial building. Marked trails on the 80 acre grounds lead past a goat pen, tipis, an archery range, an orchard, a pond and pueblo ruins to a high desert lookout point popular at sunset.

A typical Vista Clara day begins with a 6:30 wake-up followed by pre-breakfast stretching in clean active wear provided each day by the guest services department. Other activities include tai chi, yoga, aquacize, step classes, aerobic circuits, guided hikes, plus a daily massage followed by a beauty treatment. Additional treatments may be purchased. Following a fireside dinner, evenings feature light entertainment such as Indian arts demonstrations, storytelling, singing healers, and natal chart readings.

Address HC 75 — Box 111, Galisteo, NM 87540, USA

Phone 505/988-8865 or 800/247-0301. Fax 505/983-8109.

Season Year-round.

Programs 3 and 7-day holistic health rejuvenation programs.

Lodging Accommodations for up to 14 guests in 10 suites, each with southwestern decor, private bathroom and deck or open porch. Air conditioned. Limited wheelchair access.

Rates 3-day: single $904-1,350, double $751-1,121. 7-day: single $1,804-2,695; double $1,498-2,237.

Meals 3 daily meals featuring "Southwestern International Cuisine." Bake own bread. Accommodate vegetarian & special diets.

Services Swedish massage, shiatsu, clay body mask, body polishing, polarity, reflexology, paraffin hand & foot treatments, facial, and aromatherapy.

The Last Resort   Cedar City, UT

The Last Resort is a high altitude (8,700 feet) retreat on Midway Summit in the Dixie National Forest of southwestern Utah, a 3-4 hour drive from Las Vegas. On the other side of Zion National Park, Pah Tempe Hot Springs is a regular excursion destination during the resort's summer yoga retreats.

Resident retreat directors are Ed and Barbara Keays, both certified Iyengar yoga instructors. Ed is also a certified rebirther, counselor, therapist, Vipassana meditation teacher and past director of the Yoga Institute of San Diego. Barbara is also a gourmet vegetarian cook and long time student of Dr. Bernard Jensen in the fields of nutrition and natural foods cooking.

Winter silent meditation retreats employ yoga to ease muscle tensions. Summer yoga retreats include twice daily yoga classes, evening and morning meditation, spectacular hikes, plus discussions of personal growth concerns (e.g. relationships and right livelihood). A spring detoxification retreat includes light yoga, meditation, nature walks and nutrition study. A late summer natural cooking workshop includes daily morning meditation and yoga.

Address   P.O. Box 6226, Cedar City, UT 84721, USA

Phone   801/682-2289. No visits without prior arrangement.

Season   Late December through mid-September.

Programs Meditation, yoga, cooking & detoxification retreats.

Lodging   Accommodates up to 10 overnight guests in dorms & private rooms.

Rates   Meditation retreats: 5-day $320, 10-day $520, 30-day $1,250. 7-day yoga retreat $695. 10-day detoxification retreat $795. 5-day natural cooking workshop $495.

Meals   3 daily gourmet vegetarian meals. Juice fasting during detoxification retreat.

UNITED STATES   North Central Region

Heartland Spa   Gilman, IL

Eighty miles south of Chicago, The Heartland Spa is a peaceful country estate on a private lake surrounded by 31 acres of woods and miles of farmland. The lakefront mansion is connected by an underground passage to a high-tech, 3-level fitness center housed in a renovated barn. Barn facilities include massage and steam rooms, sauna, whirlpool and swimming pool. Outdoor facilities include two lighted tennis courts, parcourse, 1/4 mile track, hiking/cross-country skiing trails, and paddle boats.

All guests are furnished with casual exercise clothing, and all are encouraged to take only those classes that address his or her goals. Most guests focus on general fitness and wellness goals. Others focus on relaxation and stress management through classes such as stretch & relax, tai chi and yoga. Other classes include ballet, wushu/kung-fu and Heartland Adventure — a series of "getting to know yourself" games and outdoor challenges designed to enhance self-confidence.

Address   225 North Wabash, Ste. 310, Chicago, IL 60601, USA

Phone   312/357-6465 or 800/545-4853 (reservations).

Season   Year-round.

Programs   Weekend, 5 and 7-day personalized health & fitness programs.

Lodging   Limit of 28 guests in 14 comfortably furnished rooms with twin beds & private baths.

Rates   Weekend — double occupancy $500, single occupancy $700. 5-day double $1,375, single — $1,875. 7-day — double $1,875, single $2,575. 5 & 7-day rates include several massages and a facial. All rates include taxes & tips.

Meals   3 daily gourmet vegetarian meals with dairy products & occasional fish supplements. Also daily snacks & non-alcoholic happy hour.

Services   Complementary round-trip transportation from downtown Chicago. Also personal care services such as body composition analysis, nutrition counseling, massage, aromatherapy oil wrap, salt scrub, sea mud body masque, facial, manicure & pedicure.

Camp Al-Gon-Quian Yoga Family Week   Burt Lake, MI

Camp Al-Gon-Quian is a summer youth and family camp facility 30 miles south of the Straits of Mackinac on the southwest shore of Burt Lake. Al-Gon-Quian's 150 acres of forests, open fields and meadows support a full array of summer camp activities such as swimming, sailing, canoeing, campouts, archery, horseback riding, arts and crafts.

Yoga week is one of many youth and family camp weeks held each summer by the Ann Arbor YMCA. Adults participate in two daily Iyengar style yoga sessions led by the Y's hatha yoga instructors. There is a regular summer camp program for youths in attendance with their parents.

Address   Ann Arbor YMCA, 350 South 5th Ave., Ann Arbor, MI 48104, USA

Phone   313/663-0536.

Season   6 days in August.

Programs Iyengar style, hatha yoga family camp.

Lodging   Cabins with 8 bunks each & a nearby modern bath house. One large family per cabin. Couples & smaller families may share cabins.

Rates   Adult $340. Youth (3-12) $140.

Meals   3 daily vegetarian meals.

Camp Ronora   Watervliet, MI

On 300 acres of rolling hills, fields and woodlands, Camp Ronora is located in southwest Michigan's vineyard and orchard country 100 miles northeast of Chicago and 175 miles west of Detroit. The property contains a private lake, tennis and volleyball courts, trails for hiking or cross country skiing, a Native American sweat lodge and medicine wheel, organic gardens, horse stables and riding rings. River canoeing is a nearby option.

Originally operated as a summer camp for girls, Ronora is now managed by Darla Leggit — a former cosmetics industry executive who now leads women's workshops on the Earth based spirituality of her Shawnee ancestors. In 1993, the Camp itself organized three women's workshops plus two for both men and women on mask and shield making, astrology and tarot. Earth Wisdom (708/ 864-1130 in Evanston, IL) hosts spring and fall gatherings plus a summer weekend with well known Native American teachers. There are also a few other non-Camp sponsored retreats such as a Chicago men's gathering.

Address   9325 Dwight Boyer Road, Box 823, Watervliet, MI 49098, USA

Phone   616/463-6315 or 312/935-2713.

Season   Late April through October for public weekend programs, year-round for couples & family vacations plus private group retreats.

Programs Weekend workshops & gatherings emphasizing self-healing through Earth-based Native American ritual & wisdom. Most programs organized & conducted by Camp Ronora or Earth Wisdom.

Lodging   Accommodations for over 100 people in a 6 bedroom lodge, a 3 bedroom house, two 2 bedroom buildings, and tent sites. Firewood & linens available at extra cost.

Rates   Ronora program: $144 bunkhouse or camping, $188 shared cottage housing. Earth Wisdom program: $197-227 bunkhouse or camping, $237-267 shared cottage housing, $127-167 seniors & children.

Meals   Ronora: 5 meals (Sunday brunch) with vegetarian options. Earth Wisdom: 6 gourmet vegetarian meals with meat side dishes.

Center for Spiritual Growth   Cambridge, MN

Forty miles due north of Minneapolis, the Center for Spiritual Growth (CSG) is a nonsectarian spiritual retreat house set at the end of a meadow overlooking a marsh. The Center's peaceful grounds contain forest hiking trails and are bordered by the Rum River.

Since its inception in 1988, CSG has offered a steadily growing number of retreats designed to encourage spiritual growth in a warm and friendly environment of dialogue and quiet reflection. Some retreats are created exclusively for men, for women, or for people at life turning points. Others focus on self expressive/centering pathways such as "Creativity and Spirituality," Native American spirituality, the Enneagram, or tai chi. There are also holiday weekend and volunteer (no fee) work retreats.

The Center is directed by John Ellison and Jerie Smith, both with a background in Lutheran ministry. The retreats are facilitated by John, Jerie and other members of the CSG Advisory Community — a large and caring family of people mostly in the teaching and healing professions.

Address   35197 Wakenen Drive N.E., Cambridge, MN 55008, USA

Phone   612/689-5502.

Season   Year-round.

Programs 2 to 5-day guided, spiritual growth retreats. Also accommodate private retreats and center use by spiritually oriented groups.

Lodging   6 double & 5 single rooms, each with its own character.

Rates   Sample guided retreat rates: 3-day/3-night $95, 2-day $45-75. Private retreat $25/day.

Meals   4 or 5 meals on 2-day retreats, 8 meals on 3-day retreats, and 3 daily meals on 4 & 5-day retreats. Vegetarian options. Private retreatants BYO food. Bread, coffee & tea available for all.

Black Hills Health and Education Center   Hermosa, SD

Black Hills Health and Education Center is located in a 450 acre valley surrounded by rim-rock cliffs in southwestern South Dakota — a region where even winter weather is generally mild and sunny. The main lodge contains a whirlpool, a Russian steam cabinet, and a shower that alternates hot and cold water sprays. At least once a week, there are excursions to a large, natural indoors pool fed by a hot mineral springs.

The Black Hills Center conducts residential "Wellness Programs" designed to transform lifestyles. Each program includes an initial physical exam, daily lectures on holistic health, supervised group exercises and water therapy, massage, nutrition and stress management instruction, individual counseling and group discussions. The Center's learning-by-doing approach is also used to teach guests how to shop for and prepare nutritious meals.

The Center is operated by members of the Seventh-day Adventist Church and is affiliated with the nearby Black Hills Missionary College. The Center and the College share staff — physicians, nurses, nutritionists, therapists and counselors. There are daily morning worship services, Friday vespers, and a special community music program on each program's last Friday night.

Address   Box 19, Hermosa, SD 57744, USA

Phone   605/255-4101.

Season   Year-round.

Programs 12, 19 & 25-day "Wellness Programs" for people wishing to remain healthy and people wishing to address illness without drugs or surgery. Optional attendance at Christian services.

Lodging   12 double & single rooms, with private or shared bath. Also motor home camping facilities.

Rates   12-day single $1,550, couple $2,395. 19-day single $2,090, couple $3,150. 25-day single $2,395, couple $3,495.

Meals   3 daily buffet style, non-dairy vegetarian meals.

Onsite   Rapid City, SD

Onsite Training & Consulting is a residential outpatient treatment center for co-dependents and adult children of dysfunctional families. The programs are conducted at a motel a few miles outside of Rapid City in the peaceful and scenic Black Hills countryside of southwest South Dakota.

Onsite's most frequent offering is the 8-day "Living Centered Program" for co-dependency/family issues treatment. The second most frequent offering is the 5-day "Learning to Love Yourself" workshop, which includes teen tracks during summer months. Other 5-day workshops are "Couples Renewal," "Time Out For Women," and "Time Out For Men." For medical professionals, educators, and clergy, Onsite offers workshops combining training and "Learning To Love Yourself."

All Onsite programs are designed by Sharon Wegscheider-Cruse and John Cruse, M.D., well known authors in the recovery field. Most programs are staffed by master's degree therapists trained by Sharon in techniques such as gestalt, psychodrama, sculpting, 12-Step and experiential therapy.

Address   2455 West Chicago Street, Rapid City, SD 57702, USA

Phone   605/341-7432. Fax 605/341-4847.

Season   Year-round.

Programs 5 & 8-day workshops & treatment programs for co-dependents & adult children from dysfunctional families. Also 5 to 7-day training programs and combination training/treatment programs.

Lodging   Motel room accommodations.

Rates   1994 program rates: "Living Centered Program" $1,545; "Learning to Love Yourself" $750 or $625/person if both parent & teen/child attend; "Couples Renewal" $700/person; "Time Out For Women" $750; "Time Out For Men" $750.

Meals   3 daily buffet style meals.

Center for Exceptional Living   Elkhorn, WI

Two hours from Chicago and 45 minutes from Milwaukee, the Center for Exceptional Living Retreat Center occupies 40 acres of rolling wooded land next to Lauderdale Lakes. On the grounds are canoes, hiking paths, hot tubs, and distinctive, domed buildings formerly owned by a commune. The land's current owners are psychotherapists Judith and Bob Wright. Judith is president of Chicago's Center for Exceptional Living (CEL). Bob is president of Chicago's Human Effectiveness, Inc. Center retreats are facilitated by Bob, Judith and their staffs of professional counselors.

1993 weekend retreats included a retreat for mothers and daughters, a women's empowerment retreat, a men's spirituality retreat, and a couples retreat. Other weekend offerings were "Overcoming Soft Addictions" plus winter and spring spiritual retreats. Summer featured a two week spiritual retreat with meditation, chanting, singing, dancing, art, crafts, journal writing, team and life theme work, plus abundant outdoor recreation. CEL also leads an annual, 8 to 10-day journey to sacred places. This early fall trip was to New Mexico in 1991, Arizona in 1992 and England in 1993.

Address   Center for Exceptional Living, 333 E. Ontario, Suite 302B, Chicago, IL 60611, USA

Phone   312/664-2700 or 414/742-2110.

Season   Year-round.

Programs Weekend & weeklong spiritual attunement & self-empowerment retreats. Also an annual spiritual journey to sacred sites.

Lodging Accommodations for up to 30 overnight guests in bunkbed rooms with carpets, electricity, wood stoves & air conditioning.

Rates Summer Spiritual Retreat — 2 weeks $2,290, 1 week $1,295. Couple's weekend $750/couple. Men's weekend $525/person. Other weekends $395/person.

Meals 3 daily meals with vegetarian options.

Christine Center   Willard, WI

The Christine Center for Unitive Planetary Spirituality is located in central Wisconsin on 251 acres of former farmland. The barn has been converted to a library and meditation hall. A greenhouse stands by its side. The silo has become a chapel. And 20 hermitages plus a sauna and ofuro (a deep water Japanese bath) have been built in the nearby forest.

Founded in 1980 by a Franciscan Sisters order, the center is now an independent, ecumenical spiritual community, retreat and education center. The resident community of 2 children and 12 adults includes Franciscan Sisters and others with training in experimental and transpersonal psychology, Vipassana meditation and Sufi practices. Spiritual guidance is available in traditional religious and transpersonal/metaphysical forms.

The Ya Azim School for Spiritual Development offers 5 seminars (numbered I to V) to develop the clarity necessary to recognize Essential Self. Experiential as well as academic, these seminars make use of meditation, psychocalesthenics, body and group energetics. The School also offers a "Mystic Christianity" Bible study weekend, a weekend "Sacred Dance Retreat," and a weekend "Conscious Work Retreat." All seminars are led by Christine community members and offered several times each year.

The center supports short, private retreats; 1 to 8-day guided retreats; community life-style retreats; and long, sabbatical retreats. Life style and sabatical retreatants may participate fully in community life. A typical, community day includes periods of conscious work, group and individual meditation. On Sundays, morning communal meditation and prayer is followed after brunch by afternoon play and relaxation. Each community member also sets aside one day each week for solitude, rest and reflection.

Address W8291 Mann Road, Willard, WI 54493, USA

Phone 715/267-7507. No visits without prior arrangement.

Season Year-round.

Programs Retreats and spiritual development seminars. Retreats may be of any length. Most seminars are weekend offerings, though Seminar III is 10 days and Seminar V is 2 weeks.

Lodging   20 hermitages, each with electricity, a wood-burning stove and 1-3 beds. The 16 "rustic" hermitages do not have plumbing. The 4 "bath" hermitages each have a toilet & bath.

Rates   Seminars I, II & IV: rustic $172, bath $211. Seminar III: rustic $391, bath $508. Seminar V: rustic $602, bath $771. Weekend theme retreats: rustic $118, bath $144. Other retreat daily rates: camping $12-28, dorm $14-34, rustic $24-44, bath $37-57.

Meals   All meals made from whole grains, nuts, seeds, organic fruits & vegetables. Lunch & dinner served. Help yourself to breakfast.

Services   Spiritual guidance, reflexology, jin shin do, Rah energy balance, breathwork, sauna and ofuro.

High Wind Center   Plymouth, WI

55 miles north of Milwaukee in the Northern Kettle Moraine, High Wind is a rustic learning and retreat center consisting of residential, meeting and sanctuary facilities connected by paths across 128 acres of rolling meadows, forest and wetland fen.

The most frequently offered High Wind programs, the 5-day "Retreat Week" and the weekend "Game of Transformation," can be combined at a discounted rate into a single program. In 1993, other programs included an intensive journal workshop, workshops combining painting and movement, the one-week "Inner Dimensions of a Sustainable Culture," and one-day programs such as "Sustainable Energy Practices" and a Celtic fair.

Most programs are conducted by members of several High Wind resident families, a tight knit, non-intentional community with ties to Scotland's Findhorn community. Some programs are co-sponsored by the University of Wisconsin at Milwaukee. And some future programs will be co-sponsored by the Plymouth Institute, a new experiment in "appropriate technology" and "sustainable development" on an adjoining 144-acre trout farm.

Address   W7136 County Road U, Plymouth, WI 53073, USA

Phone   414/528-7212.

Season   May through September.

Programs 1 to 7-day personal growth retreats, creative expression & ecology workshops.

Lodging   Capacity for 15-20 overnight guests in single & double bedrooms in a solar bioshelter and a turn-of-the-century farmhouse.

Rates   Tuition, food & lodging ranges from $240-450 for weekend, 5-day & weeklong workshops. Personal retreat daily rates — single $30, double $40. Private group meeting space $60/day.

Meals   3 daily vegetarian meals.

UNITED STATES   South Central Region

Reforming Feelings   Independence, MO

The suburban Kansas City site for "Reforming Feelings" weekends is the Franciscan Prayer Center — set on an 82 acre campus of woods, trails and open fields adjacent to city parks and recreation facilities. The hilltop center includes a chapel, bookstore, library and residence hall.

Each year there are about five "Reforming Feelings I" weekends plus ten level II and III weekends. The level I weekend includes five workshops on topics such as "Understanding Self and Feeling Responsibility," "Love, Love Relationships, and Loneliness," "Happiness and Emotions, Anger and Forgiveness." Each of these workshops is followed by small group processing sessions. And each of the level II weekends is limited to 12 level I graduates, who focus entirely on experiential work.

All "Reforming Feelings" weekends are facilitated by Gail Vaughn and her staff from the nearby Reforming Feelings Counseling & Consulting center. Dr. Vaughn is a certified Neuro-Linguistics Therapist with a Ph.D. in psychology plus degrees in nursing and human relations. She specializes in counseling individuals and families for problems such as drug and alcohol abuse, adult child issues, eating disorders, child abuse, and incest.

Address   1201 West College, Liberty, MO 64068, USA

Phone   816/781-9494.

Season   Year-round.

Programs Weekend retreats on the origin & healthy expression of emotions.

Lodging   Either single or shared room accommodations, depending on size of group. Soap & linens provided.

Rates   Phase I weekend $135. Phase II or III weekend $395.

Meals   4 meals/weekend — 3 on Saturday & brunch on Sunday.

Wholistic Life Center   Washburn, MO

The Wholistic Life Center occupies 900 peaceful acres of rolling Ozark countryside in southwestern Missouri. The property contains a lake, creeks, wooded trails and abundant wildlife. Founded in 1990 to help people discover their true potential, this non-profit, non-sectarian center is staffed by 15 resident professionals including a retired psychiatrist. Programs are 3, 7, 14 and 30+ days in length.

Each day there are two sessions of light movement and stretching exercises; classes on topics such as mind/body connections, nutritional intake and balance, waste elimination, and stress reduction; recreational activities such as hiking, basketball, tennis, ping pong, volleyball, singing and dancing; and two herbally enriched jacuzzi treatments. Evenings feature open forum discussions to facilitate release of negative self concepts and unhealthy behavior patterns.

Address   Route 1, Box 1783, Washburn, MO 65772, USA

Phone   417/435-2212.

Season   Year-round.

Programs   Programs teaching a lifestyle of moderate exercise, healthy diet, positive mental attitude, emotional release, & spiritual growth.

Lodging   10 shared cabins, each with a private room.

Rates   Base rates: 3-day $325, 7-day $750, 14-day $1,400. 5-10% discounts often available. Single supplement for private room.

Meals   Tasty, healthy, non-dairy vegetarian breakfast, lunch & dinner.

Sancta Sophia Seminary   Tahlequah, OK

Sancta Sophia Seminary is located in Sparrow Hawk Village, an Ozark foothills community about two hours from both Tulsa, OK and Fayetteville, AR. The wooded 432 acre community-owned land, bordered on three sides by the Illinois River, is also the home of Light of Christ Community Church (LCCC). Sancta Sophia, a ministry of LCCC, teaches esoteric Christianity through a faculty of 30 metaphysical and healing arts practitioners.

The Seminary's graduate and undergraduate curriculum employs home study and weeklong classes, thereby allowing anyone to enrol in a 5-day class. Each class meets for 2 1/2 hours each morning or afternoon. Topics fall into categories such as "Spiritual Disciplines," "Meditation," "Dream Work," "Intuitive Development," "Numerology/Astrology," "Spiritual Healing," "Nutrition & Health."

There are frequent one and two-day weekend workshops. Each year there are also three special programs suitable for first-time visitors. The Labor Day weekend "Discover Community" program offers an inside view of Sparrow Hawk Village — a 12 year old, 100 resident, spiritual community. The four-day, "Complete MetaPhysical" weekend includes individual and group work on spiritual practices such as meditation and journal writing. The six-day "Intensive" focuses on a theme such "Opening to the Gifts of Spirit."

Sancto Sophia's dean (also LCCC's president) is Carol Parrish, Ph.D., a well known author and teacher whose life was transformed by a near-death experience at the age of 23. Carol re-defines "Holy Spirit" as "Sophia" and re-visions Christianity as the path to the "Christ-within."

Address   Sparrow Hawk Village, 11 Summit Ridge Drive, Tahlequah, OK 74464, USA

Phone   918/456-3421.

Season   Year-round.

Programs Weeklong courses, weekend workshops, & special programs (3-day Community weekend, 4-day MetaPhysical weekend, 6-day Intensive).

Lodging   Guest housing in private village homes. Also tent & cabana campsites, with nearby bathhouse, at a riverside campground.

Rates   Room, board & tuition: 3-day weekend $200; 4-day weekend $395; 6-day intensive $400. Tuition: weekend workshop $35-55; seminary week $85. Lodging: house guest $70/week, cabana camping $5/night, tent site $4/night. Seminary meals: lunch $4, dinner $5.

Meals   All meals, mostly vegetarian (some poultry & fish), included with special week & long weekend programs. Lunches available during other weekend programs & weeklong classes. Guests receive kitchen privileges or share breakfast & dinner at village homes.

Services   Spiritual healing sessions, sponsored by church donations, offered 2 days each week.

Healing Springs Ranch   Tioga, TX

A one hour drive north of Dallas, Healing Springs Ranch is a pastoral 100 acre property with a lake that allows paddleboating, fishing and canoeing. Ranch facilities include a large outdoor swimming pool, three jacuzzis, a gym and jogging track, outdoor basketball and sand volleyball courts, and a horseshoe toss. The sunny hacienda has a large living room, dance floor, non-alcoholic saloon, verandas and a deck. The Ranch's grassy fields are home for sheep, goats, horses, llamas, buffalo, and small pigs.

Guests can avail themselves of natural therapies such as stress management counseling and videos, aerobic and hydro aerobic workouts, nutritional counseling, and scented mineral baths. There are special workshops on overcoming various obsessive disorders. In addition, well known author Gary Null each year offers 4-8 weeks of workshops and seminars on holistic health and nutrition, yoga and meditation, and creative self-expression.

Address   P.O. Box 277, Tioga, TX 76271, USA

Phone   817/437-2204.   Fax 871/437-9926.

Season   Year-round.

Programs Occasional holistic health workshops & seminars. Ongoing daily program to help people cleanse, relax & balance body & mind.

Lodging   Capacity for 85 overnight guests in shared or single rooms with private bath. Also 2 large tipis.

Rates   Lodging, health facilities & sessions $55/day. Meals $20/day. Gary Null retreats $150/day, meals included.

Meals   Kitchen available for guest use. Ranch also offers 3 daily meals with both vegetarian and meat options.

Services   Massage, isolation tank, acupressure, reflexology, mud wrap, herbal body wrap, colon hydro therapy. Also airport transfers.

Lake Austin Spa Resort   Austin, TX

Lake Austin Spa Resort is a 12 acre facility bordering a 23 mile-long lake and the famous Steiner Cattle Ranch. LASR's physical facilities include indoor and outdoor pools, a 24-hour gym, lakeside exercise equipment, tennis and volleyball courts, paddleboats, sculls, a Swiss ParCourse and horseshoe pits. Hiking trails snake out over the surrounding Texas hill country. Guests are served their meals in a lakeview dining room. Winery tours and sunset cruises can be arranged.

LASR guests are offered a large daily selection of fitness and relaxation activities, holistic health classes and workshops. Fitness activities include circuit classes, cross training, rhythm and movement, Country & Western aerobics, line dancing and hill country walks. Stretching and relaxation activities include water stretch, yoga, tai chi, visualization and meditation. Classes and workshops cover subjects such as art and art therapy, cooking demonstrations, eating behaviors, body image, movement therapy, self-awareness and inner journey.

Address   1705 Quinlan Park Road, Austin, TX 78732, USA

Phone   800/847-5637.

Season   Year-round.

Programs   Regular daily program includes attendance at holistic health workshop, relaxation & fitness activities; plus use of pools, gyms, tennis courts, mountain bikes & paddle boats.

Lodging   40 cottage rooms with bed-and-breakfast style furnishings. On request, guests are matched with a roommate.

Rates   4-day rates: single $660 or $715, double $575 or $630, triple $525 or $565, quad $495. 7-day rates: single $1,155 or $1,250, double $1,000 or $1,100, triple $900, quad $855. Add 6% room tax plus $22/day service & gratuities charge.

Meals   3 daily gourmet meals. Vegetarian & other diets accommodated on advance notice. Vegetables from own organic garden.

Services   Private medical evaluation, nutrition analysis, fitness assessment, tennis & sculling lessons, counseling on behavioral issues. Various massage & therapeutic body treatments, facials, manicures & pedicures. Courtesy airport transfers.

Options Unlimited   Austin, TX

Options Unlimited was founded in 1984 by co-dependency treatment pioneers Mary Jo and Olaf Bjornstal to treat people from dysfunctional families. Participants must be free from mood or mind-altering chemicals and involved with a therapist for aftercare. Clients stay in a house in a hilly, tree lined neighborhood with parks and lakes. Each program is limited to 7 participants, who are treated by a staff of four professional counselors.

Throughout each 11-day program, clients are involved in real-life situations — going to the gym together, eating meals together, playing in the park, and attending evening 12-Step meetings in the community. Treatment modalities include humanistic, client-centered, gestalt, reality, and rational/emotive therapies. Experiential therapeutic techniques include psychodrama, guided imagery, and emotional discharge.

Address   1001 Capitol of Texas Highway, Building L, Suite 200, Austin, TX 78746, USA

Phone   512/328-0288 or 800/299-0288.

Season   Year-round.

Programs 11-day treatment programs for people from dysfunctional families.

Lodging Shared accommodations on bottom floor of a house.

Rates   Total program $2,000, including all meals & lodging.

Meals   Prepare your own breakfast. Box picnic lunch or lunch at the office, a 10 minute van ride from the house. Go out to dinner.

Texas Men's Institute   Central Texas

The Texas Men's Institute each year organizes half a dozen regional "Men's Wilderness Gatherings" plus an "International Men's Conference." Held over a weekend at a ranch or wilderness camp site, each gathering features seminars and workshops designed to facilitate emotional healing through improved self-understanding and communications. Workshop leaders include therapists, pastors, counselors and poets. Gatherings also include games, skits, stories, sweat lodges and drumming.

The Institute usually holds three annual gatherings in central Texas: a spring men's gathering, a Father's Day father/son gathering, and a fall "International Men's Conference." In 1993, a central Texas ranch was also the site of the

Institute's first "Wild Hearts Gathering" for both men and women. In other regions of America, 1993 Institute-sponsored men's gatherings included one on male/female relationships and one on healing mother/son emotional wounds.

Address   P.O. Box 311384, New Braunfels, TX 78131, USA

Phone   800/786-8584.

Season   April through September.

Programs   Weekend men's gatherings for emotional healing & spiritual growth through better self-understanding & communications.

Lodging   Cabin dorms and/or camping.

Rates $145-245 per person, all meals & camping or cabin facilities provided. $245 for father & 1 son ($100 each additional son) at father/son retreats. $350 per couple at couples' retreats.

Meals   3 daily buffet meals with vegetarian options.

UNITED STATES   Northeast Region

Figaro Yoga Cruises   Maine Coast

The Figaro is a 51 foot centerboard yawl built in 1963 for ocean racing. The USCG-licensed captains on Figaro's two annual one-week yoga cruises are Jen Martin and Barry King. Barry shares a knowledge of coastal ecology and a love of music. Jen's interests include herbalism, Native American and Eastern spirituality.

Figaro cruise mates meet in Camden, 2 hours north of Portland, for shipboard orientation and dinner on Sunday evening. The Figaro sets sail at mid-morning on Monday and arrives back in Camden five days later. Dean Lerner leads two daily Iyengar-style hatha yoga sessions. And each day there is plenty of time for explorations — visiting a fishing community, hiking the shores of an uninhabited island, rowing around a quiet cove.

Address   Box 1336, Camden, ME 04843, USA

Phone   800/473-6169.

Season   July

Programs   One-week yoga cruises.

Lodging   Accommodates 6 passengers (not including captain, first mate & yoga instructor) in 2 double cabins & 2 semi-private berths. Linens provided. "Navy" showers to conserve fresh water.

Rates $699 per 6-day cruise.

Meals   3 daily meals (vegetarian on 1 cruise, vegetarian + seafood on the other) served family style in the main saloon. Sometimes the crew eats underway to enjoy a sunset or favorable winds.

Marie Joseph Spiritual Center   Biddeford, ME

Marie Joseph Spiritual Center is run by the Sisters of the Presentation of Mary in the former Ocean View Hotel, a large white building near a sandy shore 15 miles south of Portland. During the summer, the Center is used primarily as a spiritual vacation and retreat center for women religious (i.e. nuns). During the rest of the year, the Center hosts weekend workshops and group retreats open to the public. Program participants may join the resident community of nuns in thrice daily prayer services.

Many weekend workshops focus on forms of prayer — particularly contemplative and centering prayer. There are weekend healing group retreats for women-only and for both women and men. There are also frequent Enneagram workshops. Other weekend programs have focused on devotional spirituality, such as exploring the works of St. John of the Cross and Teresa of Avila.

Address   R.F.D. 2, Biddeford, ME 04005, USA

Phone   207/284-5671. No visits without prior arrangements.

Season   October through June.

Programs   2-day weekend workshops (Friday evening to Sunday afternoon) encouraging spiritual self renewal in a prayerful atmosphere.

Lodging   Overnight guest capacity for 70 in 46 rooms.

Rates   2-day weekend workshop $75-100.

Meals   3 daily cafeteria meals in large dining room.

Services   Spiritual counseling on a donation basis.

Mystic Pines   East Orland, ME

Mystic Pines is nestled amidst 100-foot pine trees on the shore of Alamoosook Lake, a 15 minute drive from the scenic Maine coast and 35 minutes away from Acadia National Park. Facilities include dock, boats, horseshoe pits, picnic tables and grill. Leisure activities include canoeing, swimming and fishing. Hiking is "right out your front door," and the day can end at the dock watching the sun disappear over the lake.

A weeklong vacation includes 30 hours of workshops that each vacationer selects from the following menu — 1/2-day "Self Massage," 1/2-day "Attuning to Nature," 1-day "Self Healing Skills," 1 or 2-day "Whole Being Workouts" 2-day "Accessing Your Higher Self," or a 5-day comprehensive Higher Self Integration system ("Block Busters" — also available as a 2-week program). Workshop "tools" include movement & massage, dream work & visualization, memory & art work, chanting & singing, prayer, chakra & auric cleansing.

Workshops are led by healing arts practitioners JoyBeth and John Lufty-Balzer. JoyBeth is a psychic/spiritual counselor trained in social work. John is an artist and naturalist trained in social psychology. Mystic Pines does not allow pets, children, smoking, drinking or drugs.

Address   P.O. Box 19, East Orland, ME 04431, USA

Phone   207/469-7572. No visits without prior arrangement.

Season   Retreats July through Sept. Cottage rentals May through October. Year-round individual consultations & workshops.

Programs   5-day/6-night adult vacation retreats focusing on holistic health and Higher Self Integration. Non-retreatant, cottage renters can also sign up for individual, couple or small group workshops.

Lodging   3 lakeside cottages, each with bathroom and kitchen, for couples & individuals. Available for rent when retreats not scheduled.

Rates   Weeklong vacation retreats: couple $1000, individual $800, group $500/person. Weeklong cottage rental $350. Non-retreat program: 1/2-day $100, 1-day $200, 2-day $400 (divide by # of people in workshop for approx. cost/person). Individual consultation $50.

Meals   Guests mostly make meals in their cottages or dine at a local restaurant. Some meals are taken together as a group.

Services Individual Higher Self Integration consultations.

Northern Pines Health Resort   Raymond, ME

A forty minute drive north of Portland, Northern Pines has the healthy outdoor feeling of a summer camp. Cedar cabins, two lodges and a yurt are tucked beneath Rattlesnake Mountain among towering pines along the shore of Crescent Lake. The resort's 70 acres include many forest trails, a sauna, a hot tub, and a one mile lake front. Lake water temperatures rise in the summer to 75 degrees, warm enough for an evening skinny dip.

The resort offers a full menu of activities, all of which are optional. A typical day includes meditation at 6:30, stretch at 7, a 2-3 mile morning walk at 7:30, breakfast at 8:45, a class at 9:30, an aerobic workout at 11, a quiet period at noon followed by a 1 o'clock lunch, a 2 o'clock hike (snowshoeing and cross-country skiing in the winter), yoga at 4:30, supper at 6, and an evening program at 7:30. Classes and talks cover topics such as nutrition, vegetarian cooking, bowel management, biofeedback, stress management, Naturopathic and Ayurvedic medicine, tarot and astrology.

Owner/director Marlee Turner and her staff create a cheerful social environment. Marlee introduces each meal by gathering all guests in a circle, asking each to give his or her name. An expert canoeist and avid contra dancer, Marlee co-founded Northern Pines in 1980 on the health precepts she has followed since her recovery from thyroid cancer and multiple sclerosis.

Address   559 Route 85, Raymond, ME 04071, USA

Phone   207/655-7624.

Season   Year-round except the last 3 weeks in January.

Programs   Regular daily schedule of meditation, yoga and exercise periods plus various natural health classes.

Lodging   Capacity for 50 in summer & 30 in winter. Cabins, lodge & yurt with private or double rooms plus private full, 1/2, semi-private or shared bathrooms. Some accommodations have a fireplace or a private veranda. Two are wheelchair accessible.

Rates   Daily rates: double room $125-192; single room $156-229. Weekly rates: double $744-1,144; single $926-1,352. Summer season bookings must generally be made by the week. At other times, sizeable discounts can often be secured by advance reservations.

Meals 3 daily vegetarian meals, 50% fruits & salads. In summer, ingredients from own garden. 3-7 day fast option.

Services Swedish & shiatsu massage, seaweed wrap, polarity, rebirthing, aromatherapy, facial, scalp & hair treatment, flotation tank. Also Portland pick-up & drop-off service.

Poland Spring Health Institute   Poland Spring, ME

Poland Spring Health Institute is a handsome three-story house surrounded by well groomed lawns and Maine countryside 30 miles north of Portland. The Institute draws its water from the same well as the world famous Poland Spring water bottling plant. A small lake is a short walk away.

The Institute operates health regeneration programs. One-week programs include health and nutrition education, hot packs, steam baths, massage and moderate exercise. Most guests opt for the two-week program, which determines the exercise regimen on the basis of a thorough diagnostic evaluation (including an electrocardiogram). When desired and appropriate, treadmill stress testing is included in the three-week program.

Programs can be tailored to address specific guest concerns such as chronic fatigue virus syndrome, high blood pressure, hypertension, depression, diabetes, obesity, stress and arthritis. There are special smoking cessation and heart disease programs. All programs are administered by a Seventh Day Adventist staff, which invites guests to participate in short daily morning worship services and Friday vespers.

Address R.F.D. 1, Box 4300, Poland Spring, ME 04274, USA

Phone 207/998-2894.

Season Year-round.

Programs Individualized health enhancement programs with 3, 2 and 1-week options. 3-week coronary heart disease program & 2-week smoking cessation program. Optional Christian worship services.

Lodging 6 large private or semi-private rooms.

Rates 3-week: semi-private room $2,590, private room $3,105, participating married couple $4,710, married couple with non-participating spouse $4,125. 2-week: semi-private $1,790, private $2,200. 1-week: semi-private $745, private $950.

Meals 3 family style, dairy-free vegetarian meals served each day.

Services Courtesy airport & bus terminal transfers.

Ann Wigmore Foundation   Boston, MA

Housed in a handsome red brick building near Boston Commons, The Ann Wigmore Foundation is the office of living foods lifestyle creator and chief proponent Dr. Ann Wigmore. It is also the site of an ongoing 12-day "Living Foods Lifestyle" residential course. Students adhere to a living foods diet while learning nutritional theory, colon care, food growing and preparation techniques.

Each course, typically with 8-10 students, begins on a Monday with a 3 PM orientation. Students begin each day thereafter with enemas and wheatgrass juice at 7 AM, followed by light exercise or a walk outdoors. Students attend 3 to 5 daily classes on topics such as yoga, massage, painting, psychosynthesis, and "Mind As Healer." Evenings feature videos on mind/body health. Students leave on Saturday morning after a Friday graduation feast, prepared by the students themselves.

Address   196 Commonwealth Ave., Boston, MA 02116, USA

Phone   617/267-9424.

Season   Year-round except for a 2-week Christmas break.

Programs A 12-day course offered continuously throughout the year.

Lodging   Comfortable capacity for 12 overnight guests in private rooms and dormitory rooms, each with 4 or 5 beds.

Rates   Private room $1,250. Dorm $950.

Meals   3 daily live food meals: a fruit smoothie or sprouted grain cereal for breakfast; energy soup & a green salad for lunch; energy soup & fruit for dinner. Energy soup is a blended   mix   of   fruit, greens, rejuvelac, avocado, dulse and bean sprouts.

Canyon Ranch in the Berkshires   Lenox, MA

Canyon Ranch in the Berkshires is a spacious 120 acre estate of broad lawns, ponds and woods in the gentle hills of western Massachusetts. The estate's historic Bellefontaine mansion houses medical and behavioral consultation areas, a restored library and the dining room. The nearby spa complex contains exercise rooms, indoor and outdoor tennis courts, squash and racquetball courts, indoor and outdoor pools, a suspended indoor running track, plus complete body treatment and salon facilities.

The Ranch's premier offering is its "Life Enhancement Program," designed to address health objectives such as smoking cessation, weight loss, and stress reduction. Selected weeks are devoted exclusively to prevention and reversal of heart disease and healthy aging. The program includes medical evaluation and supervision, a program of daily indoor and outdoor exercise, daily meetings with behavioral health counselors, access to a broad array of professional health and personal/sports services, nutritional counseling and full use of Ranch recreational facilities.

Like its sister ranch in Arizona, Canyon Ranch in the Berkshires has been voted the world's best health spa by the readers of Conde Naste "Traveler" magazine. The magazine notes that Canyon Ranch offers "a rounded, holistic approach" with individual counseling, group workshops, plus techniques such as biofeedback and hypnotherapy. Ranch staff includes physicians, psychologists, registered dieticians, exercise physiologists, and certified health educators — a nearly three-to-one ratio of staff to guests.

Address   Bellefontaine, Kemble Street, Lenox, MA 01240, USA

Phone   413/637-4100 or 800/726-9900.

Season   Year-round.

Programs 4, 5 & 6-day "Getaway Plans;" 8-day "Total Lifestyle Plan;" 1 & 2 week "Life Enhancement Programs." Also custom tailored "Long Term Program" of at least 4 weeks in length.

Lodging   120 rooms in a New England-style Inn connected by glass-enclosed walkways to mansion & spa complex. Most rooms are garden units with private patios. Some rooms are specially equipped for the disabled. Ramp entry on all buildings.

Rates   "Life Enhancement Program" 7-night rates: single $2,580-3,130, double $2,320-2,740. 10% discount on 2nd, consecutive week. Prices do not include 18% service charge or applicable sales tax.

Meals   3 daily gourmet meals in luxurious dining room. Can accommodate supervised fasting, vegetarian & special diets.

Services Packages include a selection of professional health services (nutrition, movement therapy, exercise physiology, medical & behavioral health services) plus a selection of personal/sports services (private sports lessons, massage, herbal & aroma wraps, hydromassage, haircut, shampoo & hair styling, manicure & pedicure, makeup consultation & application).

The Cape Experience   Truro, MA

An annual mid-summer event for over ten years, The Cape Experience offers six consecutive weeks and weekends of Iyengar style yoga instruction, plus accommodations and healthy meals near Cape Cod beaches. All meals are served in the "cook house," walking distance from the two large guest houses. In their free time, guests can enjoy swimming, sailing and cycling. Evenings feature lectures and discussions.

Each week begins with a weekend of five 2-hour yoga sessions led by a nationally known guest instructor. Weekday yoga sessions are conducted from 8 to 9:30 each morning and from 5 to 6:30 each afternoon by Cape Experience director Karin Stephan and the guest teacher from the prior weekend. A long-time student of B.K.S. Iyengar, Karin is co-director of the B.K.S. Iyengar Yoga Center in Somerville, MA.

Address   Yoga/Macrobiotic Vacations, 5 Frost Street, Cambridge, MA 02140, USA

Phone   617/497-0218.

Season   Late June through early August.

Programs   6 consecutive weeklong, Iyengar style, hatha yoga vacations. Also weekend options.

Lodging   Cape Cod houses in the village of Truro.

Rates   Week $895. Weekend $325. Discounts for early registration.

Meals   Two daily vegetarian/macrobiotic meals.

Services   Shiatsu massage, rolfing, ginger compresses, yoga therapy, private & small group cooking classes, dietary & lifestyle transitioning consultations.

Gateways to Creativity   Deerfield, MA

"Gateways to Creativity" is a 5-day residential workshop where art-making is used as a catalyst for personal transformation. It is held each year on the New England country campus of Eaglebrook School, where each day begins with an optional early morning yoga session. Participants then work with a variety of art materials in an environment that encourages creative self-expression. Program benefits often include increased confidence and self-esteem, clarification of life choices, and a greater sense of inner peace.

"Gateways" is limited to 18-20 participants, none of whom need have any prior art experience. It is facilitated by Dale Schwarz and Guillermo Cuellar, directors of New England Art Therapy Institute (NEATI). Dale is a multi-media artist and registered art therapist. Guillermo's expertise includes the fields of art expression and creative behavior, Gestalt and family therapies. NEATI also offers non-residential weekend workshops.

Address   The New England Art Therapy Institute, 216 Silver Lane #25, Sunderland, MA 01375, USA

Phone   413/665-4880.

Season   Generally the last week in July.

Programs   5-day art workshop exploring creativity as a catalyst for personal transformation.

Lodging   Simply furnished, private rooms at Eaglebrook School.

Rates   1993 cost was $725 for registration prior to June 25.

Meals   3 wholesome meals each day (Sunday dinner through Friday lunch), all with vegetarian options. Home baked bread.

Insight Meditation Society   Barre, MA

Insight Meditation Society (IMS) is a Vipassana meditation retreat center set on 80 wooded acres in the quiet countryside of central Massachusetts. Retreats up to as long as 9 days are designed to be comfortable for beginners. Meditation periods alternate sitting with walking meditation, and sitting can be done on floor cushions, benches or chairs.

An IMS retreat day begins at 6 AM with 45 minutes of sitting meditation followed by breakfast and free time — an opportunity to perform one's daily 45 minutes of center maintenance work. From 8:15 to noon there are periods of meditation combined with instruction. Following lunch and a short rest break, meditation/instruction resumes from 2 to 5. After a light evening supper, there is usually a one hour evening discourse.

All retreats are led by highly qualified visiting teachers, including several current and former Buddhist monks. Three teachers, Joseph Goldstein, Jack Kornfield and Sharon Salzberg, were IMS co-founders.

Address   1230 Pleasant Street, Barre, MA 01005, USA

Phone   508/355-4378. No visits without prior arrangement.

Season   Year-round except for January.

Programs   Teacher-led Vipassana meditation retreats, usually 2, 3, or 7-9 days long.

Lodging   Capacity for 100 overnight guests. Some single rooms. But mostly double rooms, with men and women sleeping in separate quarters. Renovations have been made to accommodate the disabled.

Rates   Course rates: weekend $90; 3-day $120; 7-day $195; 8 & 9-day $250. Course fees cover only center operating costs. At the end of each retreat, students may make donations to support the teacher.

Meals   3 daily vegetarian meals.

Kripalu Center   Lenox, MA

The world's largest yoga-based holistic health center, Kripalu Center overlooks Lake Mahkeenak in the Berkshires region of western Massachusetts. Its 300 forested acres contain walking trails and a private beach for summer swimming. A spiritual community numbering nearly 350, the Center is housed in a former Jesuit monastery. Facilities include separate men's and women's whirlpools and saunas.

For a guest in the popular Rest & Renewal (R&R) program, a typical day could include early morning and mid-afternoon hatha yoga classes; a workshop on conscious living; an instructional session on meditation; DansKinetics (yoga stretches combined with aerobic dance); and an evening satsang — chanting, dancing and spiritual teaching with a senior Kripalu resident or Yogi Amrit Desai, the Center's founder and spiritual director.

Yogi Amrit Desai is also the inventor of Kripalu Yoga — a type of hatha yoga wherein postures are connected in what resembles a slow motion dance. As it is taught in the daily hatha yoga classes, Kripalu Yoga is thus an offshoot of a 6000-year-old science of personal development that regards physical health as the basis for mental and spiritual growth. These and all other Center programs are led by members of the resident staff.

Address   Box 793, Lenox, MA 01240, USA

Phone   413/448-3400 or 800/967-3577 (reservations).

Season   Year-round.

Programs   Weekend, weeklong & 2-week programs in yoga, bodywork, health & well-being, self discovery, and spiritual attunement. Month-long professional trainings in Kripalu Yoga, bodywork, and "Holistic Lifestyle Teacher Training." Also a 3-month "Spiritual Lifestyle Training" residency introduction program.

Lodging   300 guest capacity. Dorms with bunk beds. Rooms for two with double or twin beds, lake or forest views. A few rooms with private baths. Linens included.

Rates   R&R nightly rate: 3 or more midweek nights $56-136, weekend $70-170. Other program rates: 3-night $240-540, 6-night $465-1,230, 2-week $949-2,145, 1-month professional training $1,944-4,455.

Meals   3 daily vegetarian buffets, high in fiber and protein, low in fats and sweeteners. Fresh baked bread. Most meals are silent.

Services   Kripalu bodywork, energy balancing, shiatsu therapy, footcare/reflexology, and facial skin care. A daily July/August children's program for ages 4-13) and weekend childcare at other times. The permanent staff includes a holistic physician.

Kushi Institute   Becket, MA

Housed in a former Franciscan abbey on 600 acres of Berkshire meadows and woodlands, the Kushi Institute is the major eastern U.S. center for macrobiotic research and education. Michio and Aveline Kushi personally lead several of the residential programs. Mornings begin with Japanese "do-in" stretching exercises, and seminar classes open with a meditation.

The major course offerings are 6-day cooking intensives, 3-day "Way to Health" seminars, 4-day "New Medicine and Human Destiny" seminars, and 4-day "Spiritual Development" seminars. The "Way to Health" series includes cooking classes plus instruction on the diet/health relationship, oriental diagnosis, and the elements of a natural lifestyle.

The "New Medicine and Human Destiny" series explores topics such as stages in the development of sickness; the application of traditional healing methods to physical and mental problems; how character and physical constitution are influenced by climate, geographical location and birth date. The six "New Medicine & Human Destiny" seminars can be taken in any order, but each "New Medicine" seminar is limited to 16 participants.

The "Spiritual Development" series delves into the meaning of karma and the mechanism of reincarnation, the development and use of consciousness, neutralizing negative thinking patterns, and managing spiritual energy. Principle texts are the Bible and the Tao Te Ching. Prayer, meditation and chanting are practiced as well as studied. The eight "Spiritual Development" seminars must be taken in sequential order.

Address   P.O. Box 7, Becket, MA 01223, USA

Phone   413/623-5741. Fax 413/623-8827.

Season   Year-round.

Programs Macrobiotic cooking, health & spiritual development seminars.

Lodging   Main building has 10 simply furnished guest rooms, each with 1 or 2 beds and three with private bath or shower. A separate, dormitory facility can accommodate another 20-30 people.

Rates   "Way to Health" $985. "New Medicine & Human Destiny" $655/session or $1195 for 2 combined sessions. "Spiritual Development" $545/session or $995 for 2 combined sessions.

Meals   3 daily macrobiotic meals.

Services   Shiatsu massage.

Maharishi Ayur-Veda Health Center   Lancaster, MA

The Maharishi Ayur-Veda Health Center is housed in a luxurious red brick mansion set on 200 acres of well kept lawns and woodlands 30 miles west of Boston. The Center is staffed by doctors and nurses trained in both Western and traditional Indian (Ayurvedic) health practices. Dr. Deepak Chopra, the West's best known advocate of Ayurveda, teaches a half-day seminar every other month on the theory of primordial sound therapy.

The Center's basic offering is its ongoing, one-week "Perfect Health Program." This program includes an initial Ayurvedic evaluation of body type and body/ mind imbalances; a prescribed rejuvenation (Pancha Karma) program that may incorporate cleansing steam baths, herbalized oil and internal purification therapies; physiology enlivening/balancing yogic stretching and breathing exercises; primordial sound and aroma therapies; lectures and classes on topics such as diet, Ayurvedic cooking, exercise, and attuning to a "cosmic rhythm" through daily and seasonal routines.

During the "Perfect Health Program," guests may also schedule other courses: Transcendental Meditation, training for athletes in Ayurvedic three-phase workout and breathing techniques, and Five Senses therapy based on pulse assessment. Every other month, the co-director of the Center's "Physicians' Training Program" teaches a course on diagnosing self-pulse readings and designing self-treatment programs. Departing guests receive specific recommendations for designing a home "Perfect Health Program."

Address   679 George Hill Road, P.O. Box 344, Lancaster, MA 01523, USA

Phone   508/365-4549. Fax 508/368-0674.

Season   Year-round.

Programs   1-week Ayurvedic "Perfect Health Program." Optional courses available during the week: "Self-Pulse Reading," "Five Senses Therapy," "Transcendental Meditation," "Primordial Sound Theory," and "Invincible Athletics."

Lodging   Luxurious single bedrooms, double bedrooms and suites, all with air conditioning.

Rates   "Perfect Health Program": $2,850-3,950, prices varying by room type. Optional courses: "Self-Pulse Reading" $295, "Five Senses Therapy" $155, "Transcendental Meditation" $400, "Invincible Athletics" $150, "Primordial Sound" seminar $700.

Meals   3 daily vegetarian meals served in dining room or guests' rooms.

Services   Program cost includes treatments such as Marma Therapy — stimulation of vital physiological points.

New Life Health Center   Boston, MA

New Life Health Center occupies a spacious three story building in the Jamaica Plain section of Boston, a short walk from Arnold Arboretum and Jamaica Pond. The Center contains an organic vegetable garden, natural food kitchen and dining area, guest rooms, yoga and meditation hall, an infrared sauna, lecture and physical therapy rooms, and treatment rooms. Treatments include acupuncture, acupressure, cupping (for energy, blood circulation and toxin removal), moxa heat (for strengthening the immune system), herbal teas and homeopathic remedies.

The Center's one and three week resident healing programs include all of the following: an initial in-depth health evaluation by Center director Bo-In Lee; daily morning meditation, treatments (as needed) every day except Sunday and Wednesday, yoga classes 5 days a week (2 classes on 3 days); sessions (as needed) to overcome mental and emotional imbalances; lectures and workshops several times a week on diet, lifestyle, self-healing and spiritual well-being.

Bo-In Lee is a respected acupuncturist trained in India, Japan and his native Korea in the Eastern and Western healing arts, psychology and spiritual disciplines. Bo-In's staff includes five health care assistants, his wife Namye, and Asha Saxena, M.D. Namye is the creator of Mahayana Yoga, which combines yogic breathing and postures with partner work, acupressure massage and meditation. Namye also teaches fasting, diet and natural childbirth. Asha is a general practitioner and acupuncturist educated in New England and her native India.

Address   12 Harris Avenue, Boston, MA 02130, USA

Phone   617/524-9551. Fax 617/524-0345.

Season   Year-round.

Programs 7 and 21-day residential healing programs for supervised rest & relaxation vacation or to address specific health problems (e.g. chronic pain problems, pregnancy/childbirth, overweight, ulcers, substance dependencies, immune disorders, diabetes, and cancer).

Lodging   Capacity for 16 overnight guests in 12 single and double occupancy rooms.

Rates   7-day program $925. 21-day program $2,775. Additional charges for people with serious chronic illness requiring more than the regular daily treatments. Many insurance companies reimburse part or all of program costs.

Meals   3 daily meals, mostly vegetarian with occasional fish & chicken. A fasting program may be prescribed.

Services Bo-In Lee prescribes herbs, acupressure massage, and personalized corrective exercises (including relaxation techniques) to balance posture and reduce muscular tensions.

Option Institute   Sheffield, MA

The Option Institute is an 85 acre mountainside property in southwest Massachusetts, less than a 3 hour drive from both Boston and New York City airports. Housed in handsome, comfortable structures amid sweeping lawns, meadows and forests, Institute guests can enjoy swimming, cross-country skiing and hiking. Summer program participants can also enjoy the top quality theaters and festivals of the surrounding Berkshires region.

The Institute was founded in 1983 by Barry and Samahria Kaufman to help singles, couples and families learn how to increase their happiness through enhancing self-confidence and interpersonal skills. Programs include "The Happiness Option" (3-day weekend), "Loving You/Loving Me" (4-day weekend), "Empowering Yourself" (5-day), and "Living the Dream, Instead of Just Dreaming It" (4 and 8 weeks).

The Institute is operated by a full-time staff of over 40 individuals — certified Option Process mentors, apprentices and resident volunteers.

The heart of the Option Process is a non-directive dialogue technique encouraging self acceptance and suspended judgement. The various ramifications and applications of this approach are described in Barry Kaufman's eight books, the latest of which is "Happiness Is A Choice."

Address   2080 South Undermountain Road, Sheffield, MA 01257, USA

Phone   413/229-2100. Fax 413/229-8931.

Season   Year-round.

Programs 3-day, 5-day, 4-week & 8-week life enhancement workshops for individuals & couples. Custom designed programs for individuals, couples & families with children suffering from a wide range of dysfunctions. Also 3-month resident volunteer program.

Lodging   Double rooms in attractive guest houses. Weekend program participants may be housed in triple rooms. A few private rooms available on special request. Limited wheelchair access.

Rates   Program rates: 3-day $395; regular 5-day $995; personalized small group 5-day $1,275; 4-week $3,600; 8-week $6,600.

Meals   3 vegetarian meals each day.

Rowe Camp & Conference Center   Rowe, MA

Rowe Camp & Conference Center is set in northwest Massachusetts next to 1,400 acres of trust-protected Berkshire forests. The grounds include a white clapboard farmhouse, a recreation hall, camp cabins and a sauna. And the program schedule is managed by a small resident community including co-directors Prue Berry and Doug Wilson. Prue is a singer, guitar player and mother. Doug is a Unitarian Minister, comedian and political activist.

A Unitarian summer camp since 1924, Rowe Camp now offers both children's and adult camps from late June through August. There are four weeklong adult camps: "Men's Wisdom Council" for men-only; "WomenCircles" for women-only; "Recovery Camp" as a complement to various 12-Step programs; and "Liberation Camp" for singles and couples seeking better communication between men and women. "Liberation Camp" includes a program for parent-accompanied children ages 8 to 18.

Rowe Center hosts two and three-day workshops nearly every week except during camp season. Workshop topics generally involve psychospiritual healing and/or self-expression. Facilitators include well known authors, teachers, healers, political activists, and musicians from around America and beyond. Recent popular offerings were Wavy Gravy's "Clowning & Compassion," Starhawk's "Weaving Our Stories Into Ritual," and Babatunde Olatunji's "Drums of Passion & Joy."

Address   Kings Highway Road, Box 273, Rowe, MA 01367, USA

Phone   413/339-4954. Fax 413/339-5708.

Season   Year-round.

Programs Weeklong adult summer camps. Regular weekend and occasional other 2 & 3-day workshops on spirituality, healing, self expression and acceptance. A number of workshops designed for specific groups (e.g. women, men, and homosexuals).

Lodging   Capacity for 120 in farmhouse dorm rooms, dorms in heated & unheated cabins, and some private bedrooms with shared baths. Cabins near all-season bathhouse. Many cabins & dorm rooms are co-ed. BYO towels & bedding. Also campsites.

Rates   Weeklong adult camp: $325-395/adult & $200/child 8-18. 2-day program tuition $110-170. Weekend room & board $70-150.

Meals   3 daily vegetarian meals — much tastier than standard camp fare.

Aryaloka Buddhist Retreat Center   Newmarket, NH

Aryaloka is housed in a spacious building formed by two connecting geodesic domes with wood interiors. The structure includes guest quarters, a movement/ workshop room, a top floor meditation hall, a small library, and a well stocked Buddhist bookstore. The Center is 60 miles north of Boston on 13 acres of wooded property laced by paths and streams.

Anyone may participate in introductory one-day and weekend workshops offered roughly once a month on meditation and on Buddhist teachings. From time to time, there are also weeklong introductory retreats. All of these programs are conducted by resident and local teachers who comprise a spiritual community. The Center is also open for private retreats.

For those familiar with meditation and Buddhist teachings, there are occasional men's and women's meditation practice days and weekends. For men and women willing to commit to a Buddhist spiritual life by joining Friends of the

Western Buddhist Order (FWBO), there are also weekend and weeklong retreats that combine meditation, study and devotional practice. FWBO emphasizes Vipassana meditation and development of compassion.

Address   Heartwood Circle, Newmarket, NH 03857, USA

Phone   603/659-5456. No visits without prior arrangement.

Season   Year-round.

Programs Weekend & weeklong meditation retreats, working retreats and Buddhist studies workshops.

Lodging   Capacity for at least 20 overnight guests in private rooms.

Rates   Weeklong retreat $200. Weekend retreat $75. 1-day course $35. Non-program, daily guest rate (1 night & meals) $30.

Meals   3 daily vegetarian meals. Meals may be taken in one's room or in the communal dining area.

Green Pastures Estate   Epping, NH

One hour north of Boston, Green Pastures Estate is 160 acres of buildings, pastures, woodland, orchards and a garden. Founded in 1963 as the New England regional headquarters of the Emissaries, it is now a mature community of about 55 people living on property owned by the community as a whole. Major decisions are made by consensus, and most members are employed in community endeavors such as organic gardening, turkey raising, and running workshop/retreat facilities.

As a center for spiritual growth and renewal, Green Pastures hosts weekend concerts and experiential workshops conducted by outside groups. Two and three-day workshops have addressed subjects such as community building, wise woman teachings, inter-gender and relationship healing, deep ecology, "Alchemical Synergy," reiki, and bodywork. There are also occasional weeklong retreats, such as a men's "Inner King Training."

Lodging is offered as an option to weekend workshop participants and as part of the program to participants in longer retreats. In addition, people interested in exploring community living are generally welcome to live and work at Green Pastures for indefinite periods of time. All visitors are accommodated in community households, each with several individuals and families sharing living space. The entire community eats together in a large dining hall and worships together on Sunday mornings and Wednesday evenings in ever changing, cooperatively created services.

Address   Ladds Lane, Epping, NH 03042, USA

Phone   603/679-8149 or 800/888-6549 (eastern US). Fax 603/679-5138.

Season   April through December.

Programs Mostly weekend (1, 2 & 3-day) workshops on community living, holistic healing and spiritual practices. Occasional 6 to 8-day retreats. Also opportunities for community sojourn.

Lodging Single and double guest rooms in communal living facilities.

Rates 2 & 3-day weekend workshop tuition $100-160. Nightly lodging (with all meals) — shared $50, single $65. For non-overnight guests, meals are optional — breakfast $3, lunch $7, dinner $10.

Meals Communal lunch and dinner with vegetarian options. Breakfast supplies available on a "help yourself" basis.

Services Free attunements (laying on of hands) on Sunday afternoons.

Aegis at the Abode   New Lebanon, NY

Aegis is operated in a mountaintop retreat center and former Shaker village on 430 forested acres in the Berkshire Hills. During the summer, weekend and weeklong programs are conducted at the mountaintop site in classroom pavilions. The grounds also include a sweat lodge, a camp kitchen, and a dining pavilion. In cooler months, Aegis shares space with its parent Sufi community in the 150-year old village.

Summer weekend programs are on topics like "Staying Centered on the Spiritual Path" and "Sacred Circle Dance." From May through August there are usually four 5-day Sufi Studies weeks on topics like "Movement and Prayer." Each may be attended on a study/work or study/vacation basis. In August there is a one-week "Sacred Music Camp" inspired (and attended by) Pir Vilayat Inayat Kahn — Head of the Sufi Order. In winter there are monthly retreats such as "A Conscious Christmas." All Aegis programs are led by resident and visiting members of the international Sufi community.

Aegis' parent community, the Abode of the Message, consists of about 25 children and 50 adults. Each adult is free to follow his or her own spiritual path. And each day of the week includes scripture readings, prayers and chants from a different religion. There are three daily worship periods, and grace is sung before each meal.

Address R.D. 1, Box 1030D, New Lebanon, NY 12125, USA

Phone 518/794-8095.

Season Year-round with summer emphasis.

Programs 2 to 7-day programs celebrating spiritual freedom and diversity, musical expression, and healing. Each year generally includes a few programs for women-only and men-only.

Lodging Overnight guest capacity 175 in summer and 125 in winter. May-Sept: tent sites, huts and log cabins with separate wash-houses, hot showers and outhouses. Oct-April: single or shared rooms in main complex of Shaker buildings. BYO towels, linens or bedroll.

Rates   2 & 3-day programs & retreats: campsite $160-240, dorm or double $180-270, hut or single $200-300. "Sacred Music Camp": tent $280, dorm/double $315, hut/single $350, under 17 years $20/day. Sufi study/work $125/week. Sufi study/vacation $200/week.

Meals   3 daily vegetarian meals with dairy and non-dairy options.

Services   Group childcare for children ages 4 through 12.

Ananda Ashram   Monroe, NY

Ananda Ashram is located one hour northwest of New York City. The 90 acre grounds contain meadows and woodlands surrounding a lake with an island. There are nature trails, orchards, a vegetable garden, and sweat lodges used in monthly purification ceremonies. There is also a Healing Center with a eucalyptus sauna and small temple.

Overnight guest fees cover meals and all ongoing activities — daily early morning chi gung and hatha yoga sessions; frequent classes in tai chi, Kathak dance, gemstone healing, and Tui Na Chinese massage; plus daily morning and evening satsang. Satsang includes a Vedic fire ceremony, silent or guided meditation, chanting of Sanskrit hymns, devotional singing, readings on Self-realization, and question-and-answer periods.

Overnight fees also cover special cultural programs presented on most weekend evenings by resident and visiting artists. These programs include theater, musical and dance presentations. There are also seasonal parties. Rounding out the ashram experience, all overnight guests are encouraged to donate one hour each day to service.

Ananda Ashram was founded by Ramamurti Mishra, MD, now known as Shri Brahmananda Sarasvati, as the country retreat of the Yoga Society of New York. It is operated by a small resident community of families and single adults that includes the venerable Shri Sarasvati, who teaches Sanskrit as a spiritual practice and rejuvenating holistic therapy.

Address R.D. 3, Box 141 (Sapphire Road), Monroe, NY 10950, USA

Phone   914/782-5575.

Season   Year-round.

Programs Daily selection of holistic health activities plus workshops & multi-weekend courses on topics like "Laughter Meditation," "Beliefs & Health," "Acu Yoga," "Art & Healing Circle."

Lodging   Capacity for 35 overnight guests in dorms and a few semi-private rooms, all with shared bath. Also campsites.

Rates   Workshops & seminars $20-35. Multi-class courses $12-30/session ($6-9/class). Adult rates: weekday/night — camper $32, dorm $40, semi-private $46; weekend — camper $80, dorm $100, semi-private $115; 1 week — camper $185, dorm $230, semi-private $265.

Meals   3 daily lacto-vegetarian, buffet style meals prepared in various styles with fresh fruits, vegetables & accompanying salad.

Services   Swedish & deep-tissue massage, Tui Na Chinese massage, shiatsu, acupressure, cranial-sacral & polarity therapy, foot reflexology.

Awakenings   Wappingers Falls, NY

Awakenings is a New School for Women's Spirituality at Deer Hill Conference Center, a rustic 40 acre site 80 miles north of Manhattan in the Hudson River Valley. On the grounds is an outdoor pool and winter sledding. The School is designed and facilitated by Bernice Marie-Daly — an educator, psychotherapist, and author of "Ecofeminism: Sacred Matter/Sacred Mother."

Awakening's major offering is a yearlong program consisting of six weekend gatherings of the same group of women. This and the five-day summer intensive are certificate programs, with usually anywhere from ten to twenty women in attendance. Awakenings also hosts theme weekends.

All programs are communal experiences expressive of women's emerging consciousness in spirituality, justice making and the arts. Core areas of exploration include ecofeminism, the feminine Divine, the new psychology of women, women's ritual and celebration.

Address   c/o Bernice Marie-Daly, 57 Willowbrook Lane, New Canaan, CT 06840, USA

Phone   203/966-6347.

Season   Year-round.

Programs   Women's spirituality — yearlong program of weekend retreats; summer 5-day intensive; thematic weekend programs.

Lodging   Campsites, bunk houses & single rooms.

Rates   Yearlong program $2,000. 5-day intensive $500. Theme weekend $300. All fees include tuition, room & board.

Meals   3 daily meals of excellent, fresh seasonal food.

Dai Bosatsu Zendo   Livingston Manor, NY

Dai Bosatsu Zendo is the first traditional Rinzai Zen Buddhist monastery established in the West. The zendo is set on 1400 acres at the quiet edge of 30 acre Beecher Lake, the highest lake in the Catskill Mountains. The architectural style is traditional Japanese. Abbot is Eido Shimano Roshi, who also presides over midtown Manhattan's New York Zendo.

Twice each year, Dai Bosatsu hosts three-month training periods (kessei) that can be attended for two or one month periods. During each kessei, there are three silent weeklong intensive meditation retreats (sesshins). Each year there are also four "Introduction to Zen" weekends, two "Healing/ Wellness" weekends for HIV positive people, several 12-Step programs, and the August O-Bon Festival.

Guest students are expected to participate fully in the daily monastic schedule. Beginning with wake-up at 5 AM, an average day includes morning and evening chanting services; morning and afternoon work periods; plus sitting meditation (zazen) before breakfast, lunch and bedtime.

Non-student guests are welcome for visits of any length from February through mid-December. These guests may (but are not required to) participate in any daily activities. However, guests staying at the monastery are required to participate in community meals. In addition, Dai Bosatsu's Open Space Conference Center encourages unaffiliated groups to share Zen practice while pursuing their own programs.

Address   HCR 1, Box 171, Livingston Manor, NY 12758, USA

Phone   914/439-4566. Fax 914/439-3119. Call before visiting.

Season   Year-round.

Programs 100-day Zen practice periods, 5 & 7-day intensive meditation retreats (sesshins), weekend introductory workshops, private retreats.

Lodging   Accommodates up to 75 in single and double rooms in the monastery building, up to 20 in a lakeside guesthouse with separate kitchen, and up to 4 in the O-An cottage.

Rates   Kessei: 3-month $1,500, 2-month $1,200, 1-month $600. Sesshin $300. "Healing/Wellness" weekend $120. Nightly rates: guest student $35; monastery guest $50; guest house guest — single $65, double $120; O-An cottage — single $75, double $140.

Meals   3 daily vegetarian meals taken in silence.

Elat Chayyim   Woodstock, NY

Founded in 1992, Elat Chayyim is already an established spiritual retreat and healing center. The center's courses explore human spirituality and creative expression within the context of the Jewish and other spiritual traditions. The guest teachers come from throughout the U.S. Under the name Woodstock Center for Healing and Renewal, the center also offers a wide variety of Healing and Renewal (H&R) services.

In 1993, the center was housed in a leased hotel 35 minutes southwest of Woodstock, NY. This 35 acre Catskills property contains meadows, tennis courts, a volleyball court, an indoor jacuzzi, and a large outdoor swimming pool. During five and six-day retreats, the daily schedule includes pre-breakfast hikes, yoga, prayer and meditation. The day ends with a late afternoon prayer/ meditation session, dinner and evening social activities.

Retreatants may take zero, one or two courses, with each course meeting in the morning or afternoon. Typical course topics are meditation, hatha yoga, "Healing Your Jewish Self." Six-day Arts Camp courses focus on song, dance and storytelling in a spiritual context. In their free time, retreatants may join in organized hikes, tennis lessons, plus daily classes in basic Jewish spirituality. H&R services are available to all guests.

Address   P.O. Box 127, Woodstock, NY 12498, USA

Phone   914/679-2638 or 800/398-2630.

Season   June through September.

Programs   5 & 6-day spiritual & arts retreats with a weekend-only option. 2 & 3-day Yom Kippur & Rosh Hashannah retreats. Ongoing Health & Renewal (H&R) services. 5-week summer internship program.

Lodging   Rooms mostly double occupancy & air conditioned. A few single, quadruple & 5-bed family rooms. Wheelchair accessible housing.

Rates   Adult: 6-day $530-670, 5-day $480-600, (2 courses in 1 week — add $120), 3-day $245-330, 2-day $160-265, 5-day H&R $400-520, 6-day H&R $160-200. Children: 5 & 6 days $150-180, weekend $0-50.

Meals   Gourmet Kosher vegetarian cuisine — 3 meals daily.

Services   Program costs include Healing & Renewal services: physical therapy, yoga, acupuncture, massage, nutritional counseling, exercise, movement and imaginal work. Program costs also include childcare during 5 & 6-day retreats.

Foundation for "A Course in Miracles"   Roscoe, NY

The Foundation for "A Course in Miracles" is situated on the edge of Catskill Forest Park, roughly 2 1/2 hours from metropolitan New York. The center's 95 acres of lawns and forest rim the shore of Tennanah Lake, and guests are free to hike, swim or canoe between their morning and late afternoon classes. To allow undisturbed study and reflection on "A Course in Miracles" (ACIM), children and pets are not allowed at the center.

ACIM is a 1200 page manuscript of non-biblical Christian teachings scribed through a 7-year process of inner dictation to the late Helen Schucman, a professor of medical psychology at Columbia University's College of

Physicians and Surgeons. The manuscript was prepared for publication by Helen and Kenneth Wapnick, who has subsequently written 11 books on ACIM.

Before her death, Helen foresaw a teaching center for the Course. This center was founded in 1982 by Kenneth and his wife Gloria as the Foundation for "A Course in Miracles" — moved to its present location in 1988. The Foundation has a dual focus. Teaching of the Course's principles of forgiveness is accomplished primarily through workshops. Application of these principles to one's personal life is the focus of the Academy classes. Programs are conducted by the Wapnicks and the Foundation staff.

Address   1275 Tennanah Lake Road, Roscoe, NY 12776, USA

Phone   607/498-4116. Fax 607/498-5325. Call before visiting.

Season   April through early December.

Programs "A Course in Miracles" workshops of 1 to 4-days. ACIM Academy classes of 4 & 5-days.

Lodging   Total capacity for over 130 overnight guests. Academy students and personal retreatants housed in kitchenette apartments, each with a single or (for couples) queen sized bed. Workshop students housed in double occupancy rooms. All rooms have private bathrooms, and all but 7 (with shower-only) have both a shower and a tub. Linens and towels provided.

Rates   Academy tuition: 4-day $80, 5-day $100. 1-day workshop $20. Workshop tuition & meals: 2-day $103, 3-day $154, 4-day $205. Lodging: single $15 + tax; couple or double $10/person + tax.

Meals   3 daily meals, with vegetarian options, served only during workshops. Academy students and retreatants prepare meals in kitchenettes (34 units) or common kitchen.

Karma Triyana Dharmachakra   Woodstock, NY

Ninety miles north of New York City on a 20 acre site amidst meadows, forests and the Catskill Mountains, Karma Triyana Dharmachakra is a Tibetan Buddhist monastery and retreat center in the Karma Kagyu tradition. The center's resident abbot is Khenpo Karthar Rinpoche, who emigrated to the U.S. in 1976 to become spiritual director of all Karma Thegsum Choling centers. Also resident at the center is lama Bardor Tulku Rinpoche.

Each month the Center offers at least one weekend or weeklong seminar on meditation practice or Buddhist teachings. During seminars, the daily schedule is as follows: breakfast at 7:30, meditation 10-10:30, teachings 10:30-noon, meditation 3-3:30 PM, teachings 3:30-5, and supper at 6. Some seminars are designed specifically for people new to meditation and/or Buddhist teachings.

Most are taught by a resident lama. All guests are asked to donate 1 1/2 hours of daily work to help maintain the Center.

Address   352 Meads Mountain Road, Woodstock, NY 12498, USA

Phone   914/679-4625. Fax 914/679-4625. Call before visiting.

Season   Year-round.

Programs Weekend and 8-day seminars on meditation practice, Buddhist philosophy and psychology.

Lodging   Generally shared rooms. Sometimes private rooms are available. Floor and tent space also available — BYO sleeping bag.

Rates   Program rates: weekend $40-60; 8-day $200. Room & board: private $45/day, $270/week; shared $35/day, $210/week; floor or tent space $25/day, $145/week.

Meals   3 daily vegetarian meals.

Linwood Spiritual Center   Rhinebeck, NY

Two hours north of New York City, Linwood Spiritual Center is a hilltop 65 acre property looking out over the Hudson River. On the grounds is a large main building, a guesthouse, a cottage, a large outdoor pavilion, a swimming pool and tennis courts. Linwood is operated by the Sisters of St. Ursula as a nunnery and retreat center for men and women. The overall thrust of Linwood retreats tends to be toward holistic spirituality.

The center's 1-week summer Human Wellness Retreat is described by a participant as "like being at a holy spa" — combining scripture reading, quiet prayer, expressive art, journal writing, relaxation, nutrition, lifestyle discussions, stretching and massage. Weekend programs include ongoing 12-Step retreats, Enneagram study retreats, plus many theme retreats such as "The Art of Contemplation," "The Path to A Male Spirituality," and "In Praise of Mother Earth."

There are also programs that reflect the center's foundations in Catholic spiritual tradition. These include weeklong directed retreats using scripture and personal experience as material for prayer; a weeklong retreat guided by the major theme's of St. Ignatius's spiritual exercises; plus guided weekend women's retreats.

Address   139 South Mill Road, Rhinebeck, NY 12572, USA

Phone   914/876-4178. No visits without prior arrangement.

Season   Year-round.

Programs Weekend & weeklong retreats on spirituality & human development. Also guided & directed, contemplative Christian retreats.

Lodging   Single room accommodations for over 25 people. Also one double room plus a cottage suitable for private retreats.

Rates   Weekend retreat $100-150. Weeklong retreat $260.

Meals   3 daily, informal meal. 3 dining rooms allow guests the choice of eating separately in silence, eating together, or eating with the resident community.

Services   General spiritual & alcohol specific counseling. Massage available on 12-Step weekend retreats.

Living Springs Retreat   Putnam Valley, NY

One hour by car due north of Manhattan, Living Springs is a health reconditioning center on the edge of a quiet lake near the Appalachian Trail. Nestled among trees with an outdoor sundeck and a fireplace in the living room, the retreat has the cozy feel of a summer camp lodge.

The Retreat's regular "Wellness Week" includes a blood chemistry analysis, consultation with a physician, daily exercise, contrast (hot/cold) baths, steam bath, whirlpool and back massage. There are also classes and workshops on vegetarian cooking and nutrition, stress management, disease prevention, weight management, and natural remedies. Each guest's program may be tailored to focus on weight management, stress management or disease prevention. Most guests stay for a recommended two week period.

Living Springs also offers occasional "Stress Management" weekends plus a one-week "Smoker's Solution" program based on the famous 5-day Stop Smoking Plan. Guests are cordially invited (but by no means required) by the Seventh Day Adventist staff to participate in short, post-breakfast inspiration periods — song, prayer and scripture readings illustrating spiritual growth principles.

Address   136 Bryant Pond Road, Putnam Valley, NY 10579, USA

Phone   914/526-2800 or 800/729-9355 (reservations).

Season   Year-round.

Programs   "Wellness Week" & 1-week "Smoking Cessation" programs. Also "Stress Management" weekends.

Lodging   3 private rooms & 5 semi-private rooms in 2-level lodge.

Rates   Weekend: private room $350, semi-private room $290. 1-week: private $895, semi-private $695. 2-week: private $1,295, semi-private $1,095. 3-week: private $1,795, semi-private $1,495.

Meals   3 daily, buffet style vegan meals.

Services   Train station & airport pick-up/drop-off service.

New Age Health Spa　　　　　　　　Neversink, NY

New Age Health Spa is a large converted farm on 155 acres in the foothills of the Catskill Mountains 2 1/2 hours northwest of New York City. The property includes indoor and outdoor swimming pools, 5 miles of wooded trails, and an "alpine tower" — a free-standing, 50-foot high, hourglass-shaped climbing structure made of two interlocking log tripods. A barn-like building houses a full array of spa beauty treatments. There is also a mixed gender sauna and steam room.

A New Age day can begin with Zen meditation at 6:30 AM, a 3 to 7 mile power walk at 7, and yoga or tai chi at 8. Following a 9 o'clock breakfast, guests can depart for an all-day guided easy, moderate or challenging hike. Those who stay behind can select activities from the following typical daily menu: fitness lecture, equipment room instruction, body conditioning, water aerobics, stretch class, low impact aerobics, nutrition lecture, and meditation to music. Evenings generally feature a lecture and a movie.

Address　　Route 55, Neversink, NY 12765, USA

Phone　　914/985-7600 or 800/682-4348 (reservations).

Season　　Year-round.

Programs　Guests design their own holistic health program by selecting from the lectures; hikes & other fitness activities; meditation, yoga or tai chi sessions scheduled for each day..

Lodging　　Roughly 40 simply furnished cottage rooms — singles, doubles & triples. Each with private bath. No phone or TV.

Rates　　Weekly rates: single $1,099-$1,279, double $699-899, triple $599-779. Plus 15% service charge & 8% sales tax.

Meals　　3 tasty meals served daily. Choice of juice fast, vegetarian or non-vegetarian diet. Greens & vegetables from spa's gardens.

Services　Living Better: cooking & herbology classes; hypnotherapy; body fat analysis; tarot card reading; astrological, fitness & nutrition consultations. Feeling Better: aromatherapy, colonic, massage, reflexology, shiatsu. Looking Better: moor mud treatment; loofa scrub; facial; manicure; pedicure.

Omega Institute for Holistic Studies　　Rhinebeck, NY

Probably the world's largest adult summer learning center, the Omega Institute is situated in the Hudson River Valley two hours north of Manhattan. The Institute's faculty includes resident and guest teachers that are among the leading lights of the international human potential movement. The Institute's 80 acre property contains flower and vegetable gardens, tree-lined paths, plus superb recreational facilities — basketball, tennis and volleyball courts plus a lake with a beach.

All guests are required to enrol in a weekend or 5-day workshop. The course selection is broad, with workshops grouped under 5 general subject categories — self, others, expression, world, and spirit. The 25 or so subject subcategories include holistic health, relationships & family, dance/movement, caring for the earth, and spiritual retreat. Typical workshop topics are "Self-Healing," "Conscious Loving," "Joyful Dance," "Becoming One With Nature," and "Meditation for Beginners."

The Institute's most popular offering (held four times each season) is a 5-day "Wellness Week" covering diet, nutrition, fitness, exercise, lifestyle and attitude. The week includes low-impact aerobics, muscle strengthening, stretching, and creative movement. Following mornings of core program workshops, participants can opt in the afternoons for more of the same or for sessions of massage, music-making, movement or fitness activities.

An average day at Omega can begin at 6 with a yoga, tai chi or meditation session followed by breakfast from 7 to 8:15. Workshops meet from 9 to noon and from 2 to 4:30. There are optional movement classes from 12:15 to 1 and classes on movement or meditation from 5:15 to 6. The day ends following dinner with a concert, community gathering, dance or film.

Address   260 Lake Drive, Rhinebeck, NY 12572, USA

Phone   914/266-4444 or 800/944-1001 (reservations). Fax 914/266-4828.

Season   June through mid-Sept. Winter programs conducted January through mid-March at locations in Northeast & Mid Atlantic states.

Programs 8-10 workshops each week and weekend for a total of more than 200 per summer season on all aspects of holistic health.

Lodging   Capacity for more than 350 guests in tent sites, dormitories and double occupancy cabin rooms with private bath or bath shared with an adjoining room. BYO towels & linens for dorms. Some cottages & other facilities equipped for the disabled.

Rates   Separate program & lodging/meal rates. Most weekend

Programs $130-195. Most 5-day programs $230-350. "Wellness Week" $280. 10% discounts for students, senior citizens & early registrants. 2 & 5-day campsites $75 & $150. 2 & 5-day dorm $96 & $192. 2 & 5-day cabin $130 & $260 with shared bath or $160 & $325 with private bath. A few single-occupancy/parent cabin rooms.

Meals   3 daily, mostly vegetarian meals with produce from the garden.

Services   Massage, aromatherapy, sauna & flotation tanks, nutrition & stress reduction counseling available at Omega's Wellness Center. Summer day camp for pre-registered children under 14.

Phoenicia Pathwork Center   Phoenicia, NY

Phoenicia Pathwork Center is a complex of buildings set on 300 quiet acres in the Catskill Mountain Forest preserve, a 2 1/2 hour drive northwest of New York City. Recreational facilities include tennis courts, a swimming pool, mountain trails and Native American sweat lodge. A resident community maintains the facilities and administers the program schedule.

"Pathwork" is a psychospiritual healing approach based on 258 lectures channeled through Eva Pierrakos. The work includes individual sessions, group lectures and discussions, prayer and meditative exercises. Pathwork also includes Core Energetics — bodywork developed by Dr. John Pierrakos to release energy-blocking muscular tension and holding patterns. All work is facilitated by trained counselors.

Pathwork introduction weekends are offered six times each year. There are occasional 2 and 3-day Core Energetics and theme workshops. One-week Intensives are held twice each year. And every other month there is a weekend or 5-day Silent Retreat with silent sitting and movement practices, some chanting and a little teaching. Individual retreats, with optional yoga sessions, shamanic drumming, garden and sanctuary meditations, can be scheduled on a space-available basis.

Phoenicia Retreat Center also allows use of its facilities by other, like-minded groups. Three times a year the Center publishes a schedule of workshops offered by such groups that are open to the general public. Topics include organic gardening, yoga, creative writing, inner child work, women's and men's healing/empowerment, homosexual/bisexual spirituality.

Address   P.O. Box 66, Phoenicia, NY 12462, USA

Phone   914/688-2211. Fax 914/688-2007.

Season   Year-round.

Programs   Pathwork: 2 & 3-day workshops, 1-week individual Intensives. Group silent & individual retreats, Pathwork-compatible weekend workshops sponsored by other organizations. Also Work-Exchange, short & long-term residency, and 1-year (10 weekends) programs.

Lodging   Capacity for up to 170 overnight guests in 16 motel-like rooms and 42 shared bedrooms (2-4 people/room). Private rooms & cottages available for couples and retreat leaders.

Rates   Pathwork programs: introductory weekend $210; other 2 & 3-day workshops $210-415; 1-week intensive $1,600. Silent retreats: 2-day $170; 5-day $350. Individual retreat $45/day. Weekends sponsored by other organizations $170-320.

Meals   3 daily buffet meals with vegetarian options.

Shalom Mountain   Livingston Manor, NY

Shalom Mountain is a 54 acre retreat center in the Catskill Mountain foothills, a 2 1/2 hour drive northwest of New York City. Each month's 2 to 5 retreats focus on releasing blocked feelings and body/spirit integration through various means. Energy release techniques include fantasy, primal scream, role-play, gestalt and bio-energetics. Spiritual disciplines include yoga, meditation, journal-writing, dream work, fasting, worship, sacred literature, art and dance.

The basic 3-day Shalom Retreat weekend is designed to create a loving community where personal work can be initiated. Theme retreats include offerings such as "Sexuality And Spirituality," "Dancing With Our Ancestors," and "Finding Your Sacred Clown." Other programs and gatherings are limited to men, couples or therapists.

Most retreats are led by center hosts Joy Davey and Lawrence (Laurie) Stibbards. Joy is a psychologist. Laurie is a marriage and family counselor with a background in pastoral counseling. Guest retreat leaders include people trained in past life regression, Core Energetics and Bioenergetics, wilderness rites of passage, yoga, voice/song and clowning.

Address   664 Cattail Road, Livingston Manor, NY 12758, USA

Phone   914/482-5421. No visits without prior arrangement.

Season   Year-round.

Programs 2 to 7-day retreats designed to foster psychological and spiritual growth.

Lodging   12 bedrooms sleeping up to 18 people.

Rates   Couples' retreats: 7-day $1200, 3 & 4-day $700-800. Other retreats: 7 to 9-day $615-725, 5-day $500, 3-day $320-395. 2 & 3-day gatherings $65-80.

Meals   3 meals a day. Vegetarians accommodated on advance notice.

Shree Muktananda Ashram   South Fallsburg, NY

Shree Muktananda Ashram is world headquarters of the Siddha Yoga lineage and the residence of Gurumayi, Swami Muktananda's successor. She (Gurumayi) is revered as a perfect reflection of divinity by Siddha Yoga devotees, who believe that the presence of the Master enriches meditation practice and can awaken in the devotee the enlightened Master's own energy. Consequently, the ashram's most popular events are the Intensives — 2-day meditations in the presence of Gurumayi.

Other ashram programs various course taught by members of the ashram staff. These offerings include daylong and weekend silent and guided meditation retreats, five and ten-day hatha yoga classes with 1-1.5 hours of daily instruction, one hour and daylong selfless service courses, courses on chanting & accompanying instrumentation (drum, tamboura and harmonium), plus courses on Indian scriptures.

All guests are encouraged to participate in all daily community activities — morning meditation at 4:15 followed by tea and chanting before breakfast, a noon chant followed by lunch, and more chanting before and after dinner. All are also assigned daily service duties.

Shree Muktananda Ashram is a 2 hour drive northwest of New York City. The complex consists of a main building and 3 residential facilities, including 2 former hotels, all connected by shuttle bus service. Many of the rooms are occupied on a long-term basis by Gurumayi devotees.

Address   P.O. Box 600, South Fallsburg, NY 12779, USA

Phone   914/434-2000.

Season   Year-round.

Programs   Guests not involved in meditation Intensives may construct their own schedule from classes & workshops in devotional music, selfless service, hatha yoga, meditation, and Hindu scripture.

Lodging   Dorms plus some single & double rooms. Family accommodations for families with grandparents or children under 12. Wheelchair accessible rooms. Summer overflow accommodated in nearby hotels.

Rates   Programs: music, service, hatha yoga classes & workshops $10-50; short scripture classes $75-125; 1 & 2-day meditation courses $175 & $250; 2-day Intensive $400. Adult room & board: dorm $25-50/day, $150-300/week; double $50/day, $300/week; single $65/day, $390/week; 2-4 member families $45-105/day, $270-630/week.

Meals   3 vegetarian meals/day. Areas set aside for silent dining. Meat & fish available in restaurants in all 3 residential buildings.

Services   Children's programs for children ages 2 through 12. ASL interpreters & amplification system for the hearing impaired.

Sivananda Ashram Yoga Ranch   Woodbourne, NY

Sivananda Ashram Yoga Ranch is a peaceful country retreat in the Catskill Mountains 100 miles northwest of Manhattan. The main building is a turn-of-the-century farmhouse heated in the winter by a brick Bavarian type stove. Two larger, unheated buildings contain summer guest rooms and a large yoga hall. In warm weather, yoga classes are held on a large wooden platform with a scenic Catskills Mountains backdrop.

A day at the Ranch begins at 6 AM with satsang — meditation, chanting and a talk. The first hatha yoga session is at 8. After a 10 o'clock breakfast, guests are invited to donate one hour of service to the ashram community. From noon till the second yoga class at 4 PM, guests can rest, take a swim in a 1/2 acre pond, walk or cross country ski through the surrounding 80 acres of fields and forest, or thaw out in a Russian style wood burning sauna. Dinner is followed at 8 by evening satsang.

Special Ranch programs include the month-long October "Teachers' Training Camp;" a 2-week July "Teen Camp;" a 9-day "Detoxifying Fast;" weeklong "Yoga & Shiatsu" and "Naturopath Practice" programs; 4 days of "Family Fun"; and a "Sanskrit Immersion" weekend. Cultural and music programs are offered on the Memorial Day and July 4th weekends. And Native American sweat lodge and medicine circle ceremonies are conducted from time to time.

Address   P.O. Box 195, Budd Road, Woodbourne, NY 12788, USA

Phone   914/434-9242. Fax 914/434-1032.

Season   Year-round.

Programs Regular daily schedule, with mandatory attendance of satsangs and yoga classes. Special weekend, 1 and 2-week programs. Also work-study, temporary staff & residents' programs.

Lodging   40 double & 3-6 person rooms, some with private bath, in farmhouse and another building. Campsites in back field.

Rates   Adult nightly room rates: Sun-Thur — room $35, campsite $25; Fri & Sat — room $40, campsite $30; holiday weekend — room $45, campsite $35. Weeklong "Teachers' Training Camp" $1,200 all inclusive. Children's rates: under 5 free, 5-12 half-price, "Yoga for Kids" $8/child any age.

Meals   2 daily, buffet-style vegetarian meals with vegetables and greens from organic garden and greenhouse (in season).

Services   "Yoga for Kids" 8 AM to noon second Sunday of each month.

Springwater Center   Springwater, NY

Springwater is a nonsectarian meditation retreat center located on 230 acres of open fields and woods 45 miles south of Rochester in New York's Finger Lakes region. Set on a quiet hillside, the house contains a meditation room, glass-walled solarium, and a hot tub. Several miles of trails are easily accessible for walking, hiking and cross-country skiing.

Always open for private meditation retreats, the Center also conducts guided group retreats — two 4-day, seven 7-day, and one 10-day in 1993. Center director Toni Packer is present at most 7 and 10-day retreats to give talks and meet privately and/or in small groups with participants. Prior to founding

Springwater Center in 1981 with a group of friends, Toni was director of Rochester Zen Center. She has since dropped all Zen forms.

Author of the book "The Work of the Moment," Toni encourages meditative inquiry into the nature of self. All retreats are conducted in silence. Meals and work, exercise and rest, talks and meetings are all interspersed with short sittings (chairs allowed) throughout the day. Except for work periods, all activities are optional.

Address   7179 Mill Street, Springwater, NY 14560, USA

Phone   716/669-2141. No visits without prior arrangement.

Season   Year-round.

Programs 4, 7 and 10-day meditation retreats.

Lodging   16 bedrooms, each with 2 mattresses. BYO sleeping bag, or sheets & blankets, plus towel.

Rates   4-day $180. 7-day $300. 10-day $430. Rates reduced by 1/3rd for members, dues $50 per quarter.

Meals   3 daily vegetarian meals. All meal preparation & housecleaning done by participants during daily 1 hour work period.

Tai Chi Farm   Warwick, NY

Tai Chi Farm occupies over 100 acres just north of the NJ/NY border in southeastern New York. The property contains forest trails, a stream, a small waterfall and pond. A Chinese-style mountain gate, a bagua garden, pavilion, gazebo and outdoor tai chi practice area serve as gathering sites. A renovated barn containing a shrine to Zhang San-Feng (tai chi's creator and "patron saint") serves as a large indoor practice area.

Following "Early Bird" weekends in late May, the 3 month summer season gets under way with the annual Zhang San-Feng Festival on the first weekend in June. The special guest teacher at the 1993 festival came from Shanghai, China to teach the Standard Competition forms. Most of the 20-25 workshops offered over the balance of the summer are best suited for intermediate and advanced students, but all are also open to beginners.

Tai Chi Farm was founded in 1984 by Master Jou, Tsung Hwa to serve as a place for tai chi players to study and practice together. Master Jou, Tsung Hwa leads five workshops. A few workshop leaders come from as far away as California, but most are from the northeastern United States.

Address   Tai Chi Foundation, P.O. Box 828, Warwick, NY 10990, USA

Phone   914/986-9233. Best to write.

Season   Workshops mid-May through August. Open for personal retreats on weekends throughout the year.

Programs 5-day, 3-day & weekend tai chi workshops.

Lodging 8 primitive wooden cabins — no heat, electricity or running water. Hot showers on the grounds. Campsites. BYO bedding. There are also nearby motels, hotels, bed & breakfast inns.

Rates Workshop tuition: 5-day $200, 3-day $140, weekend $100, discounts for early registration. Cabin $10/night. Campsite $5/night.

Meals BYO food, campstoves & coolers. Barbecue pit. Small deli/grocery store within walking distance.

Services During Zhang San-Feng Festival weekend, all who wish to display their goods along "Tai Chi Avenue" may do so for a fee.

Wainwright House   Rye, NY

A handsome stone mansion overlooking Long Island Sound, Wainwright House is a short drive or train ride north of New York City. Wainwright's most frequent offerings are evening, daylong and weekend workshops on the arts, health and healing, psychological and spiritual development. Typical weekend workshops are "Honoring Moments of Change", "The Mysticism of Ordinary Experience," and "The Warrior's Way." Most weekend workshops offer food and lodging as an option rather than as a requirement.

Founded by the Laymen's Movement "for the purpose of bringing ethical and spiritual values into public life," Wainwright offers a yearlong "Guild for Spiritual Guidance" program. Guild participants attend two 3-day retreats plus nine 24-hour (overnight) sessions focusing on the work of Carl Jung, Teilhard de Chardin and the Judeo-Christian mystical tradition. Wainwright also offers weeklong cancer support programs and an annual "Receptive Listening Program" of one weekend each month for six months.

Address 260 Stuyvesant Avenue, Rye, NY 10580, USA

Phone 914/967-6080. Fax 914/967-6114.

Season Year-round.

Programs Occasional weekend workshops. Many single day & evening workshops. General focus on personal & spiritual growth.

Lodging Dorm & double rooms. Lodging is offered when a minimum number of 10 guests are registered in the house.

Rates Typical weekend workshop rates (excluding room & board): Friday eve/Saturday $100-120, Saturday/Sunday $130-150, Friday eve to Sunday $270. Meal rates: breakfast $6.50, lunch $8.50, dinner $13. Nightly room rates: dorm $25, double $35.

Meals 3 daily, buffet style meals.

Wise Woman Center   Woodstock, NY

Wise Woman Center is a densely wooded, Catskill Mountains goat farm, learning center, and the home of Susun Weed — an initiated high priestess of Dianic Wicca, editor of Ash Tree Publishing, and best-selling author of books on the ancient "green witch" paths to healing. The Center's 50 acres include herb gardens, meeting and moon lodge tipis, a sun deck by a large swimming pond, a river and waterfall for private swims, and many fairies.

The way of the wise woman seeks to nourish the wholeness of the unique individual through the use of compassionate intuition, personal and community ritual, and common local plants (weeds). "Problems" are viewed as solutions pointing the way to the original question, thereby allowing new answers to emerge. Center workshops, intensives, apprenticeships and correspondence courses focus on women's spirituality and women's health. Guest teachers include Z. Budapest, Vicki Noble and Grandma Twylah Nitsch.

Address Susun S. Weed, P.O. Box 64, Woodstock, NY 12498, USA

Phone 914/246-8081 (also accepts fax). Call before visiting.

Season Spring through Fall.

Programs Susun teaches herbal medicine and spirit healing through daylong workshops (usually two each month) for men & women, occasional full weekend intensives for women only, and women-only apprenticeships adjustable in length from 6 weeks to 8 months.

Lodging Dorm & campsites (BYO tent & sleeping bag). Room in house for the physically challenged. (Signing can also be arranged.)

Rates Daylong workshop $40-55. Weekend event $195-320. Apprentice: $450/week, $1400/month, or work/exchange (at 50% of highest fee).

Meals 3 daily "country vegetarian" meals.

Services Free Tuesday evening consultations on herbal medicine & wise woman ways. Also personal visits & tarot readings with Susun.

Zen Mountain Monastery   Mt. Tremper, NY

Zen Mountain Monastery (ZMM) is a building of blue stone and white oak on 230 acres in the Catskill Mountain Forest Preserve. ZMM is also a monastic training center, weekend retreat center, and residence for 20-25 male and female monks and lay-residents.

Most months, several weekend retreats are conducted by visiting Zen scholars and artists on themes of artistic expression, practical/artistic skills such as cooking and aikido, environmental and meditative awareness, and Buddhist wisdom literature. The monastery's founder and abbot, John Daido Loori, is an

American Zen master, naturalist and artist who in 1993 led a 4-day theme weekend on nature photography.

Weekend retreats begin with Friday supper and an evening orientation talk. Retreatants then conform to the Zen schedule — up at 5 on Saturday for sitting and walking meditation, a service of bowing and chanting, a silent work assignment, weekend theme classes from 10 to noon and 1:30 to 5, evening meditation and worship. A 6:45 Sunday breakfast is followed by meditation, bowing, chanting and a talk. Departure follows lunch.

There are also introductory Zen training weekends, weekend and 6-day meditation intensives, one month retreats, and extended residential programs. The introductory weekend is a prerequisite for the meditation intensives but is included in the one month retreat. One-month retreatants receive 1 or 2 days off each week and may participate in theme workshops.

Address P.O. Box 197PC, South Plank Road, Mt. Tremper, NY 12457, USA

Phone 914/688-2228. No visits without prior arrangement.

Season Year-round.

Programs Weekend retreats integrating Zen practice with a workshop theme (e.g. ecology, Zen koans, plain water cooking). Also Zen training weekends, weekend & weeklong meditation intensives, 1-month monastic trainings, 1-week to 1-year monastery residency.

Lodging 100-bed dormitory, linens & 1 blanket provided. Private or semi-private rooms usually available for residents of 1 month or more.

Rates Weekend retreat $135-185. 4 & 6-day retreats $325. Meditation intensives — $225 for entire 6 days or $45/day. Residency Program and One Month Retreat, each $575-675/month.

Meals 3 daily, primarily vegetarian meals with a vegetarian alternative when meat or fish is served. Vegetables and greens from garden.

Providence Zen Center   Cumberland, RI

Set on 50 wooded acres 15 miles north of Providence, RI, Providence Zen Center is headquarters of the international Kwan Um School of Zen — founded in 1983 by the 78th Patriarch in the Korean Chogye Order. It is also home of Diamond Hill Zen Monastery and a small community of lay Zen practitioners, who operate public walk-in and residential programs.

People new to meditation may attend monthly Sunday morning meditation instruction. Beginner meditators may also participate in meditation retreats of 2 to 7 days, committing to stay for at least one full night and day. The daily retreat schedule includes sitting, chanting, walking and bowing meditation plus talks and work practice. There are one and 2-day combination Christian-Buddhist retreats.

Diamond Hill is a long-term retreat facility and residence for monks and nuns. This facility hosts Kyol Che retreats over 3-month winter and 3-week summer periods. A Kyol Che day consists of chanting, sitting and walking meditation punctuated by short work and break periods from 4:45 AM to 9:40 PM. Non-monks may participate for a minimum of one week in the winter and a minimum of 3 days in the summer.

Address   528 Pound Road, Cumberland, RI 02864, USA

Phone   401/658-1464. Fax 401/658-1188. Call before visiting.

Season   Year-round.

Programs   Meditation & Christian-Buddhist retreats. Monthly Sunday morning meditation instruction & 1-day workshops.

Lodging   Dorms with mattresses or futons on carpeted floors. Semi-private rooms or beds for those with special needs. Men and women in separate rooms. Tent sites. BYO sleeping bag, pillow and towel.

Rates   Kyol Che retreat $250/week. Other meditation retreats $40/day. Guest stay $20/day.

Meals   3 daily buffet style vegetarian meals, eaten out of bowls, served on retreats. Short term overnight guests prepare own meals.

Karme-Choling   Barnet, VT

Set on 540 wooded acres in northern Vermont, Karme-Choling is a large meditation and Buddhist studies center. Each year the center offers at least 80 programs, most over weekends and most open to first-time visitors. The center accommodates intensive private meditation retreats. Each year it also offers several one-month group meditation retreats open to new students, who may attend for less than a month.

Weekend programs include the Gateway Series for those new to meditation and Buddhist teachings; plus offerings such as traditional Japanese archery and flower arranging that involve meditative mindfulness. Programs are conducted by both resident and visiting teachers — many from Colorado's Naropa Institute but some, such as a 23-year old abbess and several visiting lamas each year, from as far away as the Himalayas.

In August, Karme-Choling runs several camps: an 8-day "Art Celebration" with workshops, performances and exhibits; a 6-day "Teen Camp" emphasizing community, environmental education and the arts; and a 6-day "Family Camp" with daily meditation practice for parents, activities for children, and a family Rites-of-Passage ceremony for 8-year olds. The center also hosts a series of weekend Shambhala Trainings — a nonsectarian form of spiritual practice focusing on sitting meditation.

Karme-Choling is run by a non-monastic spiritual community of 50 to 60 people founded by the late Chogyam Trungpa — an ex-abbot of Tibet's Surmang monasteries, founder of Naropa Institute, and author of "Shambhala: The Sacred Path of the Warrior." The center begins each day with a 7 AM group meditation, and guests are asked to contribute 1 1/2 hours of daily work.

Address   Star Route, Barnet, VT 05821, USA

Phone   802/633-2384. Fax 802/633-3012. Call before visiting.

Season   Year-round.

Programs Weekend programs on meditation, Buddhist philosophy & psychology. Also 6-day summer family, teen & art camps; intensive private retreats; plus residency option.

Lodging   Overnight guest capacity of up to 200 at Karme-Choling and Ashoka Bhavan guest house in nearby Barnet. Basic lodging is multi-bed dorms and floor mattresses (BYO sleeping bag). Private 1 & 2-bed rooms available at extra cost. 8 cabins for private retreats. Towels & linens provided except for outdoor summer camps.

Rates   Weekend programs $70-150. 8-day summer camp $200/adult, $100/ child under 13 years old. Intensive retreats: $25/day up to 1 month, $20/day over 1 month. Residency $15/day.

Meals   3 meals, vegetarian or meat, plus a tea-time snack each day.

Services   Childcare for ages 2 to 11 included in child lodging/meal rates. Moderate cost rides to & from airports, train & bus stations.

Kushi Summer Conference   Poultney, VT

Each year the Kushi Institute holds a one-week summer conference at the picturesque campus of Green Mountain College in west central Vermont. The guest faculty of teachers, counselors and authors comes from all over the world to present workshops, classes and lectures on the macrobiotic way of life. There is also a variety of morning exercise classes plus evening entertainment such as contra dancing and a talent show.

Address   P.O. Box 390, Becket, MA 01223, USA

Phone   413/623-2103.   Fax 413/623-8827.

Season   6 days in August.

Programs Macrobiotic conference/camp.

Lodging   Accommodations for over 600 people in single rooms, double rooms and campsites.

Rates   Meals & tuition: adult $525, child 2-17 $275, child under 2 free. Rooms: adult single $275, adult double $200, child 2-17 $100. Campsites: single $75, 2 people $100, family $125.

Meals   3 daily macrobiotic meals plus Day & Night Cafe snacks.

Services   Childcare and children's camp programs at no additional cost.

ROOTS Experiential Conferences   Plainfield, VT

Mid-August 1993 marked the sixth annual convocation of ROOTS on the grounds of Goddard College, a pastoral campus in the high rolling hills northeast of Montpelier, VT. The event is staged in and around the gardens, lawns and terraces, Manor House and Haybarn Theater of a former farm estate.

ROOTS is designed to look beneath the surface of life, both individual and collective, by tuning into planetary patterns that reflect the times. Conference facilitators are eastern North American astrologers gifted in storytelling, mythmaking and psychodrama. With everyone pitching in, the gathering creates a warm and informal ceremonial forum for experiential awareness, transformation and a lot of fun.

Held during an exact conjunction of Neptune and Uranus, ROOTS '93 explored the implications of this cosmic marriage. Expanding on the theme of relationship, the conference also explored male/female, Self/community and inner psychological relationships. Activities included AstroTheater, men's and women's councils, artistic expression of yin/yang mandalas, drumming and dance, co-created ritual, and a Mayan Joining Ceremony.

Address   Helia Productions, R.R. 3, Box 928, Montpelier, VT 05602, USA

Phone   802/223-1647.

Season   Usually 5 or 6 days in August.

Programs   A depth astrology conference using ceremony and experiential workshops to suggest ways to deal with individual dilemmas while exploring the relationship between society and the cosmos.

Lodging   Simple dormitory rooms available as singles & doubles.

Rates   Tuition: full conference $230, weekend $125. Room & board: single $40/day, double $30/day.

Meals   3 daily meals — "great for both vegetarians & non-vegetarians."

Services   Participants are welcome to bring, sell & trade their wares. Post conference day for personal work with facilitators & others.

Sunray Peace Village   Lincoln, VT

Sunray Village is an annual summer encampment set on 27 acres of meadows, woods, pond and streams bordering the Green Mountain National Forest in central Vermont. The village fosters a spirit of interpersonal harmony and cooperation through Native American ceremonies, morning and evening community meditations, and the practice of working together for an hour each day before the teachings.

Annual village events include a weekend gathering of Native American elders and the one week Peacekeeper Mission — personal and planetary peace realization training based on the Native American teachings of Caretaker Mind and Right Relationship to the Circle of Life. The 1993 village presented workshops on community building and ecological architecture. The other twenty or so workshops and performances draw on Buddhist and Native American traditions plus recovery and family psychology.

The village is sponsored by Sunray Meditation Society, an international organization dedicated to planetary peace. The society's spiritual head is Dhyani Ywahoo, trained by her grandparents as the 27th generation to carry the Etowah Cherokee wisdom teachings. Tibetan Buddhist lamas have recognized Sunray as a Dharma Center and the fulfillment of prophecy.

Address   Sunray Meditation Society, P.O. Box 308, Bristol, VT 05443, USA

Phone   802/453-4610.   Fax 802/453-6096.

Season   July and August.

Programs 1 to 7-day trainings, workshops & ceremonies focusing on how to live in peace with oneself, others and the Earth. Programs led by Sunray faculty and visiting teachers.

Lodging   BYO tent & sleeping bag. Nearby toilets, sinks & hot showers.

Rates   Program fees range from $50 for a 1-day event to $370 for a 7-day program and include camping from the night before the program begins through the night before it ends. Additional camping $10/night per person. Children under 16 camp for free.

Meals   Large tent for communal cooking & dining. BYO food, cooking equipment & utensils. Meals provided during Elders Gathering.

Services   Childcare for children aged 2 to 12.

Tai Chi in Vermont   Bennington, VT

For over a decade, New York City's School of Tai Chi Chuan has hosted a 3-week summer tai chi camp at Bennington College, a hilltop campus on the edge of the Green Mountains in southwestern Vermont. The first week is reserved for beginners. The second and third weeks are designed for both beginner and advanced tai chi students. All classes are taught in light, airy dance studios by experienced tai chi instructors.

Beginners learn the theoretical and physical aspects of a daily centering/energizing/relaxing discipline that requires only 10 minutes of daily morning and evening practice. And all students follow the same schedule: morning and early afternoon classes; evening lectures and entertainments; mid-to-late afternoon free time for individual practice, "Hawaiian Swimming," rest and relaxation. "Hawaiian Swimming" is a course, derived from traditions of Hawaiian warriors, for both swimmers and non swimmers.

Address   School of Tai Chi Chuan, 46 W. 13th St., New York, NY 10011, USA

Phone   212/929-1981.   Fax 212-727-1852.

Season   3 weeks in August.

Programs Residential tai chi classes in 1 week sessions, with 3 weeks for beginner & 2 weeks for advanced students.

Lodging   Single & double rooms with shared baths in dormitory buildings.

Rates   Weekly tuition: tai chi $315, children's program $150-165, Hawaiian Swimming $40. Adult room & board: 1-week single $288, double $228; 2-week single $624, double $494; 3-week single $960, double $760. Children's room & board: 1-week $120, 2 weeks $260.

Meals   3 daily meals with extensive salad bar & vegetarian options.

Services   Program for children 3 to 14 (cost noted above) in last 2 weeks.

UNITED STATES   Mideast Region

Orbis Farm   Mauckport, IN

Orbis Farm is a retreat center and workshop facility on 75 acres of woodland 40 miles southwest of Louisville, KY. The farm has a co-created organic garden, and neighboring Mt. Tom offers miles of walking trails.

The facility is directed by Betty Cole and Helen McMahan. Betty is a long-time meditator who serves as gardener, herbalist and cook. Helen teaches tai chi, hatha yoga and meditation at both the farm and Orbis Personal Growth Center in Louisville. Farm workshops are also taught by 10-15 well qualified teachers from the U.S. lower midwest/upper south region.

Orbis Farm hosts two-night workshops on most weekends of the year. The Farm's premier offering is a series of weekends exploring Kundalini philosophy and meditation. There are frequent weekend, plus occasional five-day, workshops on hatha yoga and on tai chi. Other theme weekends focus on topics such as women's spirituality, holotropic breathwork, "Reclaiming Our Body Images," and "Paths Of Partnership."

Address   8700 Ripperdan Valley Road, SW, Mauckport, IN 47142, USA

Phone   812/732-4657. No visits without prior arrangement.

Season   Late January through late November.

Programs Yoga, tai chi, Kundalini and holistic healing workshops.

Lodging   Capacity for 20 in dormitory accommodations.

Rates   Programs: 5-night $380, 2-night $165, 1-night $90.

Meals   3 tasty vegetarian meals, fish & chicken options. Vegetables from own gardens.

Dayspring Silent Retreat Center   Germantown, MD

Just outside of Washington's northern suburbs, Dayspring Silent Retreat Center rests on a 200 acre farm amidst woods, fields and still waters. On more than 30 weekends each year, the center hosts silent residential retreats with themes such as "The Healing Space;" "Mother Earth Spirituality;" "Jesus, Dreams and Journaling." Dayspring retreat leaders come from many Christian denominations.

Retreatants begin the weekend with supper together on Friday evening. The leader then sets the theme and guides the retreatants into silence. Saturday is a time of rest, contemplation, wandering, study, or guided journal writing. There are two guided sessions of leader-provided prayer, guided meditation or scripture reading. Retreatants leave the silence with a Sunday worship service followed by a noon meal and departure at 2 PM.

Dayspring is an arm of Washington, D.C.'s Church of the Savior, recommended by author M. Scott Peck as a model for all Christian churches in requiring whole hearted membership commitment to service and building community.

Address   11301 Neelsville Church Road, Germantown, MD 20876, USA

Phone   301/428-9348. No visits without prior arrangement.

Season   February through December, August reserved for private retreats.

Programs   Guided silent retreats from Friday evening to Sunday afternoon with a different theme for each retreat.

Lodging   Capacity for 18 overnight guests — 2 leaders & 16 retreatants.

Rates   Weekend guided retreat $90. Weekday individual retreat $25/night with kitchen access, BYO food.

Meals   6 nutritionally balanced meals/weekend. A minimum of meat.

Genesis Farm   Blairstown, NJ

Genesis Farm is an Earth-centered learning center ministry of the Dominican Sisters of Caldwell, NJ. The property spans 140 acres of rolling hills, woodland, marshes, houses and farm buildings in the Delaware River region of northwest New Jersey. The Farm's organic gardens and orchards are cooperatively owned by over 100 families.

As a learning center, the Farm presents both residential and non-residential programs that assist people in making practical, positive changes in their lives that bring them closer to nature. All programs are led by the farm's resident staff and by visiting teachers active in the environmental movement.

The major residential offerings are the six-week "Earth Literacy" programs offered in the spring and fall of each year. Other residential offerings have included a 2-week program on spiritual values in an ecological age, a 5-day "Introduction to the New Cosmology," and a weekend "Environmental Sabbath: Creating Sacred Ritual."

Address   41A Silver Lake Road, Blairstown, NJ 07825, USA

Phone   908/362-6735.

Season   Year-round.

Programs   1-day to 6-week programs rooted in a spirituality that reveres the Earth as a primary revelation of the Divine.

Lodging   5 tipis and a guest house with 9 private rooms.

Rates   Sample (1993) residential program rates: weekend $125, 5-day $250, 2-week $500, 6-week $1,500.

Meals   During scheduled programs, breakfast foods are provided and 2 vegetarian meals are prepared each day.

Kerr House   Grand Rapids, OH

Kerr House is an antiques-filled Victorian mansion and yoga retreat a half hour drive from Toledo in northwestern Ohio. The director of the house is Laurie Hostetler, a lady with more than 20 years of hatha yoga teaching and lecturing experience. Each guest receives a copy of Ms. Hostetler's book on asanas. And along with breakfast served each morning in bed, each guest receives a copy of the day's schedule.

The day's first activity is hatha yoga and low impact aerobics at 8 AM, followed by a session of body treatments. Lunch is served in the Cafe. An afternoon might include counseling on stress reduction or self esteem building, followed by a walk on the Miami & Erie Canal towpath. There is another yoga session at 5 PM. The evening's candlelight dinner is served in the Formal Dining Room, often to the accompaniment of a harpist. Guests may then enjoy a whirlpool and sauna before retiring.

Most Kerr House programs are for women, though there are occasional weeks and weekends for couples or men only. Between programs, the facility may be reserved for a group or family. With three staff members per guest, the House has the relaxed formal atmosphere of an exclusive private club.

Address   P.O. Box 363, 17777 Beaver Street, Grand Rapids, OH 43522, USA

Phone   419/832-1733.

Season   Year-round.

Programs   5-day & weekend rejuvenation programs with gentle hatha yoga, body treatments, self esteem & stress reduction counseling.

Lodging   Five guest rooms, 3 suitable for couples. An 8 guest maximum.

Rates   5-day: private room $2,550, double occupancy $2,150. Weekend: $575/person, $975/couple.

Meals   Each day there are 3 excellent meals — mostly vegetarian but sometimes with fish or chicken.

Services   Programs include a generous selection of body treatments: massage, reflexology, mineral baths, herbal & body wraps, salt glow, hand & foot waxing, facials, manicure & pedicure. Additional treatments may be purchased at additional cost.

Himalayan Institute   Honesdale, PA

The Himalayan Institute rests on a plateau in the softly rolling hills of the Pocono Mountains. Its 422 acres include tennis and basketball courts plus a pond where guests can swim or, in winter, ice skate. Year round, the favorite outdoor recreation is a long walk or jog in the miles of surrounding woods and meadows, often opening on to majestic vistas.

Each month the Institute offers four to six residential seminars focusing on yoga, meditation and holistic health. Typical topics are "Finding Your Own Path in Life," "Hatha and Meditation Retreat," "Biofeedback and the Art of Self-Regulation," "Psychology of the Chakras" and "Transition to Vegetarianism." All courses are taught by Institute faculty and staff.

A guest's day at the Institute can begin with guided hatha yoga at 6:45 or breakfast from 8 to 8:30. The morning can include a course lecture and a biofeedback demonstration. After lunch there may be a guided tour of the grounds and a practicum on breathing and relaxation. Silence is observed from 5 to 6 PM and, following supper and a lecture, from 10 PM to 8 AM.

The Institute was founded by Indian yogi Swami Rama to create a bridge between Western science and the ancient teachings of the East. Its staff includes Western doctors and psychologists. Originally built as a Catholic seminary, the Institute's three story main building houses offices, classrooms, an auditorium, medical facilities, guest and resident bedrooms.

Address   R.R. 1, Box 400, Honesdale, PA 18431, USA

Phone   717/253-5551 or 800/822-4547.Fax 717/253-9078.

Season   Year-round.

Programs Weekend, 3 & 5-day courses on yoga, meditation and holistic health. Also 2 & 4-week health transformation programs, 1-3 month self-transformation programs, and residential internships.

Lodging   100 guest beds in main building. Each room has 1 or 2 beds and a sink. Linens and towels provided. Communal toilets and showers. Families with children accommodated in nearby family house.

Rates   2-day retreat $165; 3-day retreat $205; 5-day retreat $300; health transformation program $1,400-2,100/2 weeks; self-transformation program $350-425/month; residential/internship program $1,750/ year. Personal meditations retreat with meals $60/day single occupancy & $45/day double occupancy.

Meals   3 cafeteria style vegetarian meals/day, each tasty, nutritionally balanced and prepared with vegetables from the organic garden. A few tables reserved for silent meals.

Services   Stress assessment profiles and biofeedback sessions.

Kirkridge Retreat and Study Center   Bangor, PA

Kirkridge is a 50+ year old residential retreat center founded by a Presbyterian minister 85 miles due north of Philadelphia and due west of New York City. The center's 270 acre property contains seven guest quarters connected by trails and roads. The center's Lodge building is at the top of a ridge, near the Appalachian

Trail. Down in the valley, gentle pasture land surrounds the center's 180 year-old Farmhouse.

The Center is committed to addressing pressing human issues with the resources of Biblical faith. Workshop topics include "Living the Book of Acts," "Desert and Mountain Spirituality," "Literature and the Religious Imagination." Nondenominational and broadly ecumenical in spirit, Kirkridge also hosts workshops such as "Dance of the Woman's Spirit," "The Bible and Jung," and "Islamic Spirituality." Other recent topics have included mind/body healing, co-dependent and father-son relationships.

Kirkridge is further committed to integrating personal growth and social change, including giving voice to society's "outsider" groups. In 1993 there were workshops by veteran social activists William Sloan Coffin and the Berrigan brothers, workshops for sexually abused women and men, plus workshops for male and female homosexuals. Kirkridge workshops usually include small group sharing, silence and reflection, hiking, hearthside conversations, morning and evening prayers.

Address   Bangor, PA 18013, USA

Phone   215/588-1793.

Season   Year-round.

Programs 2 to 4-day workshops on personal & social transformation. Private retreats are accommodated on a make-your-own meals basis.

Lodging   Four group retreat facilities with a total capacity for more than 100 overnight guests. Also 5 private retreat accommodations, each with kitchen, bath & beds for 1 or 2 people, but no linens.

Rates   Weekend workshop $195-265. Private retreat: individual $50, couple $70.

Meals   3 daily, nutritious meals. No red meat.

Services   Pastoral counseling. Also Book Nest book store.

Kripalu Community at Sumneytown   Sumneytown, PA

On 68 acres of wooded hills less than one hour northwest of Philadelphia, Kripalu Community at Sumneytown hosts weekend workshops on yoga and meditation plus theme weekends such as "Manifesting Your Personal Destiny" and "Conscious Relationships." Most courses are taught by Kripalu Community members and visiting staff of Kripalu Center in Lenox, MA. In 1993, Kripalu Center's Yogi Amrit Desai conducted an 8-day retreat.

Kripalu Community's residents, some 6 children and 20 adults, enjoy a yogic lifestyle while pursuing schooling and careers in the surrounding area. Open and free to the public are community holiday celebrations and Saturday evening satsangs — chanting, meditation, lecture and sharing. Overnight visitors on personal retreat may participate in community projects and early morning yoga sessions.

Address   7 Walters Road, Sumneytown, PA 18084, USA

Phone   215/234-4568. No visits without prior arrangement.

Season   Year-round.

Programs 2 to 4-day workshops on yoga, meditation and lifestyle enhancement. Also personal retreats.

Lodging   Capacity for roughly 40 people in dorms, double & single rooms with shared or private bath. BYO linens, blankets & towels.

Rates   2 to 4-day workshop tuition (including meals & dorm style housing) $160-250. Personal retreat nightly rates: dorm $20, double $35, single $50.

Meals   3 vegetarian meals with mostly organically grown ingredients. Dairy and non-dairy options are available. Personal retreat visitors may use kitchen to cook own food.

Services   Private yoga classes and massage.

Pendle Hill   Wallingford, PA

At 60+ year-old Pendle Hill, a wooded 23 acre campus in the Philadelphia suburbs, education is envisioned as a means of transforming people and society. During a 9-month school year, the campus is home for a community of about 70 staff and students. Everyone has a daily kitchen job, a weekly housekeeping job, and pitches in on campus work projects for half a day each week. Each morning there is an optional worship service in Quaker format -a period of listening in communal silence for the will of God.

6 or 7 nongraded courses are offered each semester on subjects such as "Community and Compassion," "Global Spirituality and Earth Ethics," "Quakerism, Franciscanism and Creation Spirituality." Every semester includes a crafts course and the course "The Spiritual Basis of Our Work in the World." Course attendees meet as a group once each week. Term projects may take the form of written work, music or dance presentations, or craft displays created in a well-equipped crafts studio.

Pendle Hill accommodates sojourners, who may participate in community life and some classes during stays of up to 3 weeks. There are also retreats and conferences (usually weekend events) on topics such as "Healing from Life Wounds," "Tales of the Hasidism," and "A Prayer Retreat."

Address   Box T2, 338 Plush Mill Road, Wallingford, PA 19086, USA

Phone   215/566-4507 or 800/742-3150.

Season   Year-round, with a summer break in the resident study program.

Programs Resident study program, sojourns, conferences and retreats.

Lodging   Private, simply furnished study-bedrooms, linens & bedding provided. Also 2 small hermitages for personal retreats.

Rates   Resident study: full year (Oct. to mid-June) $10,500, one (10 to 11 week) semester $3,600. Daily sojourn rates: over 1 week — single $49.50, couple $79; under 1 week — single $53.50, couple $84. Theme retreat or conference weekend $135-160.

Meals   3 communal meals each day, all with vegetarian options.

Services Free 1 hour/week consultation on learning objectives is required for resident students and optional for sojourners.

Rainbow Experience   Kutztown, PA

Going on its 15th year, the Rainbow Experience is a week of non-sectarian spiritual rejuvenation and celebration at Kutztown University in the Pennsylvania Dutch countryside of Berks County, PA. Many participants opt to extend their stay at inns and B&Bs in this picturesque region of covered bridges, roadside vegetable stands, craftsmen's shops and antique markets.

Sandwiched between Sunday opening and Saturday closing, Rainbow Experience ceremonies are five days of morning and afternoon workshops, late afternoon seminars, and evening speaker programs. Nearly 50 teachers, healers and entertainers from all over North America contribute their talents to the Experience. There are also early morning tai chi sessions, morning meditations, and late evening rap sessions.

Speakers scheduled for 1994 include many well known Age of Consciousness teachers such as Jean Houston, John Milton, Joan & Myrin Borysenko. Every year, Friday evening features a healing service that extends the vision of healing from individuals to the planet as a whole.

Address   Life Spectrums, P.O. Box 373, Harrisburg, PA 17108, USA

Phone   800/360-5683.

Season   Generally the second full week in July.

Programs Workshops, seminars and talks on many topics involving holistic self-empowerment and self-realization.

Lodging   Double occupancy rooms, some air conditioned. Some private rooms. Guests may arrange for specific roommates.

Rates   Adult $430-450, ages 6-15 $340-360, ages 6-15 sharing room as 3rd occupant $260, under 6 $55. Private room supplement $80-110.

Meals   3 daily meals.

Services   Bodywork & massage. Free sessions with spiritual counselors & practitioners of a variety of other therapies.

Timshel   Montrose, PA

Timshel is a mystical retreat and study center located in the Endless Mountains of northeastern Pennsylvania. Some retreats are specifically for men or "mated lovers." Others are seasonal celebrations. Most are in the summer. And all draw on spiritual disciplines such as meditation, yoga, fasting, sacred story, and journal-writing. Each retreat is structured to encourage centering in a loving community that creates its own ritual.

Retreats are led by Jerry and Georgeanne Judd. Jerry is an ex-pastor, founder of "Shalom Retreats" and Shalom Mountain Center, and published author with a Ph.D from Yale in Psychology of Religion. Georgeanne is an artist who teaches art as meditation.

Address   R.D. 5, Box 81, Montrose, PA 18801, USA

Phone   717/934-2275. No visits without prior arrangement.

Season   February through October, but most retreats are in summer.

Programs   5 and 10-day retreats devoted to experiencing the mystical path. Usually 6 to 8 retreats each year. It is preferred, but not required, that retreatants have attended a "Shalom Retreat."

Lodging   Large house with 3 bathrooms and room for up to 15 overnight guests. Camping is not required, but all are asked to bring a tent to allow the experience of sleeping outdoors.

Rates   5-day: individual $480, couple $800. 10-day: individual $800, couple $1,450.

Meals   3 daily meals. Vegetarians accommodated on advance notice.

A.R.E. Camp   Rural Retreat, VA

Each summer, the Association for Research & Enlightenment conducts camps for children, adults and families at a secluded 50 acre site adjoining a national forest in southwest Virginia. The rustic environment includes cabins, recreation hall, arts and crafts building, meditation grove, pond, organic garden, volleyball court and soccer field.

There are three one-week family and adult camps, each with a different theme. 1993 themes were "Spiritual Breakthrough," "Embodying Your Spiritual Ideals," and "Health Connections: Body, Mind and Spirit." Each camp combines traditional summer camp activities with non-traditional activities such as daily dream exploration, meditation/quiet time, study and discussion of Edgar Cayce material.

The camp concludes with a two-week session staffed by faculty from a Virginia Beach graduate school. The 1993 session theme was "Creative Transformation." In 1993, an adult meditation retreat was offered concurrently with the final week of the University session. The meditation retreat combined mantras, chanting and meditation instruction with yoga and energy balancing techniques.

Address   A.R.E., P.O. Box 595, Virginia Beach, VA 23451, USA

Phone   804/428-3588.

Season   Late June through August.

Programs   1-week family & adult camps, a 1-week meditation retreat, a 2-week Atlantic University session. Also children's camps.

Lodging   Capacity for 110 people in screened-in cabins, each with 6 to 8 bunks. During family weeks, some families sleep in cabins but most sleep in their own tents or campers.

Rates   Atlantic University session $580, meditation retreat $180, family & adult camps — adult $180, child 10-17 $155, child under 10 $95.

Meals   3 daily, mostly vegetarian meals with fresh herbs & vegetables from the organic garden.

Fireside Retreat   Wytheville, VA

Fireside Retreat is a large, remodeled country home nestled in a quiet Appalachian Mountains valley. Its fifty acres of property include a large, in-the-ground swimming pool and cabana. The main building contains comfortable guest rooms and a great room with fireplace. There are hiking trails and trout streams amidst the mountain scenery of the adjoining Jefferson National Forest. The region is also rich in UFO sighting lore.

Retreat hosts Pam and Jim Lucas are both second degree Reiki practitioners. Pam is also a professional artist, regression hypnotherapist, long-time meditator, co-creative gardner, and gourmet cook. Guests receive instruction in both meditation and attunement to other life forms — a fish in the stream, a hawk in the sky, a tree or a rock in the forest. If they wish, they may also receive instruction in painting and hatha yoga. To insure a peaceful atmosphere, pets and children are not admitted.

Address   Star Route Box 87, Dublin, VA 24084, USA

Phone   703/228-8400 or 228-7744. No visits without prior arrangement.

Season   Year-round.

Programs   Personal & small group retreats — meditation, nature attunement & yoga instruction. Also art weekends — painting instruction for any level of experience plus meetings with local artists.

Lodging   4 large guest bedrooms with double or queen size beds.

Rates   Weekend $350. Weekday $125. Couples — 2nd person 1/2 price.

Meals   3 daily gourmet meals, vegetarian & special diets accommodated.

Services   Regressions & reiki sessions (3 recommended).

Hartland Wellness Center   Rapidan, VA

Situated on 760 wooded acres in the quiet foothills of the Blue Ridge Mountains, Hartland is a combination wellness center and missionary college operated by a team of Seventh-Day Adventist professionals — nurses, massage and hydro therapists, nutritionists and health educators. The facility includes a fully equipped cooking lab, exercise room, indoor swimming pool, sauna and sun deck. The grounds include a garden and walking trails.

Hartland's "Lifestyle to Health" programs include massage and hydrotherapy, nutrition and cooking instruction, health education, laboratory tests, and supervised exercise. They also include "God's answer to stress management" in the form of daily morning and evening gatherings that include stretches, prayer and scripture readings. There is also a Saturday morning service.

The Hartland approach has proven to be effective for weight reduction and control, heart disease reversal, hypertension reversal, diabetes control, smoking cessation, and stress resolution.

Address   P.O. Box 1, Rapidan, VA 22733, USA

Phone   703/672-3100 or 800/763-9355.

Season   Year-round.

Programs   10 & 18-day lifestyle modification programs tailor made to address each guest's specific health risks & problems. All programs include optional Christian prayer & worship services.

Lodging   15 rooms. 10 rooms have 2 beds. All have private bath.

Rates   "Lifestyle to Health" 10-day $1,500, 18-day $2,500, 10% off on 2nd family member. "Stop Smoking" 10-day $1,700, 18-day $2,700.

Meals   3 daily, non-dairy vegetarian meals.

Services   Airport, train & bus station pickup/drop-off services.

Indian Valley Retreat   Willis, VA

Thirty miles south of Roanoke, Indian Valley retreat encompasses 140 acres of rolling hills and gardens in Virginia's Blue Ridge Mountains. Owners Tom and Ise Williams support structured and unstructured individual retreats. They provide facilities for personal growth retreats led by outside groups. Each year since 1986, Ise has also hosted a "Women's Wellness Week" (WWW) in the Wise Woman tradition popularized by Susun Weed.

Generally held in late July/early August, WWW draws workshop leaders from as far away as New Orleans and New York City. The 1993 event, led by a staff of ten women, focused on healing through deepening the connection to the Earth's rhythms. Each day included free time plus several activities such as kundalini yoga sessions; sweat lodge ceremony; drumming concert; workshops on self-image, self-esteem, conflict resolution, Dreamcatchers, sacred grove, African spirituality, moontime and menopause.

Address   Route 2, Box 58, Willis, VA 24380, USA

Phone   703/789-4295. No visits without prior arrangement.

Season   Year-round.

Programs An annual "Women's Wellness Week." Also individual retreats & rental of facilities to like-minded groups.

Lodging   Dormitory style lodging in retreat cabins.

Rates   "Women's Wellness Week": entire week $350, final weekend $125-150, children's program $75/week or $12.50/day.

Meals   3 daily vegetarian meals.

Services   Massage, nutritional & transformational counseling. Children's program during Women's Wellness Week.

Monroe Institute   Faber, VA

The Monroe Institute pioneered the development of sound wave technology that alters brain waves to induce different states of consciousness. People who come to the Institute may experience these states while remaining "awake" — somewhat akin to lucid dreaming. At deep relaxation levels, "explorers" can learn consciousness-shifting techniques for purposes such as reducing stress, enhancing memory, or deepening sleep.

The Institute offers four 6-day programs. "Life Span 2000" focuses on consciousness levels of practical use during waking hours. "Gateway Voyage" takes participants through specific states of expanded awareness to deeply explore the personal self and other reality systems. "Guidelines" facilitates communication with distinct and different intelligences. "Lifeline" takes participants even further.

All explorations take place in private chambers totally isolated from light and extraneous sound. Skilled facilitators guide participants through the five or six daily 45 minute tape exercises, experiential and discussion sessions, and individual meetings.

The Institute rests on 800 acres in the rolling Blue Ridge foothills 25 miles south of Charlottesville. The property includes forest, walking trails, meditation spots along a creek and atop the ridges, and a lake where guests can swim. The

Institute was founded by Robert A. Monroe, an ex-broadcast industry executive (and engineer by training) whose life course was altered by the onset in 1958 of involuntary out-of-body states.

Address   Route 1, Box 175, Faber, VA 22938, USA

Phone   804/361-1252.

Season   Year-round with recess from mid-December to early January.

Programs 6-day programs dedicated to expanding human consciousness by inducing states of non-physical awareness through a carefully controlled brain wave-altering sound wave technology.

Lodging   Capacity for 24 guests in individual Controlled Holistic Environmental Chambers (CHECs). Each CHEC has adjustable fresh air input, adjustable (in both color and density) lighting, and night time use of speaker system for soothing sleep sounds.

Rates $1,295 per 6-day program.

Meals   3 meals per day, vegetarian option available on advance notice.

Services   Courtesy pick-up/drop-off at Charlottesville airport, bus or train stations.

Satchidananda Ashram   Buckingham, VA

Also known as Yogaville, Satchidananda Ashram is a rustic spiritual community spread on 750 acres of wooded hills in rural Virginia. Hilltop clearings offer sweeping vistas of the Blue Ridge Mountains, the James River, and the riverside Light of Truth Universal Shrine (LOTUS) — a lotus shaped temple honoring the world's major religions. Residential programs here include "For the Body, Mind & Spirit," "Raja Yoga Weekend," the "New Year's Silent Retreat," and "The Complete Meditation Workshop."

A day at Yogaville can begin at 5 AM with silent meditation, at 6:30 with yoga, or with breakfast from 8 to 9. All are welcome at the noon LOTUS meditation followed by the day's main meal. Guests are invited to practice selfless service by working alongside community members during the day. Free weekend activities may include a nature walk, an Ashram tour, a talk on Integral Yoga, guided meditation and hatha yoga classes for beginners.

Yogaville's founder is Swami Satchidananda, prolific author and recipient of the Martin Buber Award for Outstanding Service to Humanity. Reverend Satchidananda sometimes attends Saturday evening satsangs to answer questions and talk from a practical perspective spiced with Indian humor. The Yogaville community is 50 children and 250 adults. Children attend a Yogaville school. Adults are members working at the ashram, associate members with outside jobs, and others exploring the yogic lifestyle.

Address   Route 1, Box 1720, Buckingham, VA 23921, USA

Phone   804/969-3121.

Season   Year-round.

Programs Weekend and 5-day programs on holistic health, meditation and hatha yoga training. Classes taught by resident teachers.

Lodging   Capacity for 100+ guests: Inn efficiency apartments; dorms; campsites near dorm bathroom facilities; a few mobile homes for couples & families. Unmarried men & women in separate quarters.

Rates   Weekend & 5-day programs: Inn $290-590, dorm $145-295. Daily adult rates: Inn $55/one + $25/each extra, dorm $30-35, mobile home $50/couple + $25 each extra, tent $20/single & $35/couple.

Meals   3 daily vegetarian meals eaten in silence. Fruits & vegetables from Yogaville's 1 acre orchard & organic garden.

Services   A combination cafe/mini-health food store.

Sevenoaks Pathwork Center   Madison, VA

Sevenoaks is a 20+ year-old retreat center set on 130 acres in the Shenandoah foothills, less than 100 miles southwest of Washington, D.C. The property includes forest, meadows and a cleared quadrangle space surrounded by the Center's buildings. There are hiking trails, a volleyball court, and a pond where guests can swim in the summer. The grounds also contain a sweat lodge and Native American medicine wheel.

Like New York State's Phoenicia Center but on a smaller scale, Sevenoaks focuses primarily on "Pathwork" — study and practice of concepts and exercises presented in 258 lectures channeled through the late Eva Pierrakos. The Center's founder is Donovan Thesenga, a former president of the national Pathwork Foundation. Donovan and Susan Thesenga, both authors of Pathwork-related books, lead or co-lead most Pathwork programs.

Sevenoaks also offers workshops in Pathwork-compatible fields such as past-life therapy, healing relationship and building community, men's and women's empowerment gatherings, Native American and Earth-centered spirituality. In addition to the Sevenoaks staff, workshop facilitators include authors, psychotherapists and teachers from the extended Pathwork family and related psychospiritual communities.

Address   Route 1, Box 86, Madison, VA 22727, USA

Phone   703/948-6544.

Season   Year-round, with most workshops from spring through fall.

Programs 1 to 4 public workshops each month on Pathwork and related psycho-spiritual disciplines.

Lodging   Capacity for more than 40 overnight guests in shared accommodations with twin beds. Most rooms have 2 beds, and couples may receive a private room. Towels & linens provided.

Rates   Workshops: weekend $185-250, 4-day $485, 5-day $585-750.

Meals   3 daily buffet meals, with vegetarian options.

Women's Way   Albermarle County, VA

Women's Way is a group of women that runs workshops and retreats designed to foster healing and wholeness in people's lives. Most programs are held at Mountain Light Retreat Center, a 34 acre Blue Ridge Mountains property a 30 minute drive from Charlottesville. The property contains an old church used as a meditation hall, a volleyball court, a beaver pond, and open meadows on the edge of Shenandoah National Park.

Women's Way hosts a program roughly once each month. Typical workshop titles are "Freedom From Suffering," "Introduction to Meditation," "Dancing From Source," and "Art, Creativity And The Meditative Mind." Women-only weekends include "Cherishing The Body" and "Success In Motion." Women's Way also runs weeklong meditation retreats and weekend wilderness trips, conducted in an attitude of mindfulness and respect for the Earth.

Several workshops are facilitated by Women's Way Director Donna Frantzen, M.D., a psychiatrist who has departed from conventional psychotherapy to develop methods for balancing body/mind, emotions and spirit. Donna's interest in integrating psychological and spiritual growth is shared by most Women's Way facilitators — mostly Virginia therapists and artists.

Address   1647 Mulberry Ave., Charlottesville, VA 22903, USA

Phone   804/293-3699.

Season   Year-round.

Programs   Weekend & weeklong workshops & retreats focusing on body/mind healing & wholeness. Some programs for women only. Retreat center accommodates individual retreats & outside group rentals.

Lodging   Dorm capacity for 40 overnight guests.

Rates $100-225/weekend workshop. $300/weeklong meditation retreat.

Meals   3 daily meals, mostly vegetarian during meditation retreats.

Services   Therapeutic massage.

Bhavana Society   High View, WV

The Bhavana Society is a monastic retreat and meditation center built and operated in keeping with the ancient Buddhist "forest tradition." It is a secluded and heavily wooded 32 acre property with a 3 bedroom/2 bathroom house, a dining room/meditation hall and a number of small huts. The center is staffed by two American monks and Bhante Gunaratana — a Sri Lankan monk who has taught in the U.S. since 1968.

The Society hosts both 10-day and weekend retreats, but only the weekend retreats are suitable for beginners. Usually after a two hour drive from metropolitan Washington, D.C., retreatants arrive by 7 PM on Friday for orientation. Saturday begins with a 5 AM wake-up bell and 5:30 group meditation. Breakfast is at 7. Meditation resumes at 8. A three hour lunch and recess period begins at 11, followed by another hour of meditation, an hour of teacher interviews, and a 4:30 hatha yoga session.

Retreatants may talk only with teachers. Meditation periods alternate between 1 hour sittings (chairs permitted) and 1/2 hour walkings. No food is eaten after noon. Following a 6 PM tea break, the day ends with a sitting and an 8 o'clock talk. All retreat days are like the first, with weekend retreatants departing after Sunday lunch.

Address   Route 1, Box 218-3, High View, WV 26808, USA

Phone   304/856-3241. Fax 304/856-2111. Call before visiting.

Season   Year-round.

Programs Weekend and 10-day group meditation retreats — 6 of each on alternate months throughout the year.

Lodging   Capacity for over 25 retreatants in a few double rooms & small huts, each sleeping 1-3 people. Potable water & jugs available. Each hut equipped with a heater. BYO fuel, bedding & towels.

Rates   In the Vipassana tradition, all retreats (including meals & lodging) are free of charge. But donations are accepted and necessary to support this center.

Meals   Vegetarian breakfast & lunch. 6 PM tea.

UNITED STATES   Southeast Region

Hawkwind Earth Renewal Cooperative   Valley Head, AL

Hawkwind is an Earth Renewal ceremonial ground and teaching center on 77 rustic acres in the northeast Alabama mountains. It is also a folksy, down-to-earth membership organization run by John Tarwater and Charla Hermann. John is a craftsman, drum maker and ceremonial leader of Lakota/ Scottish heritage. Charla, a Wyoming native and broadcasting industry veteran, directs Hawkwind's outreach and support group programs.

Weekend workshops are usually held two or three times each month. Several programs are led by nationally known teachers such as Brook Medicine Eagle, Susun Weed, Wallace Black Elk and Brant Secunda. Other workshops are led by Hawkwind members. Men's programs include "Shield of the Warrior." Frequent women's offerings include "Quest of the Rainbow Warrior Woman."

Hawkwind hosts winter and summer spirit and healing dances, open to those who have prepared in the prescribed manner. Other Hawkwind events include "Community Quest" camps, building weekends, spring equinox and winter solstice gatherings, plus regular Saturday sweat lodge gatherings. These Saturday gatherings include a Moon Lodge for women in their bleeding time, a teaching circle, talking circle support for parents, and a pot luck dinner. Last count, there were nearly 300 regular "Sweat Hogs."

Address   P.O. Box 11, Valley Head, AL 35989

Phone   205/635-6304.

Season   Year-round.

Programs   Weekend workshops and member community events, most involving Native American medicine ceremony.

Lodging   Campsites, Hawkwind tipis & bunkhouses.

Rates   Non-member (NM) grounds fees: 1st time $15 (includes newsletter subscription), $10 thereafter. Annual member (M) fee, including 4x camping fees: individual $50, family $80. Nightly camping fees: M — your tent $3, tipi $5, bunk $8; NM — your tent $5, tipi $8, bunk $10. Weekend workshop $25-250. No charge for Native ceremonies, but love offering support is welcomed.

Meals   All meals are community potluck in the Road Kill Cafe.

Services   Day care, bodywork, massage, spiritual & healing "counceling."

Uchee Pines Lifestyle Center   Seale, AL

Fifteen miles southwest of Columbus, GA, Uchee Pines Lifestyle Center is a warm and friendly healing facility situated on 200 acres of quiet woodland. Also known as Anvwodi (Cherokee for "get well place"), the center invites guests to rediscover the natural rhythms of their bodies through rest, temperance, drinking lots of water, proper diet, sunlight, country hiking and purposeful labor — gardening, tending the orchard or chopping wood.

Anvwodi regularly offers 18-day lifestyle programs that include a physical exam, blood chemistry profiles, physiotherapy, health lectures, regular physician consultations, natural remedy and cooking classes. All lifestyle programs are customized to address each guest's goals (e.g. weight loss, smoking cessation, blood pressure or diabetes control). There are also 5-day natural health seminars plus 9 or 12-month student training programs.

Uchee Pines Institute was founded by Calvin and Agatha Thrash — both M.D.s, devout Christians, and co-authors of several books on natural remedies and preventive medicine. Respecting the healing power of faith in God, the center makes available daily morning and evening worship services, Friday and Saturday vespers, a Bible-based "Keys to Happiness" class, plus Saturday morning church services. In addition, each lifestyle program guest is assigned a counselor who can also serve as a prayer companion.

Address   30 Uchee Pines Road, #75, Seale, AL 36875, USA

Phone   205/855-4764.

Season   Year-round.

Programs   18-day, M.D.-directed programs that employ natural healing methods, including optional Christian services. Also spring & fall 5-day seminars on "Simple Remedies & Preventive Medicine."

Lodging   7 rooms with twin beds, modern furnishings & private baths. Campsites & trailer hookups available for seminar attendees.

Rates   Lifestyle program: guest $2,595, 2nd participating family member $2,395, non-participating family member $1,495. Seminar: tuition $100, meals $50, housing $75, trailer hookup $25, campsite $10.

Meals   3 daily, family style vegetarian meals free of dairy products.

Services   Seminar services at additional cost: physical exam, consultation, blood chemistry analysis, pap smear.

Anabasis   Sarasota, FL

In a quiet, campus-like neighborhood of Sarasota, FL, Anabasis offers residential programs and workshops, on-going groups and classes, plus mind/body therapies. Guests receive temporary membership privileges at the next door family YMCA. Y facilities include fitness centers; basketball, racquetball and tennis courts; indoor pool, sauna and jacuzzis. Originally created as a treatment and recovery center for alcoholics, Anabasis completed its transition to a self discovery center in 1992.

The center's major offering is a four-week "Self-Discovery Program" designed for people passing through a major life transition. Anchored in ongoing groups, classes and therapies, the program includes meditation, yoga, tai chi, diet instruction, massage, biofeedback, counseling and recovery groups. Other residential programs are "Work-Study" and "Four-Day Retreat." A Room & Board option includes meditation and movement sessions.

Each month there are also anywhere from two to six residential workshops of two to five days in length. Many led by well known human potential therapists and teachers, these programs address topics such as "Stretching the Meridians," "Breathwork," "Health Imaging," and "Creative Risk Taking." In addition, Anabasis offers workshops for professionals on therapeutic modalities such as psychodrama and creative expression.

Address   1084 South Briggs Avenue, Sarasota, FL 34237, USA

Phone   813/365-5245 or 800/329-5245.

Season   Year-round.

Programs   1-month residential program, work study program, 4-day retreat, 2 to 5-day workshops focusing on personal growth & self discovery.

Lodging   Capacity for 20 overnight guests in comfortable, 3-person rooms.

Rates   1-month program $3,500; work study program (minimum 3 months) $1,600/month; 5-day workshop $675; 4-day retreat $440; 3-day workshop $420; 2-day workshop $280; room & board $60/day.

Meals   3 daily cafeteria-style meals, vegetarian & meat/seafood options.

Services   Shiatsu, Swedish, neuromuscular & sports massage; acupuncture; biofeedback training; counseling & psychotherapy.

Hippocrates Health Institute   West Palm Beach, FL

The 30+ year-old Hippocrates Health Institute is a sub-tropical, wooded estate of winding walkways connecting two large cottages to an expansive hacienda, swimming pool and sauna. Reflecting the commitment of its director Brian R. Clement, a longtime living foods advocate, the Institute encourages guests to reach personal goals through self-healing techniques that can be maintained at home. Benefits of Institute visits have included tension release, improved digestion, greater emotional stability, reduced back pain, and reversal of degenerative disease.

The Institute's "Health Encounter" program begins with a complete health appraisal. Each day there is early morning yoga or stretching and exercise; two or three classes on subjects such as internal awareness, stress management, visualization, and positive thinking; plus afternoon aquacize in the outdoors pool. Each week there is a massage session, group discussions with a psychologist, and individual consultations with an M.D. and a chiropractor.

Address   1443 Palmdale Court, West Palm Beach, FL 33411, USA

Phone   407/471-8876 or 800/842-2125 (reservations).

Season   Year-round.

Programs   3-week health maintenance/restoration program that can be taken in 1-week pieces and tailored toward specific goals (e.g. weight reduction, cleansing, building).

Lodging   Private & shared cottage accommodations.

Rates   Minimum daily rates: shared room — 1-week $171, 2-weeks $153, 3-weeks $123; private room — 1-week $$378, 2-weeks $350, 3-weeks $280. Private rooms with shared bath are occasionally available at shared room rates.

Meals   3 daily high enzyme, organic vegetarian meals. Wheatgrass & fruit juices between meals.

Hygeia Center   Ft. Myers, FL

Hygeia is a 2 1/2 acre holistic healing center in a quiet, semi-rural Ft. Myers neighborhood. Hygeia is also the home of Dr. Matina Konstandinidis, a warm and friendly Naturopathic practitioner and Reiki therapist. Dr. Matina's background includes apprenticeship with Dr. Ann Wigmore, training in Ayurvedic and Chinese medicine, and study of the flower remedies used by the Australian aborigines. Each guest receives a health assessment and an individually designed diet, plus a herbal facial and Swedish massage.

A Hygeia day begins with wake-up stretches and a walk. Mornings are for free time at the nearby Sanibel Island beaches. The afternoon contains a gentle and contemplative yoga session led by a local teacher and, sometimes, also a tai chi session. Making dinner can be a participatory learning experience. Evenings may feature a talk by Matina, a visit to the nearby Center of Eternal Light, or relaxing at the beachside Cafe Dumont.

Address   P.O. Box 845, Estero, FL 33928, USA

Phone   813/489-3337 (also serves as fax).

Season   Year-round.

Programs   Loosely structured daily program of walks, swimming, yoga, cooking demonstrations & health lectures.

Lodging   Three single rooms, each with 2 double beds, in a private home.

Rates   Suggested donations: 7-day session $795/person; 26-day session $2,000/person or $3,000/couple.

Meals   2 daily enzyme rich vegetarian meals — mostly uncooked fruits & vegetables, some grown in the backyard. Also various fasts.

Services   Reiki, Naturopathic consultations, Australian flower remedies.

Keys Institute   Key Largo, FL

Forty miles south of Miami just off the southeast tip of Florida, Dorothy Thomas hosts some 10 to 15 growth potential workshops each winter season. The ocean side facility allows guests to enjoy a jacuzzi, salt water swimming, canoeing and paddle boating. And long afternoon workshop breaks allow time for nearby activities such as charter fishing, snorkeling and diving trips, windsurf board and sailboat rentals.

Formerly a popular Esalen Institute employee, Dorothy is able to attract top notch workshop leaders from throughout North America. Regular facilitators in recent years have included regression therapist/author Roger Woolger, Tao psychologist/author John Heider, and gestalt practitioner John Soper. Workshops led by Dorothy include a two-day "Radiance" weekend for women. Workshop participants help out by unloading group room supplies and cleaning up the workshop space on the last day.

Address   P.O. Box 3150, Key largo, FL 33037, USA

Phone   305/451-3519.

Season   Late October through early March.

Programs   2 to 4-day residential growth potential workshops involving disciplines such as bodywork, breathwork, focused awareness, gestalt, group process work, and meditation. Work-scholar opportunities require a 4 to 6 month time commitment.

Lodging   A 2-bedroom apartment & cottages accommodating anywhere from 1 to 4 (with sleeping bags).

Rates   4-day workshop — shared room $565, private room $680. 3-day workshop — share $425, private $510. 2-day workshop — sleeping bag space $250, 1-night share $295, 1-night private $340.

Meals   Daily self-serve continental breakfasts. First lunch provided. Other lunches & dinners purchased & prepared as a "structured pot luck" by the participants, who also clean up after meals.

Regency Health Resort   Hallandale, FL

A 15 minute drive from Ft. Lauderdale airport, Regency Health Resort is an oceanside body/mind health spa. Facilities include a heated outdoors pool, jacuzzi, sauna, shuffleboard, Nautilus gym with Treadmill and Stairmaster. There is also a spacious poolside/seaview wooden deck. The resort's staff includes licensed nutrition counselors, chiropractic and medical doctors.

Each Regency guest receives a program schedule with no two days alike. A pre-breakfast walk on the beach could be followed by a morning of aquacize and exercise (yoga or stretch-and-tone). Afternoon activities might include a session in hypnotherapy or creative sculpture, low impact aerobics, a food preparation class and a nutrition lecture. Evenings can feature a movie, a musical event, or a lecture. Lecture topics include behavior modification, body/mind wellness, visualization and meditation.

Address   2000 South Ocean Drive, Hallandale, FL 33009, USA

Phone   305/454-2220 or 800/695-9591.

Season   Year-round.

Programs 1-week program focusing on detoxification, fitness and nutrition.

Lodging   Ocean and non-ocean view rooms, some with living rooms and all with at least 2 double beds, at least 1 private bathroom, cable TV, a phone and air conditioning. Towels & linens provided.

Rates   Depending on room size, number of people/room (1-4) & whether or not room has an ocean view, weekly/person rates are: single $995-1,425, double $895-$1,325, triple $895, 4-to-a-room $795.

Meals   3 daily gourmet vegetarian meals. Juice or water fast option.

Services   Massage, reflexology, herbal body wrap, facial, manicure, pedicure, hairstyling.

Russell House   Key West, FL

155 miles southwest of Miami, Russell House is a gracious, European style health resort located in the heart of Olde Key West — known for its colorful characters, charming shops, art galleries, and performing arts theaters. Local sightseeing includes open-air trolley tours, a Cuban cultural center, and a maritime history museum. Key West is a casual place, swept by sea breezes and enlivened by Old Town sunset celebrations.

At Russell House, "Wellness Week" guests can enjoy the outdoor heated pool, a large Roman hot tub, a sauna and several free spa services — two 1-hour full body massages plus a deep cleaning facial. A "Wellness Week" day begins with morning stretches and breathing followed by a 2-mile walk. There are daily yoga and "aquathenics" classes plus classes during the week on meditation, creative visualization, nutrition, skin care and smoking cessation. The results? — 50% of Russell House customers are returnees.

Address 611 Truman Avenue, Key West, FL 33040, USA

Phone 305/294-8787 or (from US) 800/851-4111. Fax 305/296-7354.

Season Year-round.

Programs 7-day "Wellness Weeks" focusing on light exercise and mind/body relaxation.

Lodging 21 air-conditioned rooms with king or twin beds, CATV, separate baths & bathrobes. Large bath towels & linens provided.

Rates Weekly rates: single $1,845 or $1,395; double $1,365 or $1,065; triple $995.

Meals Juice fast or 3 daily vegetarian meals at 550, 800 or 1200 calories. All diets are 100% free of cholesterol, salt, sugar and chemicals. Special diets also available.

Services Massage, herbal wrap, aromatherapy facials, skin peels, manicure, pedicure, colon irrigation.

Sanibel Connection   Sanibel Island, FL

For over ten years, Karin Stephan has hosted an annual early winter yoga vacation on Sanibel Island — a Gulf Coast getaway forty minutes from Fort Meyer. This is a one-week vacation, but it is possible to come only for a weekend. Guest accommodations are Tortuga Beach Club condominiums, all overlooking shell filled sandy beaches. The Club allows guests free access to tennis courts, an 18-hole golf course, a swimming pool and jacuzzi.

The daily morning and evening yoga classes are taught in the Iyengar style by guest teachers and Karin — a student of B.K.S. Iyengar and co-director of B.K.S. Iyengar Yoga Center in Somerville, MA. There are 2 hours of yoga in the morning and 1 1/2 hours (2 hours on weekends) in the late afternoon. This schedule gives vacationers ample time to enjoy the beach or rent bicycles to explore the island. Evenings offer lectures and discussions.

Address Yoga/Macrobiotic Vacations, 5 Frost Street, Cambridge, MA 02140, USA

Phone 617/497-0218.

Season 7 days in early December.

Programs Iyengar style, hatha yoga vacation.

Lodging Double occupancy at Tortuga Beach Club.

Rates Week $825-925. Weekend $295-325. 5% couples discounts. $50 surcharge for beach front room with private bath & balcony.

Meals   2 large macrobiotic meals each day.

Services   Massage, ginger compresses & yoga therapy. Also private counseling on diet and life style transitioning.

Sanibel Island Yoga Vacation Retreat   Sanibel Island, FL

"Sparkling days and starry nights on magical Sanibel Island" is usually an accurate description of the annual spring Sanibel Island Yoga Vacation Retreat. Staying in condos on one of the best shelling beaches in North America, vacationers can swim, play tennis nearby, or rent bicycles to explore the island on its many bike trails. Yoga classes are taught twice daily in a bright hall, a 2 mile walk or bike ride from the housing.

The retreat has been conducted since 1982 by Bobbi Goldin, a certified Iyengar yoga teacher who directs The Yoga Institute of Miami. Bobbi is known for her ability to individualize instruction within her classes so everyone's needs are met. She is assisted on the retreat by Kandy Love. from the Health & Harmony Center in nearby Ft. Myers, Florida.

Address   The Yoga Institute of Miami, 9350 S. Dadeland Blvd. — Ste. 207, Miami, FL 33156, USA

Phone   305/661-9558.

Season   Generally the first week in May.

Programs   Iyengar style, hatha yoga vacation.

Lodging   Two bedroom, two bath beachside villas, each with A/C, TV, phone, full linens and a complete kitchen with washer & dryer. Bedrooms are double occupancy unless otherwise requested.

Rates   Yoga classes & shared room $564. Private room $210 extra.

Meals   The island has markets and restaurants to satisfy just about every taste and budget. So make your own meals at the villa or eat out. Bobbi recommends Woody's Health Food Store for its sprout sandwiches and fresh smoothies.

Shangri-La Natural Health Resort   Bonita Springs, FL

Shangri-La resides on a garden-covered 8 acre estate 22 miles south of Ft. Meyers. The local village of Bonita Springs was named after the ancient, fresh water mineral springs that feed Shangri-La's outdoor swimming pool. Two solaria allow private sun bathing in the nude. Oak Creek meanders through the grounds, and guests can row or paddle over its waters in paddle boats moored at the creekside dock. The resort's own bus is the link to nearby white sandy beaches on the Gulf of Mexico.

Shangri-La is a relaxed, informal environment where guests are on their own. Individual consultation with the resort's health director are available each morning. There are daily calisthenic and yoga classes. Other resort facilities include tennis and horseshoe-pitching courts, badminton, volleyball, tetherball and shuffleboard. There is also a jogging track and a special outdoor ping pong pavilion.

The resort was founded by R.J. Cheatham, a past president of the American Natural Hygiene Association. The late Mr. Cheatham's commitment to natural hygiene education is reflected in Shangri-La's thrice weekly evening lectures. Topics include organic gardening, sprouting, food combining and preparation, fasting, mental/emotional poise, relaxation and meditation.

Address   P.O. Box 2329, Bonita Springs, FL 33959, USA

Phone   813/992-3811.

Season   Year-round.

Programs   Daily availability of health counseling, exercise and yoga classes. Thrice weekly evening natural hygiene lectures.

Lodging   Main building contains 25 guest rooms, each with private bath. Six other buildings contain 44 motel type guest units (including 2 room suites) with private or semi-private bathrooms. All rooms are air-conditioned, heated & tastefully furnished.

Rates   Nightly rates for single & double occupancy rooms range $70-95.

Meals   3 daily vegetarian meals, all living foods except 4 nights/week when cooked food is served. Most ingredients are organic. Fruit & nuts from Shangri-La's tree gardens. Also supervised fasting.

Eupsychia Institute   Dahlonega, GA

Eupsychia Institute offers healing/training programs for professional care givers and others seeking inner healing. The programs employ breathwork, movement, guided imagery, psychodrama, artwork, meditation, journal writing, ritual, singing and drumming to address ACOA issues, codependence, birth or childhood trauma, repressed incest and abuse issues, burnout, food and process addictions (e.g. spending, gambling, sex and romance).

Eupsychia's major offering is a 14-day "Healing into Wholeness" program, which integrates the 12 Step approach with transpersonal psychotherapy. Six-day retreats have included "Transpersonal Psychodrama," "Healing the Shadow," "The Magician and the Path of Initiation." The Institute's founder and program director is teacher/author Jacquelyn Small, a former faculty member of the Institute of Transpersonal Psychology and past Training Director of the Texas Commission on Alcoholism and Drug Abuse.

Most Eupsychia programs are conducted at Forrest Hills Mountain Hideaway, 80 miles northeast of Atlanta near Dahlonega, GA. The Institute also runs weekend "Embodying Spirit" conferences in or near major U.S. cities. Most conferences are preceded by one-day integrative breathwork workshops, and conference speakers engage the audience in process work.

Address   P.O. Box 3090, Austin, TX 78764, USA

Phone   512/327-2795. Fax 512/327-6043.

Season   Intermittently throughout the year.

Programs 14-day and 6-day intensive training workshops on psychospiritual integration. Also weekend conferences with optional, pre-conference integrative breathwork workshops.

Lodging Shared accommodations.

Rates   14-day $3,095-3,195. 6-day $925-975. Conference $225. Pre-conference workshop $100.

Meals   3 daily meals.

East Coast Yoga Vacation   Highlands, NC

East Coast Yoga Vacation offers two, weeklong mid-summer vacations at The Mountain — a camp and conference center looking out over the Blue Ridge Mountains of southwestern North Carolina. Both vacations include four hours of daily yoga, guided hikes through the Botanical Garden, and general use of The Mountain facilities. But one vacation is for adults-only, and the other is for families — including a children's program of yoga, swimming, hiking, arts and crafts.

An annual event now for over five years, East Coast Yoga Vacation features well known East Coast hatha yoga instructors that are all students of B.K.S. Iyengar. Classes at The Mountain include pranayama and are divided to accommodate both beginning and continuing students.

Address   Lighten Up! Yoga Center, 60 Biltmore Ave., Ashville, NC 28801, USA

Phone   704/254-7756.

Season   Two 1-week sessions in July.

Programs Iyengar style, hatha yoga vacation.

Lodging Deluxe double rooms in lodge or rustic, 6-person cabins.

Rates   Adult rates: lodge double $850, rustic cabin $760. Children's room rates: child 0-4 years $25; child 5-9 years $135; child 10-18 years $165. Activities program for children 4-13 years $140.

Meals   3 daily vegetarian meals in a casual, private setting.

Journey into Wholeness   Western NC

Journey into Wholeness each year hosts 15-20 residential conferences, seminars and workshops designed to foster inner healing by integrating Jungian depth psychology with spiritual and religious themes. Programs are led by Jungian psychoanalysts, ministers, healers, artists and authors.

Annual 5-day programs include a February "Way of the Dream" conference plus spring, summer and fall conferences. All conferences include lectures, workshops and special events (e.g. dances, theater and films). And most conferences are preceded by a 2-day Introduction to Jung seminar with lectures, small group interaction and videos. Other annual programs are an 8-day August "Temagami Vision Quest," an "Earth & Psyche" sweat lodge weekend, a men's weekend, and a women's weekend.

Journey's five major program sites are in North Carolina's Blue Ridge Mountain region. These sites include a lakeside Episcopal conference center, a rustic Pisgah Forest retreat, and a center north of Grandfather Mountain. Two other sites are a Methodist conference center on St. Simon's Island, GA and Langskib Base Camp in the Temagami, Ontario wilderness.

Address   P.O. Box 169, Balsam Grove, NC 28708, USA

Phone   704/877-4809.

Season   Year-round.

Programs 5, 4 & 2-day conferences plus 2-day seminars integrating Jungian & various spiritual perspectives. Also weeklong vision quest.

Lodging   Generally a selection of single, double & dorm accommodations. Camp out during vision quest program.

Rates   2 & 3-day programs: tuition $150-300, food & lodging $55-250. 4 & 5-day conferences: tuition $325-350, food & lodging $130-400.

Meals   3 daily meals.

Southern Dharma Retreat Center   Hot Springs, NC

Located in the Great Smokey Mountains one hour north of Ashville, Southern Dharma Retreat Center (SDRC) hosts meditation retreats led by teachers from various spiritual traditions. Retreats range in length from a weekend to ten days, are suitable for beginner meditators, and are conducted in silence except for periods of teacher talks and teacher/student dialogue.

Typical themes for meditation retreats are "Vipassana Meditation," "Zen and Psychology," "Awareness Meditation and Yoga," and "Tibetan Buddhist Practice." SDRC teachers are Buddhist monks and other well qualified meditation instructors from all over America.

Address   Route 1, Box 34-H, Hot Springs, NC 28743, USA

Phone   704/622-7112. No visits without prior arrangement.

Season   April through December.

Programs Mostly 2 to 10-day guided meditation retreats, with an average of 2 retreats each month.

Lodging   Dormitory holds up to 24 people. There is also a small cabin and primitive creekside campsites with a nearby shower.

Rates   2 and 3-day retreats $100-120. 4-day retreat $140. 7 and 8-day retreats $260-295. Fees cover only center operating costs & teacher's travel expense. Teacher donations for the teachings are accepted at the end of each retreat.

Meals   3 daily vegan meals.

CARIBBEAN, MEXICO & BRAZIL

Sivananda Ashram Yoga Retreat   Paradise Island, Bahamas

A Paradise Island yoga camp on a beach of pure white sands and clear blue waters, Sivananda Ashram Yoga Retreat is a 4 acre paradise of disciplined relaxation. Everyone is up with the sun for meditation at 6, followed by hatha yoga on a wooden deck shaded by palms and looking out over the Caribbean. After a 10 AM brunch, vacationers may attend a noon yoga coaching class. Another hatha session begins at 4 PM. The day ends with an 8 PM meditation session and a talk on yogic practice or philosophy.

During the afternoons, guests are free to do whatever they wish — explore the island, play tennis or volleyball at the compound, swim and snorkel at the beach, or relax on an airy veranda facing the sea. It is a casual, outdoors environment. After meals, guests wash their own plates and utensils and put them out to dry on open air racks.

Though just a short walk from glamorous hotels and casinos, Sivananda Ashram Yoga Retreat is a world away in spirit. "Health is wealth, peace of mind is happiness, and yoga shows the way." That is the guiding philosophy of Swami Vishnu Devananda, founder and director of Sivananda Yoga Vedanta Centers International.

Address   P.O. Box N-7550, Nassau, BAHAMAS

Phone   809/363-2902.   Fax 809/363-3783.

Season   Year-round.

Programs   Hatha yoga retreat with regular daily schedule. Attendance required at classes and meditations. Special holiday programs. February 4-week "Teachers' Training" open to all.

Lodging   103 beds in beachside wooden cabins and main building dorms. Linens & towels provided. 50 tent sites in a coconut grove. Communal bathrooms and showers.

Rates   Daily: single $75, semi-private with ocean view $60, semi-private $50, dorm $45, tent $40. Rates $10 higher Dec 19-Jan 3 & April 9-16. "Teachers' Training": tent $1,295, dorm $1,800.

Meals   Mid-morning & evening vegetarian buffets. Snack canteen.

Services   Shiatsu and reflexology bodywork.

Yoga in the Bahamas   San Salvador, Bahamas

Yoga in the Bahamas is an annual winter program of several weeklong workshops hosted by Feathered Pipe Foundation at Riding Rock Inn, a diving resort next to a white sand beach on San Salvador Island. One of the lesser known Bahamian islands, San Salvador is served by three weekly air flights and about 20 cars.

The three 1993 workshop offerings were "Women's Wisdom," "Form & Freedom," and "The Original Yogi." "Women's Wisdom" involved exploration of women's spirituality through group discussion and spontaneous rituals. The other two workshops were Iyengar style yoga retreats, appropriate for beginners as well as experienced students. All workshops are conducted by nationally and internationally recognized teachers.

Address   Feathered Pipe Foundation, P.O. Box 1682, Helena, MT 59624, USA

Phone   406/442-8196.   Fax 406/442-8110.

Season   February & March.

Programs   One-week workshops on subjects such as yoga & women's spirituality.

Lodging   24 double-occupancy rooms.

Rates $1,500-1,700, including round-trip charter flight from Ft. Lauderdale, FL.

Meals   3 daily meals, primarily vegetarian with some fish & chicken.

Spring Getaway in Barbados   St. Philip, Barbados

For over 5 years, Karin Stephan has hosted a one-week spring yoga vacation in the Caribbean. Recently this getaway has been held at a 10,000 square foot bluff-top estate overlooking the Atlantic on the eastern coast of Barbados. Vacationers can swim in the estate's secluded pool, surrounded by coconut trees, or walk to a beach of glistening white sands only minutes away. Guests may also use the pool, tennis courts and gourmet restaurant of the neighboring Crane Beach Hotel.

Each day's morning and evening yoga classes are taught by Karin, who has studied with B.K.S. Iyengar and is co-director of B.K.S. Iyengar Yoga Center in Somerville, MA. In their ample free time, vacationers can rent mini-mokes (small, open-sided jeeps) to explore the island — its Andromeda gardens, flower forest, national park, oceanside towns, and palm-swept west coast beaches.

Address   Yoga/Macrobiotic Vacations, 5 Frost Street, Cambridge, MA 02140, USA

Phone   617/497-0218.

Season   7 days in late March/early April.

Programs   Iyengar style, hatha yoga vacation.

Lodging   Double and triple occupancy rooms at an oceanside estate.

Rates   Double occupancy $1,250; triple occupancy $1,150; 5% couples discount.

Meals   2 large macrobiotic meals each day. Gourmet restaurant nearby.

Santo Daime Transformational Retreat   Maua, Brazil

The Santo Daime Transformational Retreat is an annual, inner journey of self-discovery in the Santo Daime community of Maua, Brazil — four hours from Rio de Janiero in rolling mountains laced with waterfalls. The rhythm of village life centers around the rituals of the Santo Daime — an eclectic spiritual path focalized in the 1930s by a man named Master Irineu from the ancient shamanic practices of the Amazon rainforest.

Retreatants participate in at least six Daime rituals. These include silent, sitting concentration; singing hymns invoking the healing power of the "caboclos" — divine beings and spirit guides; and sacred dance done to the rhythm of a cycle of hymns often lasting from dusk till dawn. The retreat also includes various yoga practices to increase concentration and clear energy channels for greater receptivity to the Daime's refined spiritual energy.

The retreat leaders are Alaea and Rex Beynon, founders of a U.S. Santo Daime church. Alaea is a licensed acupuncturist, herbologist and polarity therapist. Rex is a long time meditation teacher, student of comparative religion, and director of the New England Polarity Wellness Center. Both Rex and Alaea have studied Tibetan Buddhist meditation, Taoist and Kundalini yoga, South and North American shamanic healing practices.

Address   Ceu do Beija-Flor, P.O. Box 625, Cambridge, MA 02140, USA

Phone   616/593-4329 (also accepts fax).

Season   December.

Programs   3-week Brazilian mountain village retreat rooted in the community rituals of the Santo Daime spiritual tradition.

Lodging   Simple accommodations in the Maua community.

Rates   Retreat, room, board & ground transportation between Rio de Janeiro and Maua $2,900. (Roundtrip airfare from the USA is about $950.)

Meals   3 daily vegetarian meals.

Negril Yoga Centre   Negril, Jamaica

Negril Yoga Centre provides simple, comfortable accommodations in a private and secure tropical garden setting near the village of Negril on the west end of Jamaica. Guests can enjoy the nearby beaches or join a yoga class in the open-air pavilion. Classes are taught by guest instructors or Centre director Raquel Austin. Tennis, bicycle rentals, horseback riding, country hill tours, and evening cruises can be arranged.

Address   Negril P.O. Box 48, Westmoreland, JAMAICA

Phone   809/957-4397 or 813/263-7322.

Season   Year-round.

Programs Hatha yoga — occasional workshops and daily classes.

Lodging   Capacity for over 32 guests in 11 villas, cottages & studios — all with double beds, private bathrooms with showers, ceiling fans & refrigerators. One has air conditioning, 2 have private balconies, 3 have verandas. Daily maid service.

Rates   Double occupancy nightly rates: summer $30-60, winter $35-70.

Meals   Vegetarian breakfast & dinner can be arranged. The Centre makes its own yogurt, cheeses & sprouts.

Services   Massage. Courtesy transportation to & from airport.

Rancho La Puerta   Tecate, Baja, Mexico

Rancho La Puerta is a 300 acre landscaped oasis set among rock-strewn hills and mountains near the California/Mexico border. The site was cleared in 1940 by Ed and Deborah Szekely for the Essene School of Life — initially a spartan adobe hut and campground. Renamed (in Spanish) "Ranch of the Open Door," the property later became the site of the hemisphere's first Par Course, first circuit training, and first exercise choreographed to music. This first modern health resort is also the birth place of spa cuisine.

Today the Ranch is a village-like complex of residence and administrative buildings, 3 outdoor swimming pools, 6 lighted tennis courts, volley ball courts, separate men's and women's health centers (each with sauna, steam room and whirlpool), outdoor and weight training gyms, plus six aerobic workout centers. There are also many miles of hiking trails, some that lead up nearby sacred Mount Kuchumaa. The Szekelys still own the Ranch, and there are still no phones or TVs.

During the resort's weeklong program, guests are advised to choose at least one daily class from each of five categories — aerobic workouts, anaerobic strengthening and toning, stretching and flexibility, coordination and balance, and relaxation (meditation, tai chi and yoga.) A typical day begins with a hike, includes 6 hours of classes, and ends after dinner with a guest speaker, films, billiards, cards or board games.

Address   P.O. Box 463057, Escondido, CA 92046, USA

Phone   619/744-4222 or 800/443-7565.

Season   Year-round.

Programs Regular, weeklong holistic health spa programs.

Lodging   Accommodations for up to 150 guests in studio bedroom rancheras, 1 bedroom haciendas & villa studios, and 2 bedroom villa suites. All have private bath (suites have 2). And all except the rancheras have a kitchenette, living room & fireplace.

Rates   Per person weekly rates: ranchera — single $1,700, double $1,350; hacienda — single $1,900, double $1,500; villa studio — single $2,100, double $1,700, triple $1,400; villa suites — double $2,000, 3 04 4 occupants $1,600. All rates 10% less from late June through early September. Also, roommate matching service.

Meals   3 daily vegetarian meals with fish served twice each week. Breakfast & lunch buffets, sit-down dinner with silent option. Vegetables picked daily at dawn from own 3 acre organic gardens.

Services   Courtesy San Diego airport pick-up & drop-off. Also tennis lessons, massage, herbal wrap, hair-styling, manicure & pedicure.

Rio Caliente   La Primavera, Jalisco, Mexico

In the sub-tropical forest of a Sierra Madre mountain valley, Rio Caliente occupies 24 acres that was once a spiritual center for the Huichol Indians (the "healing people"). On the grounds are four plunge pools and an Aztec steam room fed by springs of soft, odorless, volcanically heated waters. Adjacent to a quiet river, the grounds also include guest rooms with hand-crafted beds and chairs, spa facilities and an M.D.-directed mini-clinic. The altitude is 5,000 feet. Daytime temperatures are 70-85 degrees F.

The atmosphere at Rio Caliente is informal and relaxed. Dress is casual, and nude sunbathing is permitted within two enclosed pool areas — one for men and one for women. All daily holistic health and fitness programs are entirely optional. Other options include van excursions to the local market, picturesque Lake Chapala, and Tlaquepaque — Mexico's arts and crafts center. Evenings are free for conversation, a movie or a soak.

Though only one hour by microbus taxi from Guadalajara's international airport, Rio Caliente is far away from the modern world. There are no phones, and mail is extremely slow. Everyone is asked to bring a flash light and insect repellant. Clothes lines and pins are provided, though guests may pay the room attendant a small fee to wash their laundry.

Address   c/o Marian Lewis, Post Office Box 897, Millbrae, CA 94030, USA

Phone   415/615-9543.

Season   Year-round.

Programs   Holistic health and fitness spa with optional daily yoga, tai chi (in some months), meditation, hiking, and aquatic aerobics.

Lodging   48 small, single & double rooms. "Patio rooms" near dining room. Newer "pool rooms," with wooden beams & tilework, near the pools. Private baths. Limited wheelchair access.

Rates   Daily rates (tips included): patio room — for one $84; for two $140; pool room — for one $96; for two $160. Add 10% value added tax. 10% discount on stays over 30 days.

Meals   3 daily, buffet style vegetarian meals with eggs, dairy or raw foods options. Garden greens. Tropical fruits in season.

Services   Horseback riding, sightseeing trips & spa services — mudwrap, massage & beauty treatments, anti-stress & anti-aging therapies.

Ann Wigmore Institute   Rincon, Puerto Rico

The Ann Wigmore Institute offers a 12-day "Living Foods Lifestyle" program designed to rejuvenate body and spirit in accordance with the Hippocratic ideal of "Let nature be the doctor of disease." The program encourages colon care and gentle self-healing in a learn-by-doing environment. During most courses, there are 15-18 students in residence.

The Institute is housed in two white stucco buildings surrounded by coconut, papaya and banana trees in a quiet neighborhood of cottages and fishermen's homes on tropical Puerto Rico's west coast. Fifty yards away, the ocean is visible over the trees from the second story veranda of the Institute's guest residence quarters.

A day at the Institute begins with wheatgrass juice, light exercise, yoga or beach walks. Participation in certain personal growth classes (e.g. journal writing, inner child and reflexology work) is required for a diploma. Other morning and evening classes focus on nutritional theory, colon care, plus techniques for growing and preparing living foods meals. Afternoons offer free time and optional classes, including sessions on massage and relaxation techniques. Each course ends with a graduation ceremony and banquet.

Address   P.O. Box 429, Rincon, PUERTO RICO 00677

Phone   809/868-6307.   Fax: 809/868-2430.

Season   Year-round.

Programs   12-day, holistic lifestyle education program that can be repeated for a 26-day stay. Also 3-month Practitioner's Training course.

Lodging   Capacity for about 25 overnight guests in dormitory, semi-private (shared with 1 other) and private rooms. Shared and private rooms may have full bathroom, 1/2 bathroom or no bathroom.

Rates   12-day program: dorm $945; shared — no bath $1,150, 1/2 bath $1,350, full bath $1,450; private — no bath $1,350, 1/2 bath $1,550, full bath $1,750. 26-day stay: dorm $1,650; shared - no bath $2,050, 1/2 bath $2,450, full bath $2,650; private — no bath $2,450, 1/2 bath $2,850, full bath $3,250. Practitioner's Training $3,100 (including room & board).

Meals   3 daily live food meals. The staple is energy soup — a blended mix of fruit, greens, rejuvelac, avocado, dulse & pea/lentil sprouts. The regimen is complemented by fruit smoothies, nut pates, seed yogurts, coconut milk, and fresh salads.

Services Reflexology, rebirthing, massage, colonic irrigation, colonic wheatgrass implants. Free transportation to and from airports.

Omega in the Caribbean   St. John, U.S. Virgin Islands

Tucked amidst mahogany and bay trees above a secluded bay, Omega in the Caribbean is a mid winter tropical village of canvas cottages at Maho Bay Camp Resort. Part of Virgin Islands National Park, the campground's hillside boardwalks connect to miles of well-marked hiking trails along and above pristine sandy beaches.

The day begins with sunrise meditation, yoga or tai chi. Meals and workshops are in open air pavilions overlooking the sea. There are two daily 2-hour workshop periods plus informal talks or concerts in the evenings. Each week presents five or six ongoing workshops, and some weeks have a dominant theme such as song, dance or writing/drawing. During the week, vacationers may sample all workshops or focus on one or two.

During the 1993 season, the one workshop offered during all six weeklong sessions was "Creating Time for Wellness," facilitated by Omega president Stephan Rechtschaffen, M.D. Through visualization, mindfulness and awareness exercises, Stephan encourages vacationers to discover "island time — the natural rhythm that comes from living in the present moment."

When they are not in workshops, most vacationers disperse to enjoy the beaches, snorkel among Trunk Bay's coral reefs, or explore the island. Island attractions include Bordeaux Mountain's rain forest and spectacular views, the ruins of 18th-century sugar mills, and old style farms owned and worked by descendants of Danish settlers.

Address   Omega Institute, 260 Lake Drive, Rhinebeck, NY 12572, USA

Phone   914/266-4444 or 800/944-1001.

Season   6 weeks from January to mid-February.

Programs 6 weeklong vacations, each with 5 to 7 weeklong workshops led by highly qualified, visiting artists & teachers.

Lodging 96 wooden floored canvas cottages, each with 2 beds, bedding and linens, a living/dining area, lounge chairs and sofa. Boardwalks connect to toilets, showers and dining pavilion.

Rates Tuition, lodging, meals & round-trip airfare from New York City $1,285. Deduct $425 if you make your own flight arrangements. Each additional week $775. $20 each way for land transportation to & from Maho Bay.

Meals 3 lavish vegetarian buffets each day, including some fish and dairy products. Tropical fruits available throughout the day.

Services Massage & nutrition counseling. Land transport to & from Maho Bay.

CANADA

Hollyhock   Cortes Island, British Columbia

Hollyhock is a family vacation and learning center on Cortes Island, 100 miles north of Vancouver in the Georgia Strait. Handcrafted buildings blend unobtrusively into an environment of old-growth trees, flower and vegetable gardens. And across the waters to the east, the skyline is shaped by the rugged contours of the Coastal Mountains.

From spring through fall, Hollyhock hosts over 70 seminars, workshops and adventures facilitated by well known artists, authors, educators and healing arts practitioners from throughout North America and other parts of the world. Most program offerings are two to six-days long. Hollyhock adventures include "Kayaking Desolation Sound," and "Learning to Sail" (on a 30 foot sloop). Other recent offerings: "Painting and Color," "Journal Writing as a Spiritual Quest," "A Modern Shamanic Initiation," "Embracing the Transpersonal," "Creation Spirituality and the Rebirth of Nature."

Hollyhock's 1993 schedule also contained six meditation programs, including a three-week Vipassana retreat suitable for beginners. The center operates on the assumption that spiritual fulfillment may be realized by extending meditative awareness into everyday life. Hollyhock's founder/director Rex Weyler sets an example by leading six-day "Chop Wood, Carry Water" work retreats. Longer opportunities for mindfulness-in-action are the work exchange and garden apprenticeship programs. Apprentices contribute to a ten-year, labor-intensive experiment in "ecological gardening."

For children ages nine to 13, there is a one-week August Kids Camp at Coast Mountain Lodge on neighboring Read Island. And for the entire family, there are weekend and weeklong holiday packages that include all meals plus a Friday barbecue; forest hikes; area tours led by Hollyhock's resident naturalist; hot tubbing; a session in the forest bodywork studio; a guided garden tour; yoga, tai chi, meditation or a bird walk each morning; evening talks, music or stories at the beach fire circle; and swimming in the Strait's ocean waters, warmed in summer up to 72 degrees Fahrenheit.

Address   Box 127, Manson's Landing, Cortes Island, B.C. V0P 1K0, CANADA

Phone   604/935-6533.   Fax 604/935-6424.

Season   May through October.

Programs   Seminars, workshops and adventures of 2 days to 3 weeks. Topics: nature, the practical and expressive arts, psychospiritual health and meditation. Weekend, week & deluxe holiday packages. Also work exchange and apprentice programs.

Lodging   Single rooms with or without bath, double occupancy rooms, dorms that sleep 3 to 6 people, and campsites (BYO tent & bedding).

Rates   2 to 6-day program tuition $179-665. Program room & board: single private bath $89-106, single shared bath $79-96, double $69-82, dorm $59-72, tent $49-52. 5-day kid's camp $479. 1-week adult holiday: single private bath $599-699, single shared bath $529-649, double $469-599, dorm $399-499, tent $329-399. children 4-12: room & board $45-58; tenting + meals $32-37.

Meals   3 daily gourmet vegetarian meals. Seafood served twice a week and at Friday night beach barbecues with clams & oysters.

Services   Swedish, shiatsu, deep tissue and acupressure massage. Also Reiki and natural skin care. Child care can be arranged.

Institute for Embodiment Training   Cobble Hill, British Columbia

A 40 minute drive north of Victoria on Vancouver Island, the Institute for Embodiment Training encourages students to balance and expand their sense of body awareness through an integrated program of breathwork, meditation, Rolfing, light aerobic exercises, gentle stretching and improvisational dance. Each student spends about five hours with a private instructor each day for five consecutive days. During programs over five days long, weekends are set aside for self-retreat and homework assignments.

The Institute's main instructors are Will and Lyn Johnson, both with over 17 years of professional experience. Will is a certified Rolfer and the author of "Balance of Body, Balance of Mind." Trained by Judith Aston at the Rolf Institute, Lyn specializes in movement education. Will and Lyn also conduct nine-week Basic Professional Development Training programs.

Address   R.R. 2, Cobble Hill, B.C. V0R 1L0, CANADA

Phone   604/743-5971. No visits without prior arrangement.

Season   Year-round.

Programs 3-day, 5-day, 12-day and 4-week Embodiment Training programs for singles and couples in relationship.

Lodging   Guests accommodated at combination home/training center.

Rates   Individual rates: 3-day $750, 5-day $1,075, 12-day $2,050, 4-week $3,975. Couple rates: 3-day $1,425, 5-day $2,025, 12-day $3,895, 4-week $7,550. Self-retreat $50-75/night.

Meals   Guests may use a small kitchen or dine at nearby restaurants.

Kootenay Summer Residentials   Johnson's Landing, British Columbia

Looking out over Kootenay Lake from the base of Kootenay Joe Mountain, Golden Eagle Retreat Centre hosts summer residential workshops run by Naomi and Doug Mosely. Authors of the book "Dancing in the Dark — The Shadow Side of Intimacy," the Moselys have a private practice of couples counseling. Naomi also counsels families and individuals.

In 1993, the Kootenay residentials were "Going Deeper Into Self," "Couples Retreat" and "Passion Training." The common element in these workshops is bringing dark (often denied) sides of self into conscious awareness and acceptance. The Moselys also host an annual year-end Galiano Island, BC retreat with therapy, breathwork, meditation and ritual at the Bodega Inn.

Address   Summer: Box 30, Johnson's Landing, B.C. V0G 1M0, CANADA
Winter: P.O. Box 8023, Santa Fe, NM 87504, USA

Phone   Summer: 604/366-4209.

Season   Mid May to mid September.

Programs   4 to 11-day retreats focusing on discovering & working with denied feelings.

Lodging   Accommodations for up to 16 overnight guests with 2 per room.

Rates   Kootenay retreats: 4-day $795/couple; 7-day $650/ person; 11-day $995/person. 4-day year-end retreat $795/person. (Canadian $.)

Meals   3 daily vegetarian meals with meat option.

Meridian Holistic Health Centre   Victoria, British Columbia

Nestled on seven acres in a quiet part of Victoria, Meridian Holistic Health Centre shares a 12 person professional staff with a next door outpatient services clinic. The staff includes an M.D., counselors, plus specialists in several therapies — acupuncture, acupressure, chiropractory, Hellerwork, massage and Shen.

Each month the Centre offers a 5-day "Self-Healing Intensive Program" (SHIP). A SHIP day begins with a guided stretch/relaxation class followed by group sessions in communication and stress management skills; breathing, body awareness and guided visualization exercises; guided fantasy, art, ritual and dreamwork. There is an early afternoon group experiential session such as biofeedback or movement therapy. Late afternoon is free time. In the evenings, there are talks on topics related to self-healing.

Once or twice each month, the Centre also offers weekend stress management retreats with sessions similar to those in SHIP.

Address   5575 West Saanich Road, R.R. 5, Victoria, B.C. V8X 4M6, CANADA

Phone   604/727-3451.

Season   Year-round.

Programs   Weekend stress reduction workshops & 5-day self-healing intensives.

Lodging   Capacity for 10 overnight guests in semi-private rooms with shared baths.

Rates   Weekend retreat $150-198. 5-day self-healing intensive $700.

Meals   3 daily meals. Vegetarians accommodated on advance notice.

Services   Private therapy sessions (e.g. acupressure, counseling, massage). Courtesy pick-up/drop-off at airport or ferry terminal.

Salt Spring Centre   Salt Spring Island, British Columbia

Salt Spring Centre for the Creative and Healing Arts is situated among 69 acres of cedar forest, meadows, gardens and orchard on Salt Spring Island -in the Strait of Georgia just off Vancouver Island's southeastern coast. On the grounds is a wood sauna, a greenhouse, a school, and a large homey program house with oak floors, stained glass windows and sunny dining room. Swimmers can enjoy nearby Blackburn Lake.

The Centre's resident adults and children, plus others living in the area, make up the Dharma Sara Satsang Society — a community based on selfless service and Ashtanga Yoga's ancient eightfold way. Throughout the year and especially in summer, the community offers a short-term Service/Guest program (requiring 4 hours of daily work) and a Service (work exchange) program (requiring 7 hours of daily work). The community's spiritual guide and inspiration is yoga master Baba Hari Dass, who visits the community once each year during the summer retreat.

The Centre sponsors women's weekends — times for relaxation and rejuvenation with yoga and meditation classes, aerobics, nature walks and saunas. In 1993, other inner healing workshops were facilitated by a variety of healers and teachers from throughout the northwest region.

Address   Box 1133, Ganges, B.C. V0S 1E0, CANADA

Phone   604/537-2326.

Season   Year-round. No visits without prior arrangements.

Programs   Frequent women's weekends; weekends focusing on inner healing and expressive movement; a 4-day Ashtanga Yoga intensive; a community work/study week; plus ongoing work exchange and Service/Guest programs. Facilities available for rental by outside groups.

Lodging   Shared rooms for up to 20 people in main house, dorm space for an additional 6, plus summer campsites.

Rates Residential programs: Service/Guest program — $25/day 1st week; work exchange program — $10/day 1st week. (Longer residential stays possible at reduced rates). Weekend programs hosted by the Centre & other organizations $200-300, depending on the program.

Meals Vegetarian meals each day with vegetables & fruits from own gardens & orchards in season.

Services An Ayurvedic herbal steam & bodywork treatment offered throughout the year. Also polarity, reflexology & fragrant flower facial offered during women's weekends.

Serenity by the Sea   Galiano Island, British Columbia

Serenity by the Sea is an ocean bluff retreat center on Galiano Island, the forested jewel of the Canadian Gulf Islands between Victoria and Vancouver. The main house and nearby chalet were designed by resident artist Shari Street, whose paintings and stained glass creations adorn every room. Next to the house is a reflecting pond, creekside garden and "tub on the rocks."

Shari leads workshops on painting as a mode of self expression accessible to anyone, with or without prior painting experience. Her husband Chidakash, a professional massage therapist, leads retreats that employ sensory awakening techniques, body/mind rebalancing exercises, meditation, visualization and massage. Group sizes range from 4 to 12 people.

Serenity also hosts workshops conducted by visiting teachers. Topics include self expression through singing and writing, developing intuition, journal work and personal mythology, strength sourcing and life/career evaluation, yoga and massage. One personal retreat weekend is scheduled each month. Workshops are scheduled for most other weekends.

Address 225 Serenity Lane, Galiano Island, B.C. V0N 1P0, CANADA

Phone 604/539-2655. No visits without prior arrangement.

Season Year-round.

Programs 2 to 4-day residential workshops, each presenting one or two approaches to creative self-discovery. Also private retreats.

Lodging Charming bed & breakfast type single and double rooms with panoramic coastal, ocean and island vistas.

Rates Workshops $225-390. Private retreat $40-100/day depending on season & nature of accommodation.

Meals 3 daily gourmet vegetarian meals. Hot drinks available throughout the day.

Services Massage, reiki & energy balancing sessions.

Summer Yoga Intensive   Victoria, British Columbia

Each year since 1989, the Victoria Yoga Centre has hosted a 7-day intensive for teachers and students with experience in Iyengar yoga. Each day there are morning asana sessions, mid afternoon seminars, and late afternoon pranayama sessions. Seminar topics include "Patanjali's Yoga Sutras," "Bhagavad Gita," "Symbolism of the Body," and "Musculo-Skeletal & Back Problems" from a yoga perspective. Classes are held at the Victoria YM-YWCA, centrally located in one of North America's most beautiful cities.

The teachers are Shirley and Derek French, and Jessica Sluymer. Shirley and Derek are longtime students of both B.K.S. Iyengar and Swami Radha. Shirley has taught yoga in Victoria for over 20 years. Derek is a physician who teaches therapeutic yoga. Jessica is a yoga teacher with training under Swami Radha and Shirley French.

Address   Victoria Yoga Centre, 3918 Olympic View Drive, R.R. 4, Victoria, B.C. V9B 5T8, CANADA

Phone   604/478-3775 or 604/598-8277.

Season   One week in early July.

Programs   Iyengar style, hatha yoga retreat.

Lodging   Single & double rooms with shared bathrooms at the retreat site -the Victoria YM-YWCA. Similar accommodations available nearby on the attractive University of Victoria campus. Bed & breakfast available with members of the local yoga community.

Rates   Rates/room for 7 nights: Y — single $218, double $323; campus — single $229, double $335; bed & breakfast $140.

Meals   Daily cafeteria style lunch with vegetarian option. Vegetarian buffet supper & party at teacher's house on last night.

Tai Chi Summer Retreat   Nelson, British Columbia

Tai Chi Summer Retreat is a longstanding annual event at Camp Koolaree on Kootenay Lake, nestled in the mountains of southeast British Columbia. Facilities include a lodge for indoor classes and fireside socializing, a kitchen and dining area, a large meadow for tai chi practice, and a private beach for swimming and canoeing. In the area are hiking trails and a natural hot springs. Five miles to the west is the town of Nelson.

The retreat is designed to accommodate all levels of tai chi experience. The daily schedule includes forms sessions for beginner and intermediate students; weapons sessions for intermediate and advanced students; applications sessions for advanced students; plus sessions for all levels in forms, chi gung, push hands, meditation and philosophy, group sharing, healing and massage. The head instructor is Rex Eastman, who has taught tai chi since 1975.

Address Kootenay Tai Chi Centre, Box 566, Nelson, B.C. V1L 5R3, CANADA

Phone 604/352-3714 or 604/352-2468.

Season One week in August.

Programs Tai chi retreat with novice, intermediate & advanced instruction.

Lodging Tentsites & shared cabins. BYO warm sleeping bed & mattress.

Rates Tuition, meals, lodging & boat transportation $375 ($325 US).

Meals 3 daily vegetarian meals.

Thymeways   Galiano Island, British Columbia

Thymeways is the Galiano Island home-studio of Maureen and Bruce Carruthers, students of B.K.S. Iyengar and directors of an Iyengar teacher apprenticeship program. For over 20 years, Maureen has taught yoga in the Vancouver area and in workshops throughout North America. Bruce is a Vancouver physician whose therapies include health enhancing practices.

At Thymeways, Bruce and Maureen lead weeklong yoga intensives for all levels of Iyengar yoga students. They also lead weekend and weeklong "Health Enhancement" workshops that include yoga postures, silent and music meditation, breath awareness, drumming, haiku composition, mindful work, plus nutrition and exercise instruction.

Each year, Maureen teams ups with Hilda Pezarro to lead a weekend yoga workshop for maturing women. Hilda teaches both Iyengar style yoga and the Kundalini system taught by Swami Radha at Yasodhara Ashram. Thymeways also hosts weekend yoga workshops taught solely by guest teachers.

Address 790 Devina Drive, R.R. 2, Galiano Island, B.C. V0N 1P0, CANADA

Phone 604/539-5071. No visits without prior arrangement.

Season March through November.

Programs Weekend & 7-day hatha yoga & health enhancement workshops.

Lodging Rooms in house or cottage. Also tents & sleeping loft. Tents are on platforms & accommodate 1 or 2 people. Loft is above the studio & convenient to bathrooms.

Rates Guest teacher weekend yoga workshop: tuition, room & board $180. 7-day yoga workshop: tuition $350; food + tent or loft lodging $280; food + house or cottage lodging $350. Health enhancement weekend: $255 with tent or loft lodging; $280 with house or cottage lodging. Health enhancement week: $630 with tent or loft lodging; $700 with house or cottage lodging. (All 1993 rates.)

Meals 3 daily, mostly vegetarian meals. Special diets accommodated.

Yasodhara Ashram   Kootenay Bay, British Columbia

Sixty miles north of the B.C./Idaho border, Yasodhara Ashram is a 140 acre yoga retreat center and spiritual community on the shores of Kootenay Lake in the Canadian Rockies. The Ashram is distinguished by its longevity (30+ years at this spot), a Temple of Divine Light honoring the Light in all religions, and an organic farm that produces much of the Ashram's food.

Most Ashram programs range from a weekend to a week, covering topics such as kundalini yoga, spiritual aspects of hatha yoga, mantra yoga, dream interpretation, and other methods of self-investigation. "Ten Days of Yoga" is an introduction to the Ashram's major disciplines. The 3-month "Yoga Development Course" is an opportunity for life transformation and a prerequisite for teacher training courses. Those who have taken "Ten Days of Yoga" or "Yoga Development Course" are eligible for work-exchange programs. In the summer, there are also music festivals and celebrations.

All programs are based on the teachings of Swami Sivananda Radha, one of the first western women to be initiated into the Swami order. In addition to founding and presiding over the Ashram, Swami Radha is founder of the Association for the Development of Human Potential. Emphasizing self-reliance and personal effort as the path to real knowledge, Swami Radha's teachings are noted for their practical applicability to daily life.

Address   Box 9, Kootenay Bay, B.C. V0B 1X0, CANADA

Phone   604/227-9224.

Season   Year-round except September.

Programs   Workshops & courses ranging from a weekend to 3 months on many kinds of yoga, teaching certification programs, and the chance to live as a temporary resident in a spiritual community.

Lodging   Shared accommodation (usually with 1 other person) in spacious, comfortably furnished guest lodge with laundry facilities.

Rates   Programs: weekend $184, 3 to 10-day $274-784, 3-month $5,900. Non-program guest $50/day, $280/week. Part-time working guest $34/day, $188/week. Full-time work $190/day, $109/week. No fee for work-exchange (1 week minimum) during busy seasons. Guests may stay overnight at no cost on last day of program.

Meals   3 daily vegetarian meals with fish, poultry & meat dishes served several times each week. Silence observed at most meals.

Services   Private counseling. Summer children's program.

Four Worlds Summer Institute   Lethbridge, Alberta

Four Worlds Summer Institute is an experiential conference drawing on the cultural and spiritual traditions of Canadian Aboriginal societies. The annual host site is the University of Lethbridge in southern Alberta, roughly 60 miles north of the Montana border. The 1993 conference theme was "Healing Ourselves and Mother Earth."

1993 workshops included the following topics: using symbols such as the Medicine Wheel for individual and community healing; using spiritual disciplines from the Four Directions to deepen relationship with our Higher Power; understanding the healing role of vision, prophecies, sacred music, movement and ceremony; understanding and integrating holistic healing principles and processes.

Each year the conference includes daily sweat lodge ceremonies. The 1993 conference ended with an Elders' guided journey to an ancient Medicine Wheel, a tour of the Head-Smashed-In Buffalo Jump Interpretive Centre, a Pow-wow, and a closing farewell circle ceremony.

Address   Conference Services, University of Lethbridge, 4401 University Drive, Lethbridge, AB T1K 3M4, CANADA

Phone   403/329-2244.   Fax 403/329-5166.

Season   One week in July.

Programs Annual experiential conference employing Native American medicine wisdom for self healing.

Lodging   Tipis in Tipi Village near the University, shared & private room dormitory residences, 2 & 4-bedroom University apartment suites.

Rates   Per person rates: tipi $72 for the week; dorm — shared $20/night, private $28/night; apartment — $34/night.

Meals   Cafeteria style meals with large menu changing each day. Two plans for 5 days of meals — breakfast & lunch plan $62; breakfast, lunch & dinner plan $107.

Macrobiotics Canada Summer Conference   Almonte, Ontario

Each summer since 1980, Wayne Diotte and his staff have hosted a 6-day macrobiotics conference at Wayne's home/center in the village of Almonte — a farm country hamlet 30 miles southwest of Ottawa and a 5 minute walk from Canada's Mississippi River, usually warm enough for swimming by early June.

Conference activities include daily morning yoga, do-in and meditation; macrobiotic cooking classes; lectures by Wayne; three Kushi videos on health and healing; a riverside picnic; a party with dancing and guest-provided entertainment; and a farewell brunch.

Address R.R. 3, Almonte, Ontario K0A 1A0, CANADA

Phone 613/256-2665 or 613/256-4985.

Season Usually first week of July.

Programs Annual 6-day macrobiotic conference. Weekends focusing on macrobiotics, shiatsu and meditation can be scheduled on demand.

Lodging Capacity for 30-40 overnight guests in shared rooms at a nearby conference center. Single rooms at nearby bed & breakfast inn.

Rates Tuition, room & board: conference center $695, nearby B&B $790.

Meals 3 delicious daily macrobiotic meals. Over 100 dishes served. Vegetables from Wayne's organic garden.

Rates Wayne's macrobiotic consultations, private yoga sessions, massage, ginger compress, facials.

Sivananda Ashram Yoga Camp   Val Morin, Quebec

A one hour drive north of Montreal, Sivananda Ashram Yoga Camp is located on 250 acres of lawns and forest in the heart of the Laurentian Mountains. The environment is one of crisp mountain air, panoramic mountain vistas, waterfalls, forest trails, and tranquil alpine lakes. Summer guests can enjoy hiking, volleyball, and swimming in the lake or large outdoor pool. Winter guests can enjoy ice skating, cross country skiing on groomed trails, and a wood burning Russian style sauna.

A typical day begins at 6 with satsang — silent meditation followed by mantra chanting, an inspirational talk or reading, and closing prayers. Next comes a session of hatha yoga postures and breathing techniques. After a 10 AM brunch, guests are on their own until the day's second yoga class at 4. After dinner, there is meditation followed by a lecture or concert. Some summer evenings feature celebrations with bonfires, classical Indian musicians and dancers.

Summer weeks are organized by themes such as "Yoga and Communion with Nature," "Relaxation and Stress management," "Fasting and Vegetarianism." There are also theme weekends such as "Yoga & Ski" in mid-January or "Meditation and Conquest of Mind" on Easter. Christmas and New Year's weeks are periods of intensive yoga practice and spiritual celebration.

Sivananda Ashram Yoga Camp is headquarters of Sivananda Yoga Vedanta Centers International and home of the organization's founder and director, the venerable Swami Vishnu Devananda. All classes are taught by the large and well trained resident staff.

Address 8th Avenue, Val Morin, Quebec J0T 2R0, CANADA

Phone 819/322-3226.   Fax 819/322-5876.

Season Year-round.

Programs   Hatha yoga camp requiring attendance at all daily classes and meditations. Theme weekends offer special lectures. Annual, 4-week July programs are the "Teachers' Training Course" (open to all) and "Yoga Kids Camp" for children aged 7 to 13.

Lodging   2-story wood lodges with private, double and dormitory rooms. Private bath in some rooms. Towels & linens provided. Tent space on the grounds.

Rates   Nightly rates: single $58, double $48, dorm $40, tent site $34. Children under 12 pay 1/2 the daily rate. Work/study discounts available to sincere yoga students. "Teachers' Training Course" $1,200 US for campers and $1,800 US for dorm accommodations.

Meals   2 buffet style, vegetarian meals each day.

Akala Point   Tantallon, Nova Scotia

Akala Point is an environmentally conscious, hostel style retreat in Indian Harbor, NS — a 45 minute drive southwest of Halifax. The main house looks out over St. Margaret's Bay and a small rocky island. Cozy in the winter, the house's Big Room has a large brick fireplace and a cherrywood floor — used for workshops, group meditations, movement classes and music from the piano or stereo system. On the property is a sandy beach and rugged shoreline, a source of seaweed for vegetable garden compost.

Roughly twice a month throughout the year, Akala Point hosts Earth-based and "Healing Journey" theme weekends facilitated by local artists, scientists and healers. Typical themes are "Flowers that Heal," "Secrets of Organic Gardening," "Feminine Spirituality," "Creative Pause." These experiences may include guided relaxation, movement and breathing, dream work, journal writing, art, music and play. In the hostel spirit, guests are also asked to contribute an hour each day to common chores.

Address   Box 1627, R.R. #1, Tantallon, Nova Scotia B0J 3J0, CANADA

Phone   902/823-2160. No visits without prior arrangement.

Season   Year-round.

Programs   Healing Journey theme weekends.

Lodging   Cottage sleeps 20 in 8 guest bedrooms, most with 2-4 beds, plus 12 more in an upstairs dorm. Main house has a wheelchair-suitable guest room with private bath for a single or couple.

Rates   Weekends: Friday eve to Sunday noon $117, Saturday morn to Sunday noon $85, 7 nights $347. (All rates include taxes.) Private room available at additional cost. Rent or BYO towels & bedding.

Meals   3 daily vegetarian meals, with food from own organic garden.

Services   Counselling is usually available.

BRITISH ISLES

Amaravati   Hemel Hempstead, Hertfordshire, England

Amaravati Buddhist Monastery is a community of Theravadan Buddhist monks, nuns, novices and lay residents under the guidance of Venerable Ajahn Sumedho, a Westerner who lived as a monk for 10 years in Thailand forest monasteries. In the Buddhist tradition, the Monastery is funded entirely by donations. Guests may come and stay for several days (generally a one week maximum for U.K. residents) if they abide by monastery rules and routines, joining in the community's life of meditation and work.

Located in the rural Hertfordshire countryside 35 miles northwest of London, Amaravati conducts guided meditation retreats in weekend, 9-day, 13-day and 23-day formats. Every weekend retreat plus an occasional 9 or 13-day retreat is designed for beginner meditators. After a wake-up bell at 5 AM (6 AM on weekend retreats), there are 6 to 9 hours of meditation and related instruction during the day and evening. Silence is observed, and retreatants are asked to refrain from phone calls and correspondence.

Address   Great Gaddesden, Hemel Hempstead, Hertfordshire HP1 3BZ, ENGLAND

Phone   0442-842455 or 843239. No visits without advance arrangements.

Season   March through December.

Programs Weekend, 9-day, 13-day & 23-day meditation retreats. Community visits of up to several days are also possible.

Lodging   Dormitory accommodations for up to 50 guests. A few single & double rooms for people with special needs. BYO sleeping bag.

Rates   Retreatants are charged only for food — usually about #3 per day. At the end of a retreat, retreatants may contribute voluntarily & anonymously toward retreat operating costs (about #4 per day).

Meals   Daily vegetarian breakfast, noon dinner & 5 o'clock tea. No solid foods may be taken after noon.

Amrit Trust   Cornwall, England

Set in picturesque Cornwall a few minutes from the sea, Amrit Trust is a holistic yoga ashram retreat sharing the same spiritually oriented lifestyle as the Kripalu Center in western Massachusetts (USA). The Trust supports retreats structured (or unstructured) to support individual needs.

The day begins with optional, early morning chanting and meditation followed by yoga at 7 AM and breakfast at 8. Unstructured retreats allow plenty of free time for reading, journal writing, holistic lifestyle videos, or a daily walk — in the countryside or along the coastal footpath. Structured retreat topics include health and wellness, yogic spiritual practice, raw food or fruit fasting, rest and renewal, and holistic yoga.

Address 24 Tregew Road, Flushing, Falmouth, Cornwall TR11 5TF, ENGLAND

Phone 0326-377529. No visits without prior arrangement.

Season Year-round.

Programs Unstructured & structured retreats with optional yoga classes and regular meditation periods.

Lodging Simply furnished single, double (2 in 1 bed), 2 and 3-bed guest rooms. Rooms ready after 12 noon. Arrive before 8 PM.

Rates All inclusive retreat rates: 1 night #35, weekend (Fri. eve to Mon. morn) #100, 5-day #165, full week #230. B&B rates: 1 night #15, optional supper #8, optional morning yoga class #3.

Meals 3 daily vegetarian (vegan) meals. Organic produce are used whenever possible. Lunch & dinner are taken in silence. Packed lunches can be provided for beach or countryside outings.

Services Counseling & yoga therapy sessions. Truro train station pick-up/drop-off service.

The Barn   Totnes, Devon, England

The Barn is a converted old stone barn situated on hilly farmland overlooking the river Dart two miles downstream from Totnes. It was founded by the Sharpham Trust as "a working retreat center; a place where people might come, both to retreat temporarily from the world at large" and "to work practically on the land" under "the discipline of community life."

The daily schedule involves 4 to 5 hours of work. Ongoing projects include conservation, poultry and bee-keeping, organic gardening, cooking and preserving. Guest residents may also attend open evening and weekend events at nearby Schumacher College, Dartington Hall, and the Sharpham North community, a short walk across the fields. Sharpham North programs focus on Buddhism, meditation, yoga, psychology, ecology and the arts.

The Barn is a non-denominational community based on the Buddhist tradition. Each day includes three 45 minute periods of silent group meditation, and silence is observed 2 mornings of each week. There is a weekly discussion and a weekly morning of yoga. In addition, residents meet regularly with meditation teachers from the nearby Gaia House meditation center.

Address Lower Sharpham Barton, Ashprington, Totnes, Devon TQ9 7DX, UK

Phone   0803-732661.

Season   Year-round.

Programs A work retreat community allowing participation in farming and meditation activities for stays of 1 week to 6 months.

Lodging   Accommodations for 7 visiting residents in 7 private rooms.

Rates   Stays of 1 to 14 days — #8 per day. Stays of 2 to 8 weeks — #7 per day. Stays over 2 months — #6 per day.

Meals   2 communal vegetarian meals each day.

Beacon Centre   Exeter, Devon, England

A large farmhouse in the Devon Hills 3 miles from Exeter, the Beacon Centre offers residential programs an average of at least once a month throughout the year. Centre host Wendy Webber conducts focusing/listening workshops. Exeter neighbor Martyn Rudyn hosts a 5-day August "Open Spirit Dance Holiday." Offerings by other southwest England teachers are on subjects such as living foods, psychosynthesis and astrology. Guests may use the sauna and meditation sanctuary. The grounds harbor friendly animals.

Address   Cutteridge Farm, near Whitestone, Exeter, Devon EX4 2HE, ENGLAND

Phone   0392-81203. No visits without prior arrangement.

Season   Year-round.

Programs 2 to 5-day residential workshops, plus 1 & 2-day non-residential workshops, on personal and planetary transformation & healing.

Lodging   Capacity for 25 in shared rooms. Camping permitted.

Rates   Residential programs: weekend #50-70, 3-day #130-150, 5-day #220. For participants in non-residential workshops, #10 per night (BYO food & linen). Camping #2.50 per night.

Meals   Meals provided for residential programs.

Services Massage, aromatherapy, dramatherapy, counseling, hypnotherapy, focusing, crystal therapy, shamanic dance.

CAER   Penzance, Cornwall, England

CAER (Celtic for "fort") is housed in an old Cornish manor on seven acres of woods and gardens that was once the site of an Iron Age fort. On the grounds is a 2000 year old underground granite passage containing a carving of a god of healing. The surrounding area is one of lush valleys, wild moors, coastal fishing villages, and unspoiled sandy beaches.

CAER each month offers an average of four or five residential workshops facilitated by teachers, artists and healers from throughout the UK. Typical offerings — an "Enlightenment Intensive" combining meditation and communication between partners; a workshop employing the 5 rhythm work of "dancing shaman" Gabrielle Roth; and "Journeying the Sacred Patterns" to establish links with the spirit guardians of sacred places. CAER also hosts professional training workshops on counseling and group facilitation.

Address Rosemerryn, Lamorna, Penzance, Cornwall TR19 6BN, ENGLAND

Phone 0736-810530 (admin.) or 810508 (guests).

Season Year-round.

Programs 2 to 5-day workshops in 8 subject areas: personal development, gestalt therapy, spiritual approaches, expressive/creative, Native American & Celtic shamanism, humanistic psychology & shamanism, body approaches, and professional development.

Lodging Spacious and comfortable accommodations with ample bathrooms and showers, a log fire and central heating.

Rates Most workshops have a 3 tier rate structure. Weekend rates: waged #120-180, low-waged #96-145, unwaged #60-112. 4-day rates: waged #200-260, low-waged #160-192, unwaged #120-129 pounds. Free bed & breakfast on night before first workshops day.

Meals 3 daily, mostly vegetarian meals with some meat dishes for those who want them. Also can cater to most special diets.

Claridge House   Lingfield, Surrey, England

Claridge House is a Quaker Centre and healing ministry located in a small village a short drive or train ride from London. The 100-year old red brick dwelling is set on two acres of quiet, shaded lawns and gardens. The house contains comfortable lounges, a Quiet Room for meditation, a well stocked library, a music center, a piano, and no TV.

Each month Claridge House hosts several residential programs, mostly weekends but with a few 5-day holiday period offerings. Recent weekend topics have included "Exploring Past Lives;" "Use of Music and Sound in Healing;" "Healing Through the Medicine Wheel;" "Elementals, Devas & Angels." Most workshops are led by house wardins Tom and Paulin Pools, both registered healers.

The Pools also offer counseling, healing massage, and healing through laying on of hands — all free to overnight guests. Anyone may come and stay as long as s/he likes, with or without program participation.

Address   Dormansland, Lingfield, Surrey RH7 6QH, ENGLAND

Phone   0342-832150 (office) or 832920 (guests).

Season   Year-round.

Programs Weekend spiritual healing workshops.

Lodging   12 bedrooms, each with own wash basin, for single or double occupancy. Two ground floor rooms built for disabled people.

Rates   Typical program rates: weekend — single room #70-85, shared room #65-80; 5-day — single #160-165, shared #150-160. Daily guest rates: single #30, shared #28 (less #5 per week for long stays).

Meals   Daily breakfast, lunch, tea and dinner. All meals vegetarian.

Services   Healing massage, counseling, and healing by laying on of hands offered free of charge (contributions welcome). Also a courtesy train station pick-up/drop-off service on advance notice.

Craigie Lodge   St. Lawrence, Isle of Wight, England

A 3 hour trip from central London, Craigie Lodge is an elegant Victorian house, with art nouveau interior and decor, in a wooded village under the south shore cliffs of the Isle of Wight. Once the home of the celebrated writer Mrs. Pearl Craigie, the lodge is now a vegetarian guest house/ spiritual healing sanctuary under the lively and creative direction of Mrs. Angela Taylor (also an excellent cook).

Workshops by local and visiting teachers include "Mantra & Massage," "Yoga & Meditation," "Living Art," and "Cranio-Sacral Therapy." Services such as aromatherapy, reflexology, hypnotherapy and dowsing can be arranged. Mrs. Taylor also leads "Cathar Connection" trips to the Ariege district of southern France, where guests stay in an ancient farmhouse overlooking the Pyrenees and a large lake suitable for swimming, windsurfing and sailing.

Address   Undercliff Drive, St. Lawrence, Isle of Wight PO38 1XF, ENGLAND

Phone   0983-852184 (also accepts fax).

Season   Year-round.

Programs Weekend & weeklong experiential workshops encouraging harmony with the inner self. Also Cathar Connection excursions.

Lodging   Six rooms — three with showers, five overlooking the English Channel, all with wash basins and tea/coffee making facilities.

Rates   Workshops: weekend #90, 3 to 5-day #100-165. Weekly vegetarian guest house rates: bed & breakfast #115, half board #160, full board #180.

Meals   Up to 3 delicious vegetarian meals each day.

Services   Free access to a local member of Britain's National Federation of Spiritual Healers.

Creativity Holidays   Penzance, Cornwall, England

Creativity Holidays are residential courses taught in a 200-year old former farmhouse in the heart of Newlyn, a Cornish fishing village and artists' colony. The coastline here is one of sandy beaches, rocky coves and cliff walks. There is also the moorland, with prehistoric standing stones and the remains of ancient tin and copper mines. Courses are conducted in a sunny studio-workshop overlooking a secluded garden.

The center's many painting and drawing courses are taught by Mary Oliver, a Cornish artist who focuses on "the joy and sense of healing that can be obtained by looking closely at nature." She and her students also draw inspiration from music, dreamwork, visualization, and the center's books on mythology and sacred symbols. Courses such as the 2-day women's art workshops and 5-day summer sessions are suitable for beginners.

Workshops by visiting teachers cover subjects such as pottery, "Tai Chi for Health," and "Voice — The Magic of Sound" (with breathing techniques, chanting and mantras). Courses range in length from 2 to 6 full days including an additional night, with students arriving for dinner and departing after breakfast. Meals are prepared by master chef Piers Owen.

Address   Tolcarne Farmhouse, Newlyn, Penzance, Cornwall TR18 5QH, UK

Phone   0736-330284.

Season   Late February through early December.

Programs   2 to 6-day creative expression & movement workshops — painting, drawing, pottery, voice, and tai chi.

Lodging   Accommodations for 10 guests in a former farmhouse.

Rates   Weekend workshop #95. 3-day workshop #155. 6-day workshop #275.

Meals   3 meals each day, often with Mediterranean and Eastern-style vegetarian dinners. Locally caught fish optional with meals.

Services   Courtesy transport to & from Penzance railway & bus stations.

Crosthwaite Mill   Cumbria, England

A converted mill by a stream and garden in the rolling Lake District countryside of northwest England, Crosthwaite Mill is a quiet and restful place for residential courses and retreats. Activities are conducted in the mill tower — the carpeted top floor used for yoga and meditation, the second floor suitable for course meetings and concerts, the ground floor serving as a sitting room with a view of the water wheel.

The proprietors are Angela and John Pogson, who leads meditation weekends. Other residential offerings include circle dancing, crystal healing, color healing, Alexander Technique and psychotherapy workshops. The four-day Christmas at Crosthwaite holiday retreat is a time of singing, circle dancing and meditation. During the rest of the year, residential courses led by artists and healers from the Cumbrian region are offered on average at least once each month.

Address   Near Kendal, Cumbria LA8 8BS, ENGLAND

Phone   0539-568314. No visits without prior arrangement.

Season   Year-round.

Programs Residential workshops ranging in length from a weekend to 5 days on the healing arts. Also one day programs on subjects such as "Neuro Linguistic Programming," circle dancing and yoga.

Lodging   Accommodations for up to 24 people in 12 double rooms, 8 with own shower/toilet. Rooms are warm and comfortable with attractive natural wood storage units and individually chosen furnishings.

Rates   Typical course/full board rates: weekend #75; 5-day #195. Non-course nightly rates #25-28 per room.

Meals   3 daily vegetarian meals including 3 course dinner with non-alcoholic wine. Can make packed lunches & cater special diets.

Gaia House   Denbury, Devon, England

Gaia House is a meditation retreat center in the quiet and rolling South Devon countryside. The center hosts an average of about two teacher-led, residential group retreats each month except February and November. These retreats range from 2 to 10 days in length, and most are suitable for beginners. Recent retreat themes were "The Way of Zen," "Women in Meditation," and "Exploring the Way of Devotion."

Retreats begin at 7 PM on the first day and end at noon on weekdays or 3:30 on Sunday. Teachers give guidance on sitting and walking meditation through talks, individual instruction and occasional group meetings. Except for these times, all retreats are conducted in silence. Silent personal work retreats, with meditation periods and twice weekly teacher interviews, may be undertaken by people with previous retreat experience.

The center is directed by Christopher Titmus and Christina Feldman, who teach Buddhist Vipassana meditation. They are assisted by Martine and Stephen Batchelor, who can offer guidance in the Korean Zen or Tibetan Mahayana

Buddhist traditions. Retreats are also led by about 13 other teachers from England, the USA, Burma, Sri Lanka, Switzerland and Majorca.

Address Woodland Road, Denbury, near Newton Abbot, Devon TQ12 6DY, UK

Phone 0803-813188. No visits without prior arrangement.

Season Year-round.

Programs 2 to 10-day teacher-led, group meditation retreats. 20 & 30-day individual meditation intensives. Silent, personal retreats.

Lodging 3 single rooms plus 12 rooms that are generally shared.

Rates 2 to 10-day group retreat #40-140. 20 to 30-day intensive #280-308 pounds, or #140 per 10-day segment. Personal retreat — reduced fee or free when specific skills are needed.

Meals 2 or 3 daily vegetarian meals.

Gaunts House   Wimborne, Dorset, England

Gaunts Estate encompasses 55 dwellings and a church on 2000 acres of rolling Dorset farmland, woods and river moorland. Gaunts House mansion includes 8 buildings with adjacent tennis, squash and volleyball courts plus a lake where swimming and boating are permitted. Under construction is a mini-gym and walled garden. Overseeing House operations is the Glyn Foundation, a charitable trust formed to promote education in spiritual, philosophical and ecological areas.

Each month Gaunts House offers three to five residential courses and workshops, including a simple, 5-day "Gaunts Experience" stay; a 7-day "Executive Stress Program;" and a "Togetherness Week" — an energizing experience with art, dance, games, chanting, ceremony and meditation. The numerous weekend offerings include equinox and solstice celebrations with Native American sweat lodge ceremonies.

Owned by the Glyn family for over 250 years, Gaunts House is directed by Richard Glyn. But most decisions in this small community are reached by consensus. Membership consists of new arrivals and a few people from the estate's traditional rural community. Others may join after completing an "Induction Week" and a training course. The community endeavors to live in accord with "the New Way, a lifestyle of practical holism."

Address Wimborne, Dorset BH21 4JQ, ENGLAND

Phone 0202-841522. Fax 0202-841959.

Season Year-round.

Programs Residential courses and workshops, each 2-7 days long, focusing primarily on spiritual, holistic health and ecological subjects. Most programs facilitated by outside experts and teachers.

Lodging   Gaunts House comfortably sleeps 120 guests in shared rooms. The mansion has 20 shared bath and shower rooms. Other Gaunts Estate houses and cottages raise capacity to 220 guests, but some of this space is occupied by community residents. Also campsites.

Rates   "Executive Stress Program" #835, "Togetherness Week" #165, "Gaunts Experience" #125. Other programs: weekend #95-145, 4 & 5-day #185-195, week #295-415.

Meals   3 daily vegetarian meals.

Services   Free healings by trained practitioners offering a range of therapies. Also free counseling by trained counselors and untrained, caring listeners.

Grimstone Manor   Yelverton, Devon, England

Grimstone Manor is set on 27 acres of countryside at the edge of Dartmoor National Park. Facilities include a 60 foot group room, rooms for relaxing or meditation, heated conservatories, a swimming pool, jacuzzi and sauna. The manor is owned and operated by a small community — open to new members and assisted by in-residence volunteers.

Each year, Grimstone hosts about 40 residential workshops. Popular workshop themes are massage, yoga, natural health, dance and movement, shamanism and psychotherapy. Most offerings are sponsored by other organizations but may be attended by anyone. Grimstone community itself offers about a dozen workshops, generally led by guest artists and healers. All offerings are described in the manor's annual program guide.

Address   Yelverton, Devon PL20 7QY, ENGLAND

Phone   0822-854358.

Season   Year-round.

Programs   3 to 7-day workshops on creative expression, spirituality and holistic health. Also holiday family, work & play weeks.

Lodging   Can accommodate up to 36 in a mix of double and larger rooms, some with ensuite bathrooms.

Rates   Grimstone community workshop & gathering rates: 3-day typically #125-175; proportionately higher for 4 and 5-day worksops.

Meals   3 daily vegetarian meals.

Services   Free children's nursery service.

Mickleton House   Mickleton, Gloucestershire, England

Mickleton House is the central home of a Cotswold community of 50-60 adults and children. Several times each year, the House hosts two-day tai chi workshops, residential women's spirituality weekends, and residential one and three-week courses on spiritual "attunement." Attunements are offered daily at Mickleton House to enhance personal health, vision and stability. Guests may also participate with the community in its regular Wednesday evening and Sunday morning meetings.

Mickleton House is the British regional headquarters for the Emissaries, a non profit society dedicated to bringing "an integrating influence into human affairs" through the efforts of each member to project a "stable, true and loving spirit into his or her environment." There are 11 other Emissary regional centers — in the U.S., Canada, France, Australia and South Africa. The Emissaries' international spokesman is Canada's Michael Exeter, an hereditary member of the British House of Lords.

Address   Mickleton, Gloucestershire GL55 6RY, ENGLAND

Phone   0386-438727. Fax 0386-438118.

Season   Year-round.

Programs   Residential: 1 & 3-week attunement courses; women's spirituality weekends. Friday evening/Saturday tai chi workshops.

Lodging   Overnight guests accommodated both in Mickleton House and in private homes of community members.

Rates   1-week attunement course #425. Women's spirituality weekend #105. Tai chi workshop #20 including meals. Room & board available other times on a donation basis.

Meals   3 daily meals with vegetarian options.

Services   Attunements offered on a donation basis.

Monkton Wyld Court   Charmouth, Dorset, England

Set on 11 acres in a secluded valley at the Dorset/Devon border 3 miles from the sea, Monkton Wyld Court is a large stone-built Victorian rectory and several out-buildings. It is also a 52-year old, residential education center run by a 10-year old resident community of nine adults, eight children and seven volunteers. The rectory contains many guest rooms, two meeting rooms, a large sitting room with grand piano, a well-stocked library, a meditation room, plus facilities for pottery, arts and crafts.

Monkton Wyld's annual schedule is a steady stream of adult workshops punctuated by visitor periods. Workshops are facilitated by carefully selected humanistic educators from far and wide. A sampling of recent topics: "Mask Making & Masquerading," "Journey into Dreamtime," "Dancing with the Earth," and "Healing in Transforming Perception." Visitor periods include visitor weeks, family weeks, play weeks and work camps where visitors work and play alongside community members.

A day in the life of Monkton Wyld begins with a morning attunement, where community members sit on cushions and quietly hold hands in a circle. As the talking stick is passed around, each shares how s/he is feeling and outlines plans for the day. The meeting closes with people going off to their work — gardening, kitchen work and community services. There are weekly "Circle and Modern Dance" evenings plus occasional evening musical events and talks. Visitors may participate in these evening activities.

Address   Charmouth, near Bridport, Dorset DT6 6DQ, ENGLAND

Phone   0297-60342.

Season   Year-round.

Programs Experiential workshops of 2 to 7-days in length on communications and life-skills, creative arts, health and well-being. Also community visiting opportunities.

Lodging   Capacity for 34 overnight guests, usually in shared rooms though sometimes singles are available. BYO sheets or sleeping bag.

Rates   Programs: 7-day #265, 4 & 5-day #150-175, 2 & 3-day #85-120. Visitor periods: work camp #10; visitor week #70; family week — adult #100, child 5-15 yrs. #60, child 2-4 yrs. #30; play week — adult #230, child 5-15 yrs. #170, child 2-4 yrs. #110.

Meals   3 daily vegetarian meals, often with produce from the garden. Visitors help themselves to breakfast. Lunch and supper are provided, with vegan and some other special diets accommodated.

Services   Massage.

Oak Dragon Camps   Somerset, England

The Oak Dragon Project generally hosts four camps each summer, with activities centered in colorful marquees and geodesic domes. Each camp includes a potpourri of workshops, group activities and social campfire evenings. Dogs are not welcome, but children are. There are separate activity areas for kids aged 17 to 12, kids aged 11 to 5, and kids under 5.

Each camp has a theme. In 1993, the four themes were "Changing Patterns & Healing the Self," "Sacred Space for Healing," "Astrology & Divination," "Tribal Union, Drumming, Chanting, Dance." At all camps, the sense of community is enhanced by campers contributing time to kitchen, site management and children's areas.

Address   Oak Dragon Project, P.O. Box 5, Castle Cary, Somerset BA7 7YQ, ENGLAND

Phone   0816-939485 or 0269-870959.

Season   July and August.

Programs   Outdoor holistic health educational camps, each 9 to 14 days.

Lodging   Campsites with hot showers, earth toilets, water & firewood provided. BYO tent & sleeping bag. Rough weather shelter & sleeping space nearby.

Rates   9-day camp: adult #90, 5-16 yr. child #30, sub 5 yr. child #10. 14-day camp: adult #120, 5-16 yr. child #40, sub 5 yr. child #10 pounds. 1 child free for single parents.

Meals   A vegetarian cafe offer 2 daily meals. BYO crockery, cutlery & cooking gear for campfire meals.

Services   Courtesy First Aid & child care. Also alternative therapies.

Oakwood Retreats   Totnes, Devon, England

When Schumacher College (separate entry) is not in session, 5-day Oakwood Retreats are often held at The Old Postern, Dartington Hall — a secluded 14th century manor house surrounded by meadows and woodland in south Devon.

Each retreat day includes periods of guided meditation, small group sharings, a solitary walk, reflective writing, and mindful work (e.g. making lunch or tending the garden). The entire group meets once each day, sometimes for structured interaction on a particular theme. Retreatants may also meet individually with retreat leaders. Silence is observed most of the day, though evenings may include a talk or video presentation.

All retreats are led by a team of three. Retreat director Dr. Guy Claxton is a professor and author of books such as "Wholly Human." His associates are former Buddhist monk and nun Stephen and Martine Batchelor. Stephen is the author of books such as "Faith to Doubt." Martine is a meditation teacher and trained counsellor.

Address   The Old Postern, Dartington, Totnes, Devon TQ9 6EA, ENGLAND

Phone   0803-866983. Fax 0803-866899.

Season   From time to time throughout the year.

Programs   5-day structured, reflective retreats particularly well suited for people at life turning points.

Lodging   Single or twin study-bedrooms.

Rates   3 tier schedule: sponsored #345, employed & paying for oneself #245, low income or unemployed #145.

Meals   3 daily, mostly vegetarian meals: a silent, self-served breakfast; a light vegetarian lunch; a served, sociable dinner.

Open Spirit   Devon, England

Open Spirit each year conducts at least six five-day programs — two in the spring and four in the summer. The spring "Dance Holidays" are usually held at the Foxhole Conference Centre in Dartington. The summer "Dance Camps" are at Gidleigh Hall near Chagford on Dartmoor.

"Dance Holidays" include morning, afternoon and evening classes in Alexander Technique, creative dance, contact improvisation, movement awareness, massage, voice, drumming, and ways of making dance and ritual a celebratory expression of participants' lives. Each "Summer Camp" has a theme. In 1993, there were two "Arts Camps," a "Dance & Drumming Camp," and a "Healing Dance Camp."

Open Spirit is directed by Martyn Rudin, a teacher of dance and movement classes for over 20 years. He is assisted by three other teachers. Martyn and/or one or two other teachers facilitate each program.

Address   Rackclose Lane, New Bridge Street, Exeter EX4 3AH, ENGLAND

Phone   0392-422134 or 0392-496580.

Season   April through August.

Programs   5-day programs focusing on spirit-expressive dance, movement & music making.

Lodging   "Dance Holidays" — single room accommodations. "Dance Camps" — campsites (BYO tent). Bed & breakfast lodging can be arranged.

Rates   "Dance Holiday" #220. "Dance Camps": "Arts Camp" #80-120; other camps #110-150. Optional summer camp bed & breakfast lodging #10-15 per night.

Meals   "Dance Holidays" — full in-house catering at Foxhole Centre. "Dance Camps" — full in-house catering at Gidleigh Hall.

Schumacher College   Totnes, Devon, England

The campus of Schumacher College is the house and grounds of the Old Postern, previously the parsonage of the 800 acre Dartington Hall Estate. The grounds include a small vegetable garden, woodland and a large croquet lawn. The college is a short walk from the medieval courtyard of Dartington Hall and a few miles from the sea.

The college's primary purpose is to host each year a dozen or so 10 to 31-day courses in ecological and spiritual studies. The college's first course (January 1991) was led by James Lovelock, father of the Gaia hypothesis. 1993/1994 offerings addressed topics such as "Ecology of the Mind," "Ecology and Aesthetics," "Deep Ecology and Eco-Philosophy," "Creation Spirituality and the Environmental Revolution."

Each course is taught by one or two eminent Scholars-in-Residence assisted by visiting teachers. Courses regularly feature craft, drama and movement workshops. And all courses incorporate participants into a community where everyone helps out with practical daily activities such as cleaning, cooking and gardening. There are daily periods of communal meditation and reflection plus opportunities for expressive and creative activities.

Attracted by the college's commitment "to explore the foundations of a more balanced and harmonious world-view," course participants have come from over 45 countries and have ranged in age from 17 to over 80. Long term residence is a possibility for those who have completed a course.

Address The Old Postern, Dartington, Totnes, Devon TQ9 6EA, ENGLAND

Phone 0803-865934. Fax 0808-866899.

Season Year-round.

Programs 10 to 31-day residential courses on eco-spirituality, eco-technology and eco-economics.

Lodging Comfortable single rooms, each with a wash basin. Room sharing can be arranged on request.

Rates 11-day course #520. 12-day course #650. 17-day course #780. 22 to 24-day courses #950-1,000. 30 & 31-day courses #1,080-1,200. Courses over 3 weeks long often divisible into 2 parts that can be taken separately. Scholarships often available.

Meals 3 varied vegetarian meals each day.

Self-Realization Healing Centre   Yeovil, Somerset, England

Self-Realization Healing Centre is a 17th century estate a short walk from the shops of Queen Camel village. The estate's quiet grounds include a therapy pool. The Centre is operated as a charitable trust by a resident spiritual family of eight adults including Mata Yogananda, who provides instruction and guidance in meditation. Residents and guests meditate together at each end of the day and sit in silent communion before lunch.

Each month, the Centre offers weekend workshops that can be attended on a residential or non-residential basis. Typical weekend workshop topics are "Intuitive Living & Being," "Yoga and Relaxation," "Meditation Refresher," and "Animal Healing." There are three-day residential Christmas and Easter celebrations. There are also occasional five-day residential workshops on "Meditation," "Spiritual Advancement," and "Creative Self-Development."

The Centre's major offerings are multi-week courses in "Healing" (4 weeks over 18 months) and "Progressive Counseling" (7 weeks over 2 years). These are residential programs requiring that each week be attended in proper sequence. Throughout the year, the Centre also offers morning and evening classes on health, meditation, hatha yoga, and spiritual knowledge.

Address   Laurel Lane, Queen Camel, near Yeovil, Somerset BA22 7NU, ENGLAND

Phone   0935-850266. Fax 0935-850234. Call before visiting.

Season   Year-round.

Programs   Weekend and 5-day workshops on meditation (the most important part of the Centre's work), yoga, relaxation, spiritual science, healing and self-development. Also 3-day holiday retreats.

Lodging   Can accommodate up to 17 overnight guests in single & double rooms, some with private baths.

Rates   Weekend & 3-day courses & retreats — #67-77 (including room & board). 5-day residential courses #230-250. Non-course visitor room & board — night #25-27, week #174-187.

Meals   3 daily vegetarian meals, special diets accommodated.

Services   Intuitive counseling and healings — for both people and animals.

Chrysalis   County Wicklow, Ireland

Chrysalis is a personal growth/spiritual retreat center occupying an 18th century house on three secluded acres in the picturesque Glen of Imaal 32 miles from Dublin.

The center each month offers several residential workshops led by teachers and healers from the British Isles and America. Recent weekend offerings included "Yoga," "Meditation," "Art & Dreamwork," and "Celebrate the Art in You." There are also occasional four to eight-day programs such as "Spiritual Quest & Human Growth" and "Expand Horizons Through Psychodrama."

At least once each month, Chrysalis also offers one-day workshops on topics such as "Vegetarian Cooking," "Food & Healing," and "Dealing Creatively with Stress." Guests attending these workshops are welcome to stay over night, dinner included, at reasonable bed & breakfast rates.

Address   Donoughmore, Donard, County Wicklow, IRELAND

Phone   045-54713. No visits without prior arrangement.

Season   Year-round.

Programs   1-day (Tuesday or Wednesday) and weekend workshops & retreats. Occasional 4, 5 & 8-day retreats.

Lodging   Accommodates 18 guests in 3 single rooms & 3 dorms. BYO towel.

Rates   1-day workshops #25-30, weekend workshops & retreats #75-100, 4 to 8-day workshops & retreats #125-255.

Meals   Overnight program guests receive 3 daily vegetarian meals, often with organically grown produce from local gardens.

Lios Dana Holistic Health Centre   County Kerry, Ireland

Lios Dana is a holistic health center located in southwest Ireland on the Dingle Peninsula seacoast, about 2 hours from Cork or Limerick. The center overlooks Inch Strand, 3 miles of sandy beaches with Macgillycuddy's Reeks (Ireland's highest mountains) rising to the southeast across the bay. Lios Dana's hosts are Michael Travers and Anne Hyland. Michael is an artist who gives art sessions to help free creative expression. Anne is a shiatsu massage practitioner and a Kushi-trained macrobiotic cook.

During most months, Centre staff and visiting teachers conduct several 2 to 6-day workshops and "Natural Living Programs." Recent workshop titles included "Yoga Holiday Week," "The Healing Voice," "Moving Experience," and "Macrobiotic Cooking." "Natural Living Programs" include instruction in shiatsu, macrobiotics, aikido, meditation and yoga. The Centre also runs a 2-year shiatsu apprenticeship program and can be used for individual/couple holiday stays or private group retreats.

Address   Inch-Annascaul, County Kerry, IRELAND

Phone   066-58189. No visits without prior arrangement.

Season   February through mid-July, September through December.

Programs   Weekend, 3-day and 6-day holistic health workshops.

Lodging   Can accommodate up to 20 guests in simply furnished bedrooms.

Rates   Full board & workshops: weekend & 3-day #96, 6-day #185.

Meals   3 daily meals. Macrobiotic, vegetarian, whole food & seafood dishes. Home made bread.

Services   Shiatsu massage.

Meitheal   Inch Island, County Donegal, Ireland

Meitheal is the Celtic word for "cooperative working effort." It is also a community of 11 adults and 5 children on the 5 acre site of an old British navy fort on an island a few miles west of Derry. Like Scotland's Findhorn community, Meitheal respects inner guidance through meditation, attunements and consensual decision making. Community members are self supporting, though they sometimes pay for a long term guest with healing, gardening or building skills through which the community can grow and learn.

Meitheal's weekend workshops celebrate and explore song, dance, bodywork, herbal and flower essence remedies, gardening and crafts. A new tradition is seasonal celebrations conducted around standing stones sculpted by visiting Slovenian artists Marko and Martina Pogacnik. The stones have been placed on energy lines and power points to serve as what Marko calls "lithopuncture" — acupuncture on the body of the Earth. Meitheal camps and programs are drawing growing crowds, so the community is pleased by English medium Kathy Hughes' prediction that its expansion plans are timely.

Address   Inch Fort, Inch Island, County Donegal, IRELAND

Phone   077-60323.

Season   Year-round.

Programs   Weekend workshops & seasonal celebrations, holiday family camps, short & long term guest stays.

Lodging   Campsites, local B&B accommodations, a few rooms for guest stays.

Rates   Weekend workshops & celebrations (lunch but no lodging included): #30-45. Family camp weekends (BYO food & tent): people over 12 years old #7, 2-12 years old #5, under 2 years old free. Short term guest #50-100 per week.

Meals   Short & long term guests receive 3 daily vegetarian meals. Much of the food is from the community's own organic gardens.

Services   Massage, shiatsu, reflexology, Reiki, herbal & Bach flower remedies, chakra balancing, and crystal healing.

Centre of Light   Struy, Inverness-shire, Scotland

The Centre of Light is a healing center 10 miles west of Inverness in the Scottish Highlands. The property contains an organic garden, cottage, wooden chalets and healing/meditation room overlooking the River Glass from an area of heather, lakes and forest. The Centre's three person staff includes Centre founder (1986) Linda Christie — a healer trained in Reichian therapy, rebirthing, reiki, hypnotherapy and kinesiology.

The Centre's major scheduled offerings are weeklong group workshop retreats, each including one-on-one counseling, interactive group work, and ample time for individual processing/reflection. The Centre also conducts individual retreat and healing weeks, with no more than three individual retreatants staying at the Centre at any one time. Individual retreats focus on clearing the light body and connections with nature.

Address   Tignabruaich, Struy, by Beauly, Inverness-shire IV4 7JU, SCOTLAND

Phone   046-376254. No visits without prior arrangement.

Season   Year-round.

Programs   Weeklong group workshops teaching self healing techniques. 1993 workshop themes: "The Mirror Within" & " Alignment To The Light."

Lodging   Capacity for 6 guests in twin-bedded wooden chalets. Towels & linens provided.

Rates   Group workshop #425 per person.

Meals   3 vegetarian meals, organic whenever possible.

Findhorn Foundation   Forres, Grampian, Scotland

The Findhorn Foundation is an international spiritual community 25 miles east of Inverness on the North Sea coast of Scotland. The Foundation's primary educational activities are residential conferences, special events and workshops on personal growth, healing and creative expression. Offerings include Findhorn's own "Game of Transformation" and weeklong retreats on Scotland's holy island of Iona. All programs are "focalised" by well-trained community members and visiting staff.

Findhorn's founders, Dorothy Maclean, Eileen and Peter Caddy, were directed by Eileen's inner guidance to settle in 1962 in a trailer park near a windswept beach. The Findhorn Foundation now has 140+ resident members, not including 260-280 people who remain financially independent while living nearby as members of the greater Findhorn spiritual community.

Findhorn's method of government reflects the belief "that our identity is Divinity, our purpose is service, and our power is co-creation through love." Most Findhorn decisions are reached by a process of 1) group discussion, 2) a short meditation, with each person silently inquiring what is best for the group as a whole, and 3) each person sharing what s/he experienced in meditation. A clear consensus generally emerges.

Findhorn's attitude of love and respect extends to its relationship with the natural world. The community's focus on co-creation with nature was born out of messages from the plant world, received in Dorothy's Maclean's meditations, giving practical advice on garden care. The resulting garden, with giant cabbages and roses blooming in the snow, made Findhorn famous throughout the world.

In recent years, Findhorn's creativity has flowered in organizational endeavors. Believing that trees are valuable for the balance they provide to the Earth's ecosystem and to human emotions, Findhorn is directing a project to restore the Caledonian Forest. Another project is construction of a Findhorn "eco-village" to replace the trailer caravans. In 1992/93, Findhorn also led a 7-week, spiritually oriented tour of India.

Address   Cluny Hill College, Forres IV36 ORD, SCOTLAND

Phone   0309-672288 or 0309-673655 (reservations).

Season   Year-round.

Programs Weekend, one and two-week workshops of three general types: personal and spiritual growth; creative expression; health and healing. Also a 1 to 3-day short-term guest program, 1 week departmental guest program, and 4 to 12-week living-in-community guest program. Guest programs involve participation in the community's daily work, meditations and other activities.

Lodging   Ample accommodations, mostly shared, at the Findhorn Bay Caravan Park and Findhorn-owned Cluny Hill College in nearby Forres. Special accommodations for non-ambulant guests in wheelchairs.

Rates   Weekend workshop #60-140. 1-week workshop #225-400. 2-week workshop #525-625. Short-term guest #12 per day (includes lunch & dinner, lodging at local B&Bs). Departmental guest week #160-250. Living-in-community guest: 1st month #490-590, 2nd #460-560 pounds, 3rd #420-520.

Meals   3 daily vegetarian meals.

Lendrick Lodge   Callander, Perthshire, Scotland

Lendrick Lodge is situated in the Trossachs, about 20 miles from Sterling in central Scotland. The Lodge is associated with LIFE Foundation School of Therapeutics and directed by yoga teacher Sadie Mulvaney. Lodge facilities include a yoga room and a meditation sanctuary, where daily morning and evening group meditations are open to guests.

Lendrick's major residential programs are its two summer, 7-day yoga weeks. 1993's guest yoga week instructors came from Ireland and the USA. One week featured guest Reiki teachers from the Findhorn Community. The other featured guest shiatsu and movement therapists. Both weeks explore the philosophy as well as the postures and breathing techniques of yoga. Each year there is also at least one weekend yoga workshop.

Address   Brig o'Turk, Callander, Perthshire, SCOTLAND

Phone   087-76263.

Season   February through December.

Programs Yoga weekend workshops & weeklong vacations.

Lodging One single & 7 double rooms, all with shared bathrooms.

Rates Weekend #65-70, week #180.

Meals 3 daily vegetarian meals.

Newbold House　　　　　Forres, Grampian, Scotland

Newbold House is an elegant, 100-year old mansion set on 7 acres of woodlands in the outskirts of Forres, a 15 minute walk from the Findhorn Foundation's Cluny Hill College. The estate's ancient trees and walled garden create a contemplative atmosphere for a small Scottish/German/ English community that operates its own workshops while remaining part of the neighboring Findhorn community.

Meditation is a popular subject for Newbold workshops. Other subjects include tai chi, past life regression, holotropic breathwork, inner child and relationship healings. Workshops are facilitated by Newbold community members, members of the larger Findhorn community, and by visiting teachers on occasion. In 1993, a Newbold resident led a one-week hiking retreat on the wild island of Mull off the west coast of Scotland.

Participation in community life is an important part of all workshops, and an "Open Community" week is offered at least once a month — often at times of seasonal celebrations. Newbold also welcomes community guests and short-term members with a minimum 3-month commitment. Community members do not have fixed work schedules and work unpaid — "affirming rather that in alignment to the laws of spirit and nature our needs will always be met."

Address St. Leonard's Road, Forres IV36 ORE, SCOTLAND

Phone 0309-672659.

Season Year-round.

Programs One & 2-week workshops, "Open Community" weeks, community guest arrangements, and short-term (3-month) community memberships.

Lodging Capacity for 35 members and guests, generally in shared accommodations.

Rates Workshop contributions are worked out at the end of a stay in a meeting with a staff member.

Meals 3 daily vegetarian meals.

Samye Ling Tibetan Centre   Langholm, Dumfriesshire, Scotland

Located in the rolling hill country of southern Scotland, Samye-Ling is the site of the only Western Buddhist Temple built in accord with traditional Tibetan architecture. The Centre is a major repository of Tibetan cultural artifacts. It also owns Scotland's Holy Island, currently being reforested as the first step toward the conversion of this ancient Celtic retreat into a sanctuary for people of all faiths.

Samye Ling's abbot, Dr. Akong Tulku Rinpoche, is a Tibetan doctor, Buddhist master and head of Samye Ling and Samye Dzong centers throughout Europe and South Africa. Over the Christmas/New Year holiday week, the Abbot and his qualified students conduct a course in therapy, including psychotherapy and bodywork, plus basic Buddhism and meditation. The Centre's staff also conducts 3-day to 4-week courses over Easter and during the summer.

In addition, Samye Ling each month hosts one or two weekend therapy workshops taught by visiting teachers on subjects such as art therapy, tai chi, aromatherapy, dance and body movement, compassion and meditation. Participants in all courses may stay at the Centre overnight. Anyone else may do so too, joining in with daily worship and study activities, as long as they and their children respect the meditative atmosphere. Visitors are also expected to contribute a few hours each day to community chores.

Address   Eskdalemuir, Langholm, Dumfriesshire DG13 OQL, SCOTLAND

Phone   0387-373232. Fax 0387-373223.

Season   Year-round.

Programs Courses in meditation, healing and values based on Tibetan Buddhist teachings. Also weekend therapy workshops taught by visiting teachers drawing from various healing traditions.

Lodging   Tent space, dorms, double & single rooms.

Rates   No charge for Centre-led courses, but donations appreciated. Suggested donation of #25 for weekend therapy workshop. Nightly food & lodging: own tent #8.50, Centre tent #12, dorm #12, double room #14, single room #16. Children — 5-12 yrs. 1/2 rates, under 5 free. Food/lodging fees #2/day higher during Centre courses.

Meals   Vegetarian breakfast, lunch and evening soup. Some non-vegetarian food is available in the cafe.

Healing Space Summer Camp   South Pembrokeshire, Wales

Healing Space Summer Camp is an annual one week tent camp near the sea in the Pembrokeshire National Park of South Wales. Facilities are simple — wood fired showers, undercover group space and cooking area, and compost loos. Campers can swim in the sea, walk in the wilds, and sing around evening campfires.

This is a combination healing and family vacation camp that welcomes both children and a playful spirit. Camp hosts are Ella and Andy, professional practitioners of rebirthing, deep tissue bodywork and massage, regression, and karmic astrology. Healing and release work includes sweat lodges, hot and cold water rebirthing, and supportive group process.

Address Ella & Andy Portman, Well House Cottage, Well House Lane, Glastonbury, Somerset BA6 8BL, WALES

Phone 0458-834332.

Season Last week in July.

Programs One week healing & family vacation camp.

Lodging Camping. BYO tent.

Rates Adult #160. Child #50.

Meals 3 daily vegetarian meals, simple & mostly organic.

LIFE Foundation School of Therapeutics   North Wales

LIFE Foundation School of Therapeutics conducts weekend and five-day dru yoga, tai chi, stress management, meditation, and holistic health retreats at its Snowdonian Mountains and Bangor retreat centers in North Wales. It also offers weeklong retreats on Bardsey Island, a holy place and bird sanctuary off the tip of the Lleyn Peninsula.

LIFE was founded by Dr. Manny Patel, who leads a five-day "Pathfinders" self-empowerment retreat. Other special programs include a summer five-day "Family Break" (with a program for children) plus a three-day International Yoga, Health & Ecology conference featuring some 30 workshops. There is also a one-year basic and advanced "Holistic Health Care in Practice Course" and the three-year "Dru Yoga Diploma Course." These on-going courses are taught at weekend retreats meeting every three months.

Address c/o 15, Holyhead Road, Bangor, Gwynedd LL57 2EG, WALES

Phone 0248-370076 or 601095. Fax 0248-602900.

Season May through November.

Programs 7, 5 & 2-day yoga, meditation & holistic health retreats.

Lodging A range of facilities from dorms & shared rooms with bunkbeds to double rooms with en suite bathrooms & sauna facilities.

Rates Weekend #69. 5-day retreat #196, or #250 with Manny Patel. Weeklong island retreat #180.

Meals 3 daily vegetarian meals.

Spirit Horse Nomadic Circle   Mid Wales

Spirit Horse Nomadic Circle each year hosts one or two one-week Irish "walkabouts" plus at least a half dozen camps — each 3 to 8 days long. Most encampments are sited in a secluded valley near Machynlleth, mid Wales. Children are welcome but dogs are not allowed in deference to the valley's 5,000 sheep.

Camp elements include song, dance, story, ceremony, sweat lodge and meditation. Recent camp themes were "Shamanic Contemplation," "Awakening to the Tao," "Poetry and the Wild." 1993 workshop leaders included tai chi/Taoist meditation teacher Empty Cloud and Japanese poet Nanao Sakaki.

Frequent Spirit Horse tribe members are drummer Jessica Palin of Salsa Band Candela and singer/musician Anthony Johnstone of the band Zambula. 1993's two "walking encounters with Ireland" were in Counties Clare and Galway.

Spirit Horse is the creation of Shivam O'Brien and Erica Indra. Shivam is a tent-maker, carpenter, storyteller, musician, and personal growth workshop leader. Shivam's spiritual teacher is an English-born shamanic lama, who leads 10 and 14-day Spirit Horse yogic encampments. Erica is a Hungarian-born healer, psychic, counselor, massage and bodywork therapist, and mother of three.

Address   Shivam O'Brien, 19 Holmwood Gardens, London N3 3NS, UK

Phone   0813-463660. Best to call before May.

Season   May through September.

Programs Irish "walkabouts" and Welsh theme encampments loosely structured around performing arts, spiritual and personal growth activities.

Lodging   Camp space for some 20-40 people in a colorful collection of large bedouin tents, tipis, yurts & celtic benders. Most campers bring their own tent for personal space & storage.

Rates   3 to 5-day camp #120-125 (#50 for occasional self-catered camp). 7 to 10-day camp — adult #220-250, child #60-100. 14-day camp — adult #320, child #70.

Meals   3 daily, mostly vegetarian meals prepared in a large kitchen tent equipped with gas stoves. Everyone pitches in with fetching water, gathering and chopping firewood, cooking, and washing up.

CONTINENTAL EUROPE

Le Ble En Herbe Healing Centre   Creuse, France

Nestled in the foothills of the Massif Centrale, Le Ble En Herbe ("The Ripening Seed") is a rural holistic retreat set on 7 1/2 acres of gardens, fields and woods. The general locale is La Creuse, central France — a region known for its lakes, rolling fields, quiet country lanes, wild flowers, butterflies and birds of prey. At Le Ble En Herbe, a peaceful and nurturing atmosphere flows from living simply and in harmony with nature.

The heart of the Centre is an old stone house, home to Maria Sperring — gardener, masseuse, student of yoga and tai chi — and various friends and helpers. The Centre welcomes visitors for camping or home stays. It also offers 6-day courses led by guest teachers on a range of subjects such as yoga, dance, shiatsu, sound and singing. A small and tranquil green space where time is measured in circadian rhythms, Le Ble En Herbe limits course camps to no more than 15 guests.

Address   Puissetier, La Cellette, 23350, FRANCE

Phone   55 80 62 83.

Season   April to September.

Programs 6-day course camps focusing on expressive & reflective healing.

Lodging   Farmhouse room or camping (BYO tent or van). Also WWOOF (Working Weeks On Organic Farms) — work exchange for food & lodging.

Rates   Typical weekly rates (all meals included): course tuition #150, camping 600 francs, room 850 francs.

Meals   3 daily vegetarian meals. Fresh organic produce from the garden.

Yoga Retreats in Southern France   Nice, France

Two weeklong Yoga Retreats in Southern France are held each summer at Le Domaine des Courmettes, a country estate overlooking the French Riviera from a 2400 foot altitude at the base of the Alps. On the 1500 acre property are caves, Roman roads, an ancient forest, and a stone village. A one hour walk leads to Tourrettes-Sur-Loup, the medieval "City of Violets." And a winding 45 minute drive leads to the beaches of Nice and Cannes.

Retreat students are divided into two groups, each with a maximum of 20. Classes are given in English, beginning each day with optional early morning yogic breathing practice. A late morning hatha yoga session explores the classic poses. A late afternoon session focuses on supported, restorative poses and deep relaxation, ending with a quiet meditation sitting. Students are on their own in the early afternoons and evenings.

Retreat directors are Francois and Deborah Raoult, students of B.K.S. Iyengar and directors of Center for Aplomb and Yoga (Rochester, NY). The Raoults both have a strong interest in "aplomb" — structural alignment. Deborah also has a background in prenatal yoga. The Raoults were joined at Le Domaine des Courmettes in 1993 and 1994 by Judith Hanson-Lasater, a long-time teacher at the Iyengar Yoga Institute in San Francisco.

Address   Center for Aplomb and Yoga, 30 Arlington Street, Rochester, NY 14607, USA

Phone   716/244-0782.

Season   June & July.

Programs   Iyengar style, hatha yoga vacation.

Lodging   Accommodates up to 40 guests in simple, comfortable semi-private rooms with 2 or 3 beds; dormitory style rooms; and campsites.

Rates   Rates for pre and post-March 31 registration: private room $875-945, dormitory $825-895, camp site $775-845.

Meals   3 daily vegetarian meals prepared by a French cook with produce from the estate's organic garden. Nearby gourmet restaurants.

Lesvos Yoga Vacations   Lesvos, Greece

Two of the world's best known yoga teachers, Angela Farmer and Victor van Kooten, each year host several 19-day yoga vacations on the Greek island of Lesvos — 200 miles northeast of Athens. Classes are conducted in the Yoga Hall at Molivos, a hillside fishing village on the northwest end of the island. The surrounding rugged hill country, dominated by a medieval castle, is suitable for walks and hikes. Three miles northeast of Molivos are the pebble beaches of Eftalou, with a natural hot spring and Turkish coast horizons extending to the north and to the east.

Victor and Angela have developed their own style of yoga — one that emphasizes breath, quiet preparation and moving gently through the asanas. They also use imagery and self exploration to encourage students to surrender to the flow of movement that arises from within. Each day except Sunday, there is a 3 hour morning asanas/movement class and a 1 1/2 hour evening yogic breathing session and meditation.

Address   Richard Farmer, 8088 Rae Leigh Place, Saanichton, BC V0S 1M0, CANADA; or Patricia Schneider, 139 East Dennis Street, Yellow Springs, OH 45387, USA

Phone   Canada: 604/652-9901 (also serves as fax). USA: 513/767-7727.

Season   May, June & (in some years) fall.

Programs 19-day hatha yoga vacations.

Lodging   Many alternatives: hotels, guest houses, rooms in local houses. Accommodations are simple & clean. Some have cooking facilities. Many students book a room for 1 or 2 nights, evaluate options, then rebook elsewhere — often sharing with another student.

Rates $800 for yoga instruction. Comfortable accommodations available for $15-25/day. Meals & snacks usually no more than $20/day.

Meals   Hotel restaurants, tavernas, coffee bars and a bakery. For meals at "home," local markets offer fresh fish, fruit and vegetables.

Practice Place   Crete, Greece

The Practice Place is a stark white structure perched on the cliffs above the bay of Agios Pavlos on the pristine southern coast of Crete. The structure consists of guest rooms, two indoor studios and several terraces — all overlooking the ocean. The crystal clear waters of the bay below wash against miles of empty beaches ringed by high mountains. The nearest village is Saktouria, offering spectacular vistas 3 1/2 miles up the road.

Each year the Practice Place offers 13 two-week sessions, each with 20-25 hours of Vinyassa Yoga practice plus 20-25 hours in one of two other disciplines. Most sessions offer tai chi. Other options include massage, Iyengar Yoga, Alexander Technique, shiatsu, ceramics and swimming skills. A typical day can begin at 7 with tai chi, followed by Vinyassa Yoga at 8:30. Breakfast at 11. There is free time until 6, when the other disciplines are taught. Dinner is at 8:30.

Most vacationers come to learn and practice Vinyasa Yoga, which combines the discipline of classical hatha yoga with the excitement and fluidity of dance, aerobics and body sculpting. The Vinyasa Yoga instructors are Derek and Radha, native Brits who spend 3 to 4 months each year refining their practice under the tutelage of Pattabhi Jois in Mysore, India. All other disciplines are taught by experienced practitioners from the US and UK.

Address   Derek & Radha, 17 De Montfort Road, Merley, Wimborne, Dorset BH21 1TG, ENGLAND

Phone   0202-842853.

Season   April through mid-October.

Programs 16 two-week sessions combining Vinyassa Yoga practice with practice of another body/mind discipline. Each vacationer may choose his/her degree of program participation.

Lodging   18 twin and triple-bedded guest rooms, each with twin beds, private bathrooms and ocean views.

Rates   Per person program rates: twin-bed room with private balcony #485, twin-bed room opening onto terrace #425, triple-bed room opening onto terrace #385. All terraces & balconies overlook ocean. Lower rates for unprogrammed, vegetarian vacation.

Meals   2 large & tasty buffets plus a packed lunch each day. All meals are vegetarian, with vegan and macrobiotic options. Teas, coffee, cookies and toast are available throughout the day.

Skyros Holidays   Skyros Island, Greece

Skyros Holidays are a summer mecca for international holistic health and personal growth vacationers. The tranquil island setting includes secluded sandy beaches, large pine forests, and cobblestone-paved villages where hand-carving and embroidery are the major livelihoods. Skyros Holidays are held at two island locations — Atsitsa and Skyros Village. All vacations are two weeks long and led by a visiting faculty of about 90 teachers.

Atsitsa, home of Skyros holistic health vacations, is a seaview country center on Atsitsa Bay nine miles from Skyros Village. Atsitsa vacationers choose up to three courses each week from over 20 options such as meditation, yoga, tai chi, art/art therapy, dreamwork, voice/singing/ music, theater/mime, healing and rituals. Classes are conducted in the late mornings and late afternoons.

Skyros Holiday's large villa at Skyros Village houses Skyros Centre, Skyros Institute and the Writers' Workshops. The villa's back garden opens on to views of the mountains and the sea, and the beach can be reached by foot in 10 minutes. And as at Atsitsa, Village vacationers join in communal activities such as meal preparation, house cleaning, short daily "home groups," and community get-togethers.

Skyros Centre programs offer three hours a day of experiential personal development courses drawing on approaches such as gestalt, psychodrama, bodywork and psychosynthesis. The focus is on working through emotional blocs in small groups, which switch facilitators for the second week. Those who wish may also take early morning or late afternoon classes in yoga, tai chi, massage, dance, music, art or theater.

Skyros Institute offers training courses in disciplines such as Alexander Technique, gestalt counseling, dance therapy and massage. Institute courses are suitable both for professionals and those wishing to develop personal skills. Writers' Workshops focus on writing from a variety of perspectives — as art, as craft, as therapy, etc. Both Institute and Writers' Workshop courses meet for four hours each day.

Address   92 Prince of Wales Road, London NW5 3NE, ENGLAND

Phone   0712-674424. Fax 0712-843063.

Season   April through October.

Programs 2-week sessions structured as holistic health vacations (Atsitsa), personal development courses (Skyros Centre), writers' workshops, and personal development/holistic health training courses (Skyros Institute).

Lodging Atsitsa — shared accommodations for up to 100 in 2 houses and 2-person huts. Skyros Village — accommodations for up to 55 in villagers' homes & modern houses with shared or single rooms.

Rates   Depending on dates, rates for 2-week sessions range from #395-645. Single supplement #80.

Meals   Atsitsa — 3 daily meals, primarily vegetarian with occasional fish or meat. Skyros Centre, Writers' Workshops & Institute — 2 daily, primarily vegetarian meals with dinner (or lunch) usually eaten at inexpensive, local tavernas.

Ananda Assisi   Assisi, Italy

Ananda Assisi is situated on a panoramic ridge 10 miles from Assisi in the peaceful Umbrian countryside. The grounds include a large stone house that serves as the guest reception center, a secluded villa surrounded by a small park, and several guest houses. The villa is used for classes and spiritual practices — given or translated in Italian, German and English.

Like California's Expanding Light at Ananda retreat, Ananda Assisi is run by a resident spiritual community following the spiritual practices of the late Paramhansa Yogananda. The daily schedule includes a pre-lunch meditation, morning and late afternoon sadhana (energization exercises, yoga postures, chanting and meditation), plus evening programs. There are also morning and afternoon classes during theme retreats.

Theme retreats are scheduled throughout the year (steadily during the summer) for weekend, weeklong, 2 and 3-week periods. Weekend and weeklong programs generally focus on meditation, overcoming negative emotions, and practical metaphysics. There is a 2-week intensive on "Hatha Yoga & Healing," plus two 3-week intensives — "How to Heal Yourself & Others," and "Yogananda's Interpretation of the Bhagavad Gita." There are also holiday programs that integrate Eastern and Western spiritual perspectives.

Address   Casella Postale 48, I-06088 Santa Maria degli Angeli (PG), ITALY

Phone   742 811212. Fax 742 811124.

Season   Year-round except 2 weeks in January & 2 weeks in June.

Programs Weekend, weeklong, 2 and 3-week retreats focusing primarily on meditation, yoga and yogic spiritual practices. Work/study and personal retreatants also welcome.

Lodging   Double occupancy rooms (some with private baths) & dorms in guest houses (1 with a kitchen). Also tent & camper sites.

Rates   Lodging, meals & classes: Daily — campsite 40,000 Lire, dorms & shared rooms 50-75,000 Lire; 2-week program — camping 560,000 Lire, room 840,000 Lire; 3-week program — camping 740,000 Lire, room 1,100,000 Lire; family week — 1/2 price for children ages 3-14, children under 3 free. Annual registration fee 20,000 Lire.

Meals   3 daily vegetarian meals.

Bunga Raya Yoga Retreat Center   Bacchereto, Italy

Bunga Raya Yoga Retreat Center is Dona Holleman's home/yoga studio — a reconstructed 400 year old farmhouse surrounded by olive groves and woodland a short walk from the village of Bacchereto and a 40 minute drive out of Florence. The house includes a spacious kitchen, dining room and yoga room. When Dona is not traveling, the house is open for yoga students to pursue individual study. It is also the site of annual 7-day courses in April, June and December for groups of up to 16 people.

Dona has studied with B.K.S. Iyengar and taught Iyengar style hatha yoga for over 30 years. She has also written books and produced home-made video tapes on yoga asanas. Focusing on intermediate-to-advanced practice, Dona expects her students to have at least one year of Iyengar yoga experience.

Practice at Bunga Raya consists of pranayama and asana in the morning, head and shoulders balance in the evening. This totals about three hours of yoga each day for individual yoga studies guests. During the weeklong courses, practice periods are somewhat longer.

Address   Dona Holleman, Via Madonna Del Papa 9, Fi. 50040, Bacchereto, ITALY

Phone   055 8717057 (also accepts fax). Call before visiting.

Season   Year-round.

Programs Weeklong Easter, June & Christmas Iyengar style, hatha yoga courses. Individual yoga study stays available at other times.

Lodging   Reconstructed farmhouse accommodating up to 16 overnight guests.

Rates   7-day course 650,000 Lire. Individual yoga study 60,000 Lire/day.

Meals   Guests can dine out or cook their own meals in the farmhouse kitchen. Small village food stores are a 15 minute walk away.

Cortijo Romero   Granada, Spain

Cortijo Romero is a converted farmhouse and human potential center in the foothills of the Sierra Nevada a few miles from the rugged Mediterranean Sea coast. On the peaceful grounds is a garden, an orchard, and an outdoor swimming pool close to the shade of verdant palms. The climate is mild and the nearest major city is Granada with its cultural legacy of Moorish Spain. Set in a region believed to be among the most spiritually uplifting in Europe, Cortijo Romero honors the transformative power of love.

The center's weeklong courses cover a range of subjects such as massage, meditation, yoga, movement, voice and artistic expression. Facilitators include center staff and other experienced workshop leaders. A typical day includes a 10 AM community attunement, group time in the morning and late afternoon, and free time in the afternoon and early evening. During the week, there is also a full day picnic lunch excursion to the mountains.

Address   Wendy Moffatt, 24 Grange Ave., Chapeltown, Leeds LS7 4EJ, UK

Phone   0532-374015.

Season   Year-round, but light programming during winter months.

Programs   Weeklong programs focusing on holistic healing & personal transformation. Open to outside group rentals in winter months.

Lodging   Accommodates up to 17 guests in simple, comfortable twin-bedded rooms, each with an en-suite bathroom.

Rates   1-week program tuition, room & board #305.

Meals   3 daily vegetarian meals with locally grown foods including eggs & dairy products. Cater to special diets. Guests help clean up after meals. Tea & snack facilities available on 24 hour basis.

Services   Courtesy pick-up/drop off at Malaga Airport, 2 1/2 hours away.

Zenith Institute Summer Camp   Tessin, Switzerland

The Zenith Institute each summer hosts a retreat encampment in south central Switzerland, halfway between Lukmanier Pass and the town of Olivone at an altitude of roughly 4,900 feet. The camp is pitched amidst mountain meadows and pine forests against a backdrop of rugged snow capped peaks.

During the five week encampment, Pir Vilayat Inayat Khan leads three weeklong meditation camps — one in English, one in French, and one in German. Each of these camps is followed by a group retreat camp at a separate location a few minutes walking distance from the main encampment. Individual retreats are also possible throughout the five week period.

In 1993, weeklong theme camps included a "Sacred Music Retreat," a "Zira'at Camp" (Sufi teachings and spiritual practice), a "Retreat in the Christian Mystical Tradition," plus retreats on painting and acting. Hatha yoga and cooking classes are offered throughout the summer.

The Institute is an independent outreach of the Sufi Order International.

Address   For information: CH-6853 Ligornetto, SWITZERLAND
During the camp: CH-6718 Olivone, SWITZERLAND

Phone   Best to write.

Season   5 weeks in July and August.

Programs   Weeklong camp retreats, each on a particular subject. Meditation is the major subject. Other subjects include Sufi teachings, sacred music, painting & acting. Also work camp & work study.

Lodging   BYO tent or rent a large, white tent & platform. A few shared bedroom & dorm spaces available in a nearby hostel.

Rates   380 Swiss Francs for 1st week of attendance. Price is 10% less for each subsequent week of attendance. Weekly tent rental 110 SF. Hostel nightly rates — dorm 8 SF, room 20 SF.

Meals   3 daily vegetarian meals.

Services   A children's camp program offered throughout the summer.

INDIA, AUSTRALIA & NEW ZEALAND

Chenrezig Institute   Queensland, Australia

Chenrezig Institute is a Tibetan Buddhist community, retreat and study center high in the rain forests of the Blackall Ranges 60 miles north of Brisbane. The Institute's 160 acre property contains a community of nuns, a lay community, a collection of Tibetan art and architecture, and magnificent vistas of the "sunshine coast."

Visitors are encouraged to attend morning and evening meditation sessions. Meditation instruction and personal counselling are available on request. Visitors may also attend some of the regular classes taught by resident lama Geshe Tashi Tsering. One-day and weekend introductory meditation and Buddhist philosophy courses are taught by Western monks and nuns. There are also special courses for people with life-threatening illnesses.

Visitors who stay beyond two weeks participate fully in community life — attending daily teachings and meditations, participating in weekly work days, attending bi-weekly community meetings and monthly retreats. After several months of continuous residency, visitors may apply for residency.

Address   P.O. Box 41, Eudlo, Queensland 4554, AUSTRALIA

Phone   074 450 077. Fax 074 450 088.

Season   Year-round.

Programs Courses on meditation, Tibetan Buddhist philosophy & psychology, related Western approaches. For all levels of students.

Lodging   Usually shared rooms. Single rooms during slow periods. Also campsites & small, single room retreat huts.

Rates   Tuition: some courses & regular classes free to Centre guests; other courses usually $20-25/day. Lodging: daily — shared $17/ person, single $25, hut $17, campsite $10/person; weekly — shared $85/ person, single $125, hut $85, campsite $50/person. Meals: breakfast $3, lunch $5, dinner $2.

Meals   3 daily vegetarian meals.

Hippocrates Health Centre of Australia   Queensland, Australia

Located south of Brisbane on the semi-tropical Gold Coast of Queensland, the Hippocrates Health Centre of Australia is a member of Dr. Ann Wigmore's international network of living foods centers. The weekly health education program runs from Sunday evening to Saturday morning. Centre director Ronald Bradley recommends a stay of at least three weeks so that eating and lifestyle changes can be thoroughly mastered for continuing use at home.

Hippocrates is a learn-by-doing environment. Food-related instruction covers permaculture, sprouting, food dehydration and preparation, kitchen equipment, wheatgrass, rejuvelac, food combining and menu planning. Other instruction covers gentle stretching exercise, meditation, visualization, relaxation, positive thinking, goal setting and affirmations. All students receive a free textbook plus free time to use the swimming pool, jacuzzi, steam room and tennis court. They can also hike in the nearby rain forest.

Address   Elaine Avenue, Mudgeeraba 4213, Gold Coast, Queensland, AUSTRALIA

Phone   075 302 860.

Season   Year-round.

Programs   A weekly living foods lifestyle program.

Lodging   Private, motel type rooms.

Rates   1 week $995. 2 weeks $1,895. 3 weeks $2,795.

Meals   3 daily vegetarian meals of fresh, raw foods. A juice diet is recommended for the first 3 days.

Services   Program includes 2 free hours each week of naturopathic services. Students may choose from therapeutic massage, body scrub, aromatherapy, iridology, facial, manicure and/or pedicure.

Ontos Health Retreat   Victoria, Australia

Ontos is a 700 acre health resort and organic farm one hour by car from Bairnsdale in the Snowy River Wilderness region of eastern Victoria. The gently rolling property includes orchards, vegetable gardens, a volleyball court, a children's adventure playground, and a lake for swimming. Guests can also enjoy hiking and excursions to local natural attractions such as the Buchan Caves, the Little River Waterfall and Gorge.

Ontos resembles its international sister community, America's Satchidananda Ashram, in the nature of its daily schedule — talks, group meditations, hatha yoga and guided relaxation sessions. There are organic farm tours, and children are welcome except during "Adult Holiday" weeks (about four times each year) and "Integral Yoga" weeks (usually twice a year).

Address   Buchan P.O., Victoria 3885, AUSTRALIA

Phone   05 155 0275.

Season   Year-round.

Programs   Frequent weekend & multi-week holiday programs featuring special children's activities. Occasional Integral Yoga weeks.

Lodging 16 self-contained motel units with central heating, toilet & shower, linen service, and up to 6 beds. 2 room cabins with potbelly heater, front & back verandas, bunk beds sleeping 6, but no linens & separate shared bathroom blocks. Also campsites.

Rates Program rates same as regular rates. Individual nightly rates: motel unit — single adult $90, adult shared $75, 5-15 year child $30, 3 & 4 year child $15; cabin — single adult $75, adult shared $65, 5-15 year child $30, 3 & 4 year child $15; camping — adult $40, 5-15 year child $20, 3 & 4 year child $15.

Meals 3 daily vegetarian meals with organic ingredients from Ontos' orchards and gardens.

Services Massage and twice-a-week Bairnsdale train pick-up. Afternoon & evening children's programs during school vacation periods.

Atmasantulana Village   Maharashtra, India

Atmasantulana Village is a holistic living, healing and learning community located in the countryside between Bombay and Pune. It is surrounded by mountains, close to the Indrayani River, and next to the Maharashtra Tourism Development Corporation (MTDC) Holiday Resort. Over its 10 year life, the Village has planted more than 4,000 trees of about 200 varieties.

The Village welcomes visitors for holiday stays, which include food, accommodation and participation in the community program. The program includes daily kriya yoga and yogic breathing sessions; several lectures each week on topics such as oriental therapies and spiritual philosophy; plus frequent cultural programs, especially music and dance.

The Village's Shri Balaji Health Foundation conducts a one-month course in Ayurveda that covers holistic living, naturopathy, ayurvedic analysis based on body type, ayurvedic physiotherapy, pancha karma, ayurvedic diet and cooking, herbal cosmetics, meditation, yoga and the art of living. The course includes about 5 hours of daily class work plus visits to Ayurvedic medical centers.

Atmasantulana was founded by Shri Balaji Tambe and his wife Dr. Veena Tambe, both doctors of Ayurveda and Naturopathy. Shri Balaji has pioneered the development of music therapy; light-and-sound therapy; and cosmology-based counseling based on a holistic understanding of the relationship between personality and the universe. Shri Balaji is also an artist and composer.

Address Bombay-Pune Road, near MTDC Holiday Resort, Karla 410 405, Maharashtra, INDIA

Phone 232 & 203.

Season Year-round (including the July-Sept. rainy season).

Programs Holiday stays with participation in community program of yoga & holistic health education. Also 1-month Ayurveda course.

Lodging Capacity for up to 100 in single & double Village guest houses. Bungalows may be rented at the neighboring MTDC Holiday Resort.

Rates Holiday stay: 13,000-17,000 rupees (roughly $500) per month. Short course in Ayurveda: 29,000 rupees (about $950) per month. Rates include meals, lodging, course fees & community program.

Meals 3 daily vegetarian meals.

Services Pancha Karma therapy — including steam treatment, massages, oil treatments, diet and cleansing of the gastro-intestinal tract.

Osho Multiversity   Maharashtra, India

Osho Multiversity is operated on 27 lush acres in metropolitan Pune by Osho Commune International — a "buddhafield" (meditative energy field) for spiritual growth. Commune members work on the campus in an attitude of mindfulness in exchange for room and board. Multiversity students may participate in the community's six daily one-hour meditations. They may also attend evening, community gatherings for meditation, celebration and an Osho video discourse.

Multiversity programs are "designed not to teach, but to awaken each person to new dimensions of awareness and clarity." Most programs incorporate some form of therapy — to free people from their repressed emotions and fears. According to the late Osho Rajneesh, this freedom "clears the ground for a tremendous transformation from mind to no-mind" through meditation. Meditation is integrated into all of the programs, and an intensive "Meditation Camp" is held on the second weekend of each month.

The late Osho Rajneesh envisioned modern man as "Zorba the Buddha" — an integrated material/spiritual being. To address guests' material needs, the Commune operates several restaurants such as Osho Cafe and a lively night spot called Meera Bistro. There is disco dancing and nightly movies. And the Commune's Club Meditation features an olympic-sized pool, sauna, hot tubs, "zennis" and volleyball courts, plus a beauty salon.

Osho Commune also contains gardens abounding in tropical trees and plants, peacocks, ponds, swans, waterfalls and sculptures. Classes are conducted in pyramid-roofed structures connected by marble pathways. The campus has its own central reservoir, organic gardens, central air conditioning plant and waste re-cycling center, and a hygiene lab that regularly tests all food and water. There are both allopathic and alternative medical clinics, and admission into the grounds is restricted to people with an HIV-negative certificate (testing available at the Commune) less than 30 days old.

Address   Osho Commune International, 17 Koregaon Park, Pune 411 001, Maharashtra, INDIA

Phone   91-212-660963. Fax 91-212-644181.

Season   Year-round.

Programs Daily classes and 1 to 90-day sessions & programs by 9 Osho faculties: School of Creative Arts, Center for Transformation, International Academy of Healing Arts, Meditation Academy, School of Mysticism, School for Centering, Institute for Tibetan Pulsing Healing, School for Zen Martial Arts, Academy for Zen Sports and Fitness. Work-study possibilities for committed meditators.

Lodging   Day visit & program guests may secure nearby hostel or hotel accommodation, or rent nearby apartments. Work-study residents housed in shared Commune accommodations.

Rates   Guided tour 10 rupees. All-day pass 20 rupees. Meals 200-250 rupees/day. A good hotel room 425-475 rupees/night. Multi-day programs 2,200-2,600 rupees/day. Work study 12,100 rupees (roughly $400) per month including room & board.

Meals   Vegetarian meals available in 2 large cafeterias, 2 bistros, a restaurant and a cappuchino bar.

Services   Massage, full body scrub, waxing, facial, manicure, haircut.

Sivananda Yoga Vedanta Dhanwantari Ashram   Kerala, India

The Sivananda Yoga Vedanta Dhanwantari Ashram is set amidst 12 acres of tropical splendor in the foothills of the Sahyadri Mountains on India's southern tip. Yoga students from all over the world practice their asanas beneath palm trees on the shore of a quiet lake. Simple accommodations at the side of the main ashram look out over the lush valley below.

Those who come for a two-week Yoga Vacation observe the following daily schedule: 6 AM meditation, chants and a talk; 8 o'clock pranayama and asana instruction; 10 AM brunch; 11 o'clock practice of selfless service by helping out around the ashram; 1:30 PM tea; 2 PM short talk; 4 o'clock hatha yoga session; 6 PM dinner; evening meditation, chanting and a talk.

The 4-week "Yoga Teachers' Training Course" (TTC), generally offered in January, provides a thorough grounding in yogic science, philosophy and practice. TTC students have the same schedule as Yoga Vacationers with the addition of Bhagavad Gita study at noon and a 2 PM lecture on subjects such as anatomy, physiology and Vedanta philosophy. TTC graduates qualify for a 4-week February "Advanced Teachers' Training Course" and a 10-day Sadhana (intensive practice) workshop later in the year.

Immediately after TTC, the ashram usually conducts a February pilgrimage to the temples and holy places of South India. Most years, there is also a September pilgrimage to Badrinath and Gangotri in the Himalayas.

Address   Neyyar Dam P.O., Trivandrum Dt., Kerala 695 576, INDIA

Phone   047254 493 (within India).

Season   Year-round.

Programs "Yoga Vacations," beginning 1st & 15th of each month, with mandatory attendance of all classes & meditations. "Teacher's Training Course," "Sadhana Workshop," "Advanced Teacher's Training Course." 4-week April/May "Children's Yoga Camp."

Lodging   Red shuttered, white walled huts with spiritual murals and 2 cots. Some have a bathroom. BYO bedding, towels and asana mat.

Rates   "Yoga Vacation" nightly rates — room with bath 200 rupees, room without bath 150 rupees. "Teacher's Training Course" — campsite $1,000, room without bath $1,200, room with bath $1,400.

Meals   2 buffet style, vegetarian meals each day.

Tauhara Centre   Taupo, New Zealand

Tauhara Centre is a northern New Zealand retreat and conference center overlooking Lake Taupo and Mt. Tauhara. The lake offers summer swimming and other water sports. Nearby are hot mineral springs and pools, ski resorts, and hiking trails with many panoramic vistas. Climbing Mt. Tauhara is a half-day "tramp."

The Centre offers frequent weekend workshops on topics such as meditation, complementary health, relationships and sacred dance. There are also storytelling, women's spirituality and family festival gatherings. Tauhara is also always open to private retreatants.

Address   P.O. Box 125, Taupo, NEW ZEALAND

Phone   07 378 7507. No visits without prior arrangement.

Season   Year-round.

Programs Mostly weekend holistic health & ecumenical workshops. Some weeklong workshops. Also accommodates private retreats.

Lodging   Shared (4 bed) rooms, a self contained apartment, a cottage and a chalet (reserved for private retreatants). Also campsites.

Rates   Weekend workshops & retreats (meals included) $90-180. Adult private retreat nightly fees: camping $12, shared $24, double $33, single $44. Children's lodging at 1/3rd adult rates. Meals — breakfast $6, lunch $8, dinner $14, 1/2 price for children.

Meals   Professionally catered for organized events. Also a small kitchen for private retreatants wishing to cook their own meals.

7 Multiple Site Vacations & Retreats

This chapter contains profiles of organizations that offer programs at two or more sites in different states, provinces or nations. The profiles are listed in geographical order within each of three categories: "Two or More Continents," "Europe" and "North America." As it happens, all of the organizations profiled under "Two or More Continents" have at least one program site in the United States and at least one on another continent.

Dance of the Deer Foundation   Two or More Continents

The Dance of the Deer Foundation was founded in 1979 to support the Huichol Indians and to preserve their shamanic traditions. It is directed by Brant Secunda, who completed a 12 year apprenticeship with the late Huichol shaman don Jose Matsuwa. A small tribe living in Mexico's Sierra Madre Mountains, the Huichols are believed to be the last North American tribe to have maintained their pre-Columbian traditions.

In recent years, Dance of the Deer programs have included a summer solstice weekend seminar in the Catskill Mountains, a 5-day Mt. Shasta pilgrimage, an 8-day event at Montana's Feathered Pipe Ranch, a 6-day seminar in the Bavarian Alps, a 16-day spring retreat in central Europe, and a 10-day pilgrimage and seminar in a secluded villa on Mexico's Pacific coast.

Program participants experience vision quests, Huichol ceremonies, and the sacred Dance of the Deer. They learn shamanic health and healing practices, including the use of dreams for life guidance and empowerment. They also learn how to approach sacred places and to bring the life• balancing power of those places into their hearts.

Address   P.O. Box 699, Soquel, CA 95073, USA

Phone   408/475-9560.

Season   Generally May through November.

Programs Experiential shamanism seminars and pilgrimages to beautiful, sacred places of power.

Regions   Central western Mexico, the USA (California, Montana & New York), and Europe (southern Germany, southern France or northern Italy).

Rates   Weekend $199. 5 or 6-day program $350-500. 8-day program $890. 10-day program $1,299. 16-day program $1,500.

Global Fitness Adventures   Two or More Continents

Global Fitness Adventures are designed by ex spa resort physical director Kristina Hurrell as "catalysts to an awakening" that are "part stress management, part nutrition and wholly vacation." Also a former top European fashion model, actress and photographer, Kristina carefully chooses vacation spots with a "fresh, clean, tranquilizing beauty true to the promise of vibrant health and adventure."

A Global Fitness day begins with a pre-breakfast yoga/stretch class and meditation. The rest of the morning is dedicated to an 8-18 mile hike, snoeshow or cross country skiing outing. Early afternoon is usually a time for massage and leisure activities such as volleyball, swimming, and siesta. Late afternoon features muscle toning and stretch classes, often preceded or followed by a horseback ride. Evening activities include sweat lodge, drumming and dance, visualizations, and holistic health lectures.

A co-leader on many Global Fitness Adventures (particularly those at Aspen) is Rob Krakovitz, M.D., an authority on detoxification techniques, high energy personal diets and nutritional supplements. Global Fitness meals are spa cuisine (vegetarian with some fish) with full vegetarian options.

Address   P.O. Box 1390, Aspen, CO 81612, USA

Phone   303/920-1780.   Fax 303/927-4793.

Season   Year-round.

Programs 7, 8 & 13-day vacations designed to extend physical limits, de-stress body & mind, and invite greater peace & joy into life.

Regions   1993 scheduled vacations were in Bali (1); Dominica, Caribbean (4); Palm Springs, CA (5); Sedona, AZ (6); Aspen, CO (10); and Emerald Lake, Canada (2). Also custom designed adventures in Europe, Central America, Africa, the Himalayas, and Siberia.

Rates   7 & 8-day vacations $1,800-1,975. 13-day Bali vacation $3,100. Rates include all lodging, meals, massage, classes, activities, sightseeing arrangements, fitness evaluation, and home maintenance program. Air fare not included.

International Meditation Centers   Two or More Continents

The worldwide network of six International Meditation Centers (IMCs) includes four centers in English speaking countries — the U.S., the U.K., and two in Australia. The U.S. center is in rural Maryland north of Washington,

D.C. The U.K. center is west of London in Wiltshire. The two Australian centers are near Perth and Sydney.

All IMCs host monthly 10-day meditation retreats, and most also offer occasional weekend retreats. All retreats have a uniform schedule: 4 AM wake-up, 4:30-6:30 meditation and teacher talk, group and individual meditation periods during most of the morning and afternoon, 6 PM teacher talk, and 7:30-8:30 group meditation. During meditation periods, students may get up to quietly stretch or walk around.

On 10-day retreats, the first five days focus on calming the mind by attention to breath and the last five days focus on developing awareness by moving attention throughout the body. All IMC meditation teachers have been trained by Sayamagyi Daw Mya Thwin and Sayagyi U Chit Tin, who have practiced and taught Vipassana meditation for over 30 years in the Burmese Theravada Buddhist tradition of their teacher — the late Sayagyi U Ba Khin.

At all centers, lodging is provided in separate men's and women's dorms; ample food is provided at a daily, vegetarian breakfast and lunch; and there are also daily tea breaks in the evening and early morning.

Address   446 Bankard Road, Westminster, MD 21158, USA
Splatts House, Heddington, Calne, Wiltshire SN11 OPE, UK
Lot 2, Cessnock Road, Sunshine, NSW 2264, AUSTRALIA
Lot 78, Jacoby Street, Mahogany Creek, Western Australia 6072

Phone   US: 410/346-7889. Fax 410/346-7282.
UK: 0380-850258. Fax 0380-850833.
NSW, Australia: 49 705 433. Fax 49 705 747.
Western Australia: 09 295 2644. Fax 09 295 3435.
No visits without prior arrangement.

Season   Year-round.

Programs   10-day & weekend retreats in concentration & insight meditation. All retreatants are expected to adhere to the daily schedule & observe Noble Silence (refraining from all unnecessary talk).

Regions   U.S. (Maryland), U.K. (Wiltshire), Australia (near Perth & Sydney). Also centers (non English speaking) in Burma & Austria.

Rates   U.S. — 10-day retreat $225-300, weekend retreat $50. Australia - 10-day retreat $250 (Australian), weekend retreat $50.

Light Institute of Galisteo   Two or More Continents

The Light Institute runs residential 3-day and 6-day group Intensives on the campus of Nizhoni School for Global Consciousness at SunRise Springs, NM — 15 miles southwest of Santa Fe. Each Intensive includes multi-incarnational sessions, yoga and Tibetan exercise classes, a firewalk seminar, workshops and a cranial — a session that stimulates the body's master glands to release physical tensions and emotional holding patterns.

Participants receive shared accommodations and gourmet vegetarian meals.

As an intensive form of guided individual retreat, the Institute also offers over thirteen 4-day spiritual growth programs, each addressing a separate theme. Individuals new to this process begin with two programs that focus, respectively, on opening to the Higher Self and dissolving projections of self-image on to parents. Each of these programs consists of an emotional body balancing session followed by 3 multi-incarnational sessions. Each session takes about three hours on a separate day.

Most 4-day spiritual growth programs are conducted at the Institute's Galisteo, NM headquarters site, which does not provide meals or lodging. Some of these programs are also conducted in Europe by facilitators visiting from New Mexico. Most European programs are at Le Relais, a renovated 12th century post house inn in the Charente region of southwest France. Le Relais offers both meals and lodging. Some "sessions" programs are also conducted in other continental European countries.

The Institute's founder, Chris Griscom is a multilingual healer and teacher who conducts seminars throughout the world. Chris's work is inspired by her 6 near-death experiences, 9 years in the Peace Corps, mastery of esoteric acupuncture, and her Higher Self. Chris has written 9 books.

Address   North America: HC75, Box 50, Galisteo, NM 87540, USA
Europe: Boite Postale # 6, 16390 Saint Severin, FRANCE

Phone   U.S.: 505/983-1975. Fax 505/989-7217.
France: 45 98 07 21. Fax 45 98 92 03.

Season   Year-round.

Programs 3-day & 6-day residential Intensives plus 4-day spiritual growth ("sessions") programs designed to heal, clear & expand consciousness. Intensive themes include "Clearing Your Parents," "Death & Samadhi," and "Initiate Your Life Purpose."

Regions   New Mexico (USA), southwestern France, and from time to time in Germany, Switzerland, Holland & Denmark.

Rates   U.S.: 6-day Intensive $2,300-2,500; 4-day spiritual growth sessions — adult $1,000, young person (12-16) $500, child (5-11) $250. Europe — 4-day spiritual growth sessions $1,500; Le Relais (France) B&B 165 francs, B&B + dinner 280 francs.

Person Centered Expressive Arts Program — Two or More Continents

The Person Centered Expressive Therapy Institute (PCETI) offers residential programs in expressive arts therapy. Roughly 60% of program attendees come for the purpose of professional training. Others attend for the personal therapeutic value of the work.

The Level I program focuses on the use of the expressive arts — movement, painting, writing and sound — in a non-judgmental, person-centered environment. Level II extends the experience to include relationship and community. Level III leads to a deeper understanding of body and psyche.

All Levels are offered at a 10 acre retreat center near hot springs, redwood forests and the Pacific coast 1 1/2 hours north of San Francisco. All levels are also offered at an English country manor between Liverpool and Manchester. Programs have also been offered on the U.S. East Coast.

The Institute's founder is Natalie Rogers — daughter of the well known author and humanistic psychologist Carl Rogers and a respected author/ psychotherapist in her own right.

Address   Person Centered Expressive Therapy Institute, P.O. Box 6518, Santa Rosa, CA 95406, USA

Phone   707/526-4006 or 800/477-2384.

Season   July (California) and August (U.S. East Coast & England).

Programs   7, 10 & 11-day Level I, II & III experiential expressive arts trainings. Levels I & II are prerequisites for Level III. All 3 levels are prerequisites for Level IV interns.

Regions   Northern California (Sonoma County), northeastern U.S. (PA & NY), and England (Greater Manchester).

Rates   U.S.: Level I, tuition $525, room & board $330; Level II tuition $790, room & board $550; Level III, tuition $875, room & board $660. England tuition, room & board: Level I, 500 pounds, Level II 700 pounds.

RIGPA Retreats — Two or More Continents

The RIPGA Fellowship is an international, non-profit organization founded to support the teaching of Tibetan Buddhist spiritual practices such as meditation, Tonglen, Ngondro and Dzogchen. RIGPA's founder is Tibetan lama and meditation master Sogyal Rinpoche — raised and tutored by three of Tibet's greatest 20th century Buddhist masters, educated in comparative religion at Cambridge University, author of "The Tibetan Book of Living and Dying," and teacher throughout the Western world for over 20 years.

With the assistance of other lamas, Sogyal Rinpoche each year hosts several long (2 to 12-week) European retreats. Most attendees are people in RIGPA courses or study groups organized by the many Western RIGPA city centers coordinated by the Centre in London. But others are welcome. In the U.S., Sogyal Rinpoche and senior Rigpa students also lead several 10-day retreats. A number of RIGPA centers also organize weekend retreats.

The longest RIGPA retreats are usually held at Lerab Ling — a secluded 360 acre site 40 miles northwest of Montpelier in southern France. From its highest point, Lerab Ling opens onto views of the distant Pyrenees. Other long retreats are held at Dzogchen Beara, a 250 acre farm looking out over the North Atlantic from the cliffs above Bantry Bay in southwestern Ireland. Dzogchen Beara also accommodates unprogrammed holiday stays and use by non-RIGPA retreat groups. The major U.S. retreats are generally held at rented facilities in northern California and New England.

Address   U.S.: P.O. Box 7866, Berkeley, CA 94707, USA
U.K.: 330 Caledonian Road, London N1 1BB, ENGLAND
Ireland: Dzogchen Beara, Garranes, Allihies, West Cork, IRELAND
France: Lerab Ling, L'Engayresque, 34650 Roqueredonde, FRANCE

Season   Throughout the year.

Phone   U.S.: 510/644-3922.
U.K.: 0717-000185.
Ireland: 027-73032.
France: 67 44 41 99.

Programs   10-day to multi-month long retreats to deepen meditation practice & expand understanding of Tibetan Buddhist teachings. In several major cities, RIGPA centers also offer 5-week, non-residential "Foundation" courses on meditation & compassion.

Regions   Retreats conducted in France, Ireland & the U.S.

Rates   Sample 1993 rates: 16-day summer Ireland retreat 398 Irish pounds; 10-day summer & fall U.S. retreats $425-680, prices varying by site & type of accommodations.

Woman Within   Two or More Continents

Woman Within conducts 2 1/2-day women's initiation workshops designed to help women reclaim those parts of their feminine nature that they have denied. Each workshop draws on a variety of experiential therapies — group and dyad exercises, meditations, visualizations, art, movement, and journal writing. At most workshops, the number of participants is exceeded by the number of staff members — all workshop graduates with additional training.

Woman Within workshops are generally held in secluded, residential facilities. For example, the Wisconsin site is a rustic lakeside camp. The 1994 schedule included 10 weekends at Lake Delavan, WI (40 miles from Milwaukee and 80 miles from Chicago); 5 weekends near Ontario, Quebec; 4 weekends near Houston, TX; 2 weekends each in the Washington, D.C. and Minnesota areas; plus weekends in the vicinity of London, England.

Address   7186 Driftwood Drive, Fenton, MI 48430, USA

Phone   313/750-7227. Fax 313/750-8386.

Season   Year-round.

Programs   2 1/2-day Woman Within (WW) initiation workshops. Also 3-day trainings for WW graduates wishing to staff WW workshops.

Regions   USA: Southeastern Wisconsin; Ontario, Quebec; Houston, Texas; Minnesota; Washington, D.C. Also London, England.

Rates   1993 rates: standard $500-600; women over 65 $400-500.

Friends of the Western Buddhist Order   Europe

Friends of the Western Buddhist Order (FWBO) was founded in 1967 by Sangharakshita, an Englishman who had lived 20 years in the East as a Buddhist monk. In the U.K., FWBO operates several country retreat centers — the Waterhall Centre in Essex, the Rivendell Retreat Centre in East Sussex, the Taraloka women's center in Shropshire, plus men's centers in north Wales and Norfolk.

All FWBO centers offer retreats suitable for beginner meditators and those new to Buddhist teachings. All also offer retreats for experienced meditators and students of Buddhist texts. Retreats are generally a weekend or a week in length. Some retreats focus on a theme such as yoga, motherhood, artistic expression, or center upkeep (i.e. a work retreat).

Each center serves three daily vegetarian meals and provides shared accommodations. (Vajraloka also has single rooms.) Men and women are housed in separate quarters at the two mixed gender centers. The addresses of all four country retreat centers may be obtained from the London Buddhist Centre — listed below.

Address   London Buddhist Centre, 51 Roman Road, London E2 OHU, ENGLAND

Phone   0819-811225. No visits without prior arrangement.

Season   Year-round.

Programs   Weekend and weeklong meditation & Buddhist teachings retreats.

Regions   England & Wales.

Rates   Nightly rates range by income anywhere from $18-30.

Rainbow Circle Camps   Europe

Annual events since 1988, Rainbow Circle Camps are operated by a totally volunteer staff of administrators, teachers and facilitators at rural sites rented from farmers in England and Wales. Each camp provides a play space for toddlers, a children's area, communal spaces for adult socializing and workshops, well being and first aid centers, and emergency cover. Some camps also have a sauna. No dogs are allowed.

Regular, annual offerings are the 10-day "Green Gathering & Creative Crafts Camp," the 8-day "Astrology & Self Discovery Camp," and the 8-day "Healing Camp." In 1993, other camps were the 2-day "Voice Liberation" and "Roots of Change" (exploring anger) weekends; the 3-day "Forest Fayre" and "Celebration of Life" long weekends; a 7-day "Healing Skills Training Week"; and an 8-day "Dance and Spirit Camp."

Address   Tim & Cherry Holland, Fivestones, Main Road, Whiteshill, Stroud, Gloucester GL6 6AU, ENGLAND

Phone   0453-759130.

Season   May through September.

Programs   2 to 10-day camps dedicated to planetary healing, personal awareness and inner growth.

Lodging   Campsites. BYO tent, sleeping bag & cooking equipment. Camp provides hot showers, earth privies, firewood & water.

Rates   Bottom & top of sliding scale range: weekly income under #50 — weekend #30, week #50, season ticket #60; weekly income over #400 — weekend #50, week #160, season ticket #280. Children free.

Meals   On site vegetarian cafe. Campers may also cook own meals.

Sivananda Yoga Retreats   Europe

England's Sivananda Yoga retreats are an abbreviated, English countryside version of the vacations available at North American and Indian Sivananda Yoga Ashrams. Each spring/summer season there are 5 or 6 retreats, each 2 to 7 days long. Attendance averages 40-50 people, with classes divided into groups by experience level. Instructors are from the staff of London's Sivananda Yoga Vedanta Centre. Beginners are welcome.

The day begins at 6 AM with meditation, chanting and a talk followed at 8 by hatha yoga. After the 10 o'clock brunch, retreatants are free to relax or go for a walk in the country. A 2 PM talk is followed at 4 by another session of asanas and pranayama. The day ends following a 6 o'clock dinner with meditation, chanting and a lecture. The two daily meals are vegetarian. Participation is required in all scheduled activities.

Address   Sivananda Yoga Vedanta Centre, 51 Felsham Road, London SW15 1AZ, ENGLAND

Phone   0817-800160. Fax 0817-800128.

Season   April through July.

Programs   Hatha yoga retreats.

Regions   England & Scotland. 1993 English retreat locations were Honiley Hall, Warwickshire; Dartington Centre, Totnes, Devon; and The Old Red Lion, Castle Acre, Norfolk. The Scottish retreat location was Orcharton House, Castle Douglas, Scotland.

Rates   Typical cost: #175 for a 4-day retreat.

Spring Grove   Europe

Spring Grove leads spiritual retreats in England, Germany, Switzerland, Austria, France, and Italy with one or two each year in Assisi, Italy — home of St. Francis and St. Clare. Usually an Assisi retreat can be conveniently combined with a Spring Grove retreat at another European holy site (e.g. the Taize community of French monks). All trips encourage an experience of inner peace and contemplative, spiritual community.

Spring Grove was created by Bruce Davis to assist people who are seeking spiritual respite. Bruce is a psychologist, spiritual guide and counselor, university professor of East-West spirituality, and author of books such as "Monastery Without Walls" and "My Little Flowers." Outside of Europe, Bruce also conducts retreats in India and the U.S. San Francisco Bay area.

Address   P.O. Box 807, Fairfax, CA 94930, USA

Phone   415/453-7799.

Season   Summer & fall.

Programs   2 to 9-day contemplative retreats at European holy sites. All retreats are conducted in English, but most attendees are from continental Europe.

Regions   Recent retreat sites: Assisi, Italy; Taize & Lourdes, France; Glastonbury, England; Medjugorje, Yugoslavia.

Rates   Assisi retreats: 6-day $650, 9-day $975. 1993 5-day Taize retreat $575 (or $1,095 in combination with 6-day Assisi retreat). Costs include meals, lodging & local transportation.

Yoga With Danielle   Europe

Each summer since 1988, Danielle Arin-Strutt has hosted two yoga vacations in her native France. Depending on the vacation, guests have no classes on Wednesday afternoon and/or Sunday. There are otherwise three daily classes totaling 5 1/2 to 6 hours of instruction. Sometimes classes are divided into groups by level of experience. Otherwise, all classes are taught by Danielle — a woman with 17 years of full-time yoga teaching experience.

The early summer Normandie vacation is at Le Moulin Foulon — a country location 48 miles from the English Channel. In the vicinity are castles, medieval towns, historical churches and France's largest Buddhist center. The late summer vacation alternates between Provence and the French Riviera. The 1992 Riviera site was a country house in the foothills of the Alps 6 miles from the Mediterranean. The 1993 Provence site was a restored monastery near historical Salon-de-Provence, 30 miles from Marsielle.

Address   Yew Tree Cottage, Spinfield Lane West, Marlow, Bucks SL7 2DB, ENGLAND

Phone   0628-486698.

Season   June through early September.

Programs   7 to 11-day yoga vacations with gourmet vegetarian cuisine and (depending on group size) single or shared rooms.

Regions   France — Provence (or French Riviera) & Normandy.

Rates   1993 room, board & tuition rates: 1 week Provence stay #280, 11-day Normandy stay #430.

Buddhist Society of Compassionate Wisdom   North America

Under the guidance of Zen Buddhist monk Samu Sunim, the Buddhist Society of Compassionate Wisdom operates temples in Chicago, Ann Arbor and Toronto. Visitors can usually arrange in advance to stay at any of these temples — participating in morning and evening meditation and chanting practice but otherwise free to rest or pursue their own spiritual path.

Each temple conducts Friday/Saturday overnight introductory meditation courses. Course graduates and other experienced meditators may participate in one, two and five-day intensive meditation retreats plus the annual two-month summer retreats at the Chicago and Toronto temples.

The daily summer retreat schedule is as follows: morning meditation at 5:30 AM, jogging and exercise at 7:30, breakfast at 8, sutra study from 10 to noon, lunch at 1 followed by a period of rest, manual work from 2:30 to 5:30, tea at 6, chanting and meditation from 7 to 9 PM.

Temple accommodations are modest — typically shared rooms convertible to dorm space with futon floor beds during introductory meditation weekends. The suburban Ann Arbor facility has a few single rooms. At all temples, there is a daily vegetarian breakfast and lunch plus evening tea.

Address   Chicago: 1710 W. Cornelia, Chicago, IL 60657, USA
Ann Arbor: 1214 Packard Road, Ann Arbor, MI 48104, USA
Toronto: 86 Vaughan Rd., Toronto, Ontario M6C 2M1, CANADA

Phone   Chicago: 312/528-8685. Ann Arbor: 313/761-6520.
Toronto: 416/658-0137. No visits without prior arrangement.

Season   Year-round.

Programs Introductory meditation courses; 1, 2 & 5-day intensive meditation retreats; 2-month summer retreats that may be attended for as short a period as three days.

Rates   Visitor $35/night. Introductory meditation retreat $140. Intensive meditation retreat: 1-day $60; 2-day $100; 5-day $200. Summer retreat — 3 days $75, 1 week $150, 1 month $400.

Center for the Dances of Universal Peace   North America

The Dances of Universal Peace were created by the late Samuel Lewis, an American Sufi teacher, as a synthesis of folk art and spiritual practice. From an initial body of about 50 dances, the collection has grown over the past 20 years to more than 500 dances drawn from a rich multitude of spiritual traditions. Now danced around the world, the Dances are celebrated every month by 40 to 60 grassroots groups in the U.S. alone.

In 1993, the International Center for the Dances of Universal Peace sponsored three camps open to beginners — a 7-day early July "Midwest Dance Camp" near Frontenac, MN; a 7-day late July North Pacific "Dance to Glory" camp at Breitenbush Hot Springs, OR; and a 7-day late August "East Coast Dance Camp" near Portland, CT. Meals are vegetarian. And all camp teachers are members of the Dances' Mentor Teacher Guild.

All dance camps are described in the Center's annual "Whole Dance Catalog," which also lists many other weeklong and weekend events throughout America and abroad. Other major 1993 Center-sponsored events included a 20-day dance pilgrimage to the Middle East; a 7-day Taos, NM retreat for advanced dancers; and three Pescadero, CA weekend dance retreats open to all.

Address   International Center for the Dances of Universal Peace, P.O. Box 626, Fairfax, CA 94978, USA

Phone   415/453-8159.

Season   Year-round but primarily July through October.

Programs Dance camps and Dance leader trainings.

Regions 1993 weeklong camps held in Oregon, Minnesota and Connecticut.

Rates 1993 camp rates: Oregon: tuition $365; room & board $360 (limited tenting for $325). Minnesota: tuition $300; room & board — villa $270, dorm $210, tent $175. Connecticut: tuition $300; room & board $175 for cabins or tents.

Donna Farhi Yoga Retreats   North America

Donna Farhi is a San Francisco Bay area Registered Movement Therapist and yoga teacher, certified in the Iyengar tradition. Donna's annual teaching activities include weekend yoga intensives conducted around the country, weekend and weeklong retreats at Rainbow Ranch, and weeklong retreats in Mexico. Donna's weeklong retreats generally allow a 2 or 3-day partial attendance option. At the retreats, Donna teaches two daily classes.

In 1993, Donna and Rainbow Ranch hosted a weekend women's retreat, a weekend mixed gender retreat, and a weeklong women's retreat. Near the hot springs town of Calistoga, Rainbow Ranch occupies 80 panoramic acres on the top of Mayacama mountain — a 1 1/2 hour drive north cf San Francisco. The Ranch contains a lake and hiking trails, a large outdoor swimming pool, and a large redwood lodge with hardwood floors for yoga practice. Retreatants share rooms and enjoy tasty vegetarian meals.

In southern Mexico, Donna hosted two 1993 six-day retreats. The February retreat was at the beachside Catalina Hotel in the Pacific Coast fishing village of Zihuatanejo. The November (Thanksgiving period) retreat was at a retreat center in Tepotzlan — a quiet and traditional village in a verdant valley ringed by jagged cliffs 37 miles northeast of Cuernavaca.

Address P.O. Box 460428, San Francisco, CA 94146, USA

Phone 415/821-2979.

Season Mexico — late fall & winter. California — January & summer.

Programs Weekend, 6 & 7-day yoga retreats.

Regions Southern Mexico & northern California.

Rates 6 & 7-day retreats $640-850 ($200-340 for 2 or 3-day partial attendance option). California weekend retreat $235. Rates do not include airfare or ground transportation costs.

Down To Earth   North America

Down To Earth conducts workshops in the canyons of Arizona and New Mexico, where participants are encouraged to explore their connections to the land and to express those connections in the form of art. Some workshops focus on the therapeutic value of the creative experience. Others focus on learning the skills of pastel painting, papermaking and collage.

All workshops are facilitated by two registered art therapists — pastel landscape artist Jane Schoenfeld and papermaker/collage artist Ellen Schechner-Johnson. Room and board is provided by Triangle T Guest Ranch in Dragoon, AZ and Ghost Ranch Retreat Center in Abiquiu, NM. Enrollment is limited to 20 participants per workshop.

Address   P.O. Box 5912, Santa Fe, NM 87502, USA

Phone   505/986-1108.

Season   February through June.

Programs   4 to 7-day workshops of two types: art therapy, and landscape painting. All levels of art experience welcome at all workshops.

Regions   High desert of southern Arizona & northern new Mexico.

Rates   Tuition, meals & double occupancy accommodations: 4-day $450, 5-day $465-555, 7-day $690.

Eastwest Retreats   North America

Eastwest conducts two annual retreats combining Holotropic Breathwork and vipassana meditation. One retreat is held on a New England campus. The other is in southern California's Joshua Tree desert. The daily schedule includes morning lectures and meditation; afternoon breathwork and mandala drawing; evening meditation and small group discussions. Each participant works with a partner and silence is observed (except during sessions) throughout each retreat. Rooms are shared. Meals are vegetarian.

Each retreat is led by Jack Kornfield, Stanislav and Christina Grof. Jack is a clinical psychologist and vipassana meditation teacher trained as a monk in Thailand, Burma and India. Stan is a psychiatrist, scholar and the inventor of Holotropic Breathwork — a method of inner self-healing that explores early life, perinatal and transpersonal memories and images. Founder of The Spiritual Emergence Network, Christina is a research specialist in the relationship between mystical states and clinically-defined psychosis, addiction and spiritual emergence.

Address   P.O. Box 12, Philo, CA 95466, USA

Phone   707/895-2856.

Season   Late summer (east) & fall (west).

Programs   6-day retreats combining instruction & practice of Holotropic Breathwork and insight meditation (vipassana).

Regions   Southern California desert & central New England.

Rates   Each retreat $775.

Iyengar Yoga Retreats   North America

Annual weeklong Iyengar Yoga Retreats are held in Baja, Mexico and Maui, Hawaii. The Baja retreat is in May at the Hotel Cabo San Lucas Resort, a 2,500 acre estate on historic Chilene Bay. The Maui retreat is in July at the Hana-Maui, a luxurious 50-acre beachside hotel surrounded by 4,700 acres of working ranch lands. Other, annual weeklong retreats usually include another in Mexico (in Tepoztlan in 1993 and Tulune in 1994) and a Rocky Mountains "Yoga & Ski Vacation" (at Crested Butte, CO in 1994).

All retreats are led or co-led by Elise Miller, a certified Iyengar yoga teacher in the San Francisco Bay area since 1976. Also a hypnotherapist with an MA in Therapeutic Recreation, Elise combines yoga instruction with private counseling for back problems and other sports related injuries.

The Maui retreat is co-led by Lolly Font, Director of the California Yoga Center. The 1994 Rocky Mountain retreat was co-led by Karin Stephan, co-director of the B.K.S. Iyengar Center of Somerville, MA.

At each retreat, yoga sessions are held in the early morning and late afternoon. This allows vacationers plenty of time to rest or enjoy activities such as swimming, hiking, horseback riding or skiing. Packages generally include breakfast and a dinner option with a menu oriented toward fruits, vegetables and fish.

Address   Elise Miller, 1081 Moreno Ave., Palo Alto, CA 94301 USA

Phone   415/493-1254.   Fax 415/857-0925.

Season   Usually May through October.

Programs   One-week, Iyengar style, hatha yoga retreats.

Regions   Mexico, Hawaii & Rocky Mountains.

Rates   Retreat fee, lodging, most meals & yoga instruction $875-1,495. Round trip transportation to retreat site is not included.

Miracles Community Network   North America

The Miracles Community Network (MCN) hosts two annual conferences on "A Course In Miracles" (ACIM). Each conference features some 20 to 30 facilitators, speakers and entertainers in experiential workshops, roundtable discussions, informal group meetings and evening entertainment. Workshops generally focus on skills such as "Inner Listening" and "Forgiveness" that involve the understanding and application of ACIM principles. MCN sometimes offers a pre-conference program and invites attendees to stay for a few days after each conference to become involved in planning the next event.

At conference and retreat centers in the Sangre de Christo Mountains of northern New Mexico, MCN also conducts a weeklong summer institute plus two weeklong winter retreats. The institute includes ACIM workshops, musical events, a special children's program, and time to explore the region. Each winter retreat is led by a spiritual director, who guides retreatants in meditation, prayer, group singing, dancing and healing ceremonies. Miracles Community Network also publishes "Miracles Magazine."

Address   P.O. Box 418, Santa Fe, NM 87504, USA

Phone   505/989-3656.   Fax 505/982-4159.

Season   Events throughout the year.

Programs 5-day "Course In Miracles" conferences plus a 7-day summer institute, each with many workshops. Also weeklong winter healing & devotional retreats.

Regions   Past conference sites: Vermont, New York, Virginia, Colorado & California. Summer institute & winter retreats in New Mexico.

Rates   Winter retreat fee of $750 includes meals & shared rooms. Conference tuition of $300 & institute tuition of $350 both include meals. Hotel accommodations generally $45-80/night. All meals with vegetarian options.

Painting From The Source   North America

"Painting From The Source" workshops and vacations are "about painting purely for the joy of exploration and expression," explains artist and practicing psychotherapist Aviva Gershweir. Aviva hosts weekend workshops about 7 times each year at her Spencertown, NY residence, a Berkshires retreat with simple accommodations for 11-15 overnight guests. She prefers that people attend a weekend workshop before attending a 7-day intensive.

Spring and summer intensives are held in New Mexico at the 200 acre Synergia Ranch, an artists' community 20 miles south of Santa Fe on the rim of the Galisteo Basin. Synergia's facilities include single guest rooms opening onto adobe courtyards, spacious studios, outhouses, and a communal shower house. The surrounding high desert scenery includes gardens, orchards, and clear vistas of the Sangre De Cristo Mountains.

For the first time, a "Drawing From The Source" weekend workshop was also held in early 1994 in New River, Arizona — 20 miles north of Phoenix in the colorful Sonora Desert.

Address   Aviva Gershweir, RD 2, Box 197 A-1, Ghent, NY 12075, USA

Phone   518/392-2631 or 718/454-2231.

Season   From time-to-time throughout the year.

Programs Weekend & weeklong self-expressive painting retreats.

Regions   The Berkshires (Spencertown, NY), the New Mexican Galisteo Basin, and Arizona's Sonora Desert.

Rates   Weekend in the Berkshires: $250 for workshop, materials, 2 nights & 4 vegetarian meals. 7-day Synergia Ranch intensive: $600 for workshop & materials plus $280 for room & full board (vegetarian with some fish). Arizona weekend $330 all inclusive.

Rites of Passage Island Retreats for Women   North America

Rites of Passage Island Retreats for Women are held in early spring and fall on Nantucket and two southwest Florida coast islands — the private island of Useppa and Cayo Costa (due west of Fort Myers). Each year there are usually four 5-day retreats and two weekend retreats. Retreatants are housed in cottages (on Nantucket), private homes and at camp grounds.

All retreats give women the opportunity to gather and celebrate the changes in their lives through ritual, drumming, chanting, vision telling, guided meditations, campfire sharings, and full moon circles. Useppa retreats include workshops on co-dependency issues. There is also time for recreational activities such as tennis, swimming or a walk on the beach.

Retreats are led by Lynda McHugh, experienced in 12-Step and women's group processes. Co-facilitators sometimes include therapists and counselors.

Address   547 North Yachtsman Drive, Sanibel Island, FL 33957, USA

Phone   813/472-3276.

Season   March/April, October/November.

Programs 5-day & weekend women's self-empowerment workshops.

Regions   Southwest Florida coast islands & Nantucket (an island off the south Cape Cod coast of Massachusetts).

Rates   5-day workshops: Nantucket $645, Useppa $450. Weekend workshops on Cayo Costa $195. Rates include three daily vegetarian meals, lodging, and boat transportation to & from the mainland.

Sacred Circle   North America

The Sacred Circle conducts programs that integrate seasonal celebration and medicine wheel teachings into an experience of personal and collective wholeness. The creator and primary facilitator of Sacred Circle gatherings is Susan Rangitsch, an experienced group process leader who developed a model for transpersonal group facilitation as the core of her doctoral dissertation. Sacred Circle co-facilitators often include a ceremonial drummer, a Reiki practitioner and/or a Jungian therapist.

About half of the programs are held at Circle Arrow Ranch and Feathered Pipe Ranch in western Montana. These include three annual events: a summer solstice gathering, a "Women's Harvest Celebration," and training in "The Art and Practice of Creating and Sustaining Sacred Space Within Community."

Programs scheduled for 1994 also included a weeklong vision quest in Arizona, a workshops at Chinook Learning Center in Washington state, and two workshops at Phoenicia Pathwork Center in new York state. Rooms are shared, and meals are vegetarian or have a vegetarian option.

Address   Dr. Susan Rangitsch, 400 Cote Lane, Missoula, MT 59802, USA

Phone   406/542-2383.

Season   February through October.

Programs   4 & 5-day gatherings & workshops for emotional & spiritual healing. Also 9-day transpersonal group facilitation training.

Regions   Western Montana, upstate New York, and Washington's Puget Sound.

Rates   4-day summer gathering $295. 4 or 5-day workshop $385-585. 9-day training with follow-up consultation and direction $1,295.

Shared Heart Foundation   North America

The Shared Heart Foundation is Barry and Joyce Vissell — a medical doctor and a registered nurse. The Vissells are parents of three children, authors of several books, and leaders of workshops on relationship, parenting and healing. Each year since 1987, they have conducted a 7-day "Living From the Heart" Hawaii retreat for couples, individuals and families. Barry and Joyce now lead similar retreats — using group process, guided visualization, yoga, ritual and circle dances — throughout the U.S.

The Vissells' 16 acre combination home/center overlooks Monterey Bay and Peninsula from the Santa Cruz Mountains. The property includes a hot tub, indoor showers, camping sites, RV parking spots, and nearby toilet facilities. In the area are remote beaches and redwood forests. During the warm months, the home/center hosts weekend workshops, a 7-day "Creating More Fulfilling Relationships" retreat, 10-day "Shared Heart" and couples trainings. Meals are vegetarian, and special dietary needs can be met.

Address   P.O. Box 2140, Aptos, CA 95001, USA

Phone   408/684-2130 or 800/766-0629. Call before visiting.

Season   Year-round (April through September at home/center).

Programs   Weekend, 5, 7 & 10-day workshops, retreats & trainings dedicated to awakening people to more loving relationships.

Regions   Mostly Hawaii, central California coast, and other West Coast locations. A few East Coast & Mid West retreats.

Rates   Home/center rates: weekend workshop $135-160, week retreat $495, 10-day training $850. 7-day Hawaii retreat (air fare not included): shared room $690-840, campsite $630-730.

Tai Chi in Paradise   North America

The Pacific School of Tai Chi conducts annual retreats in Costa Rica, Hawaii and the northwestern U.S. The Costa Rica site is a beachside Caribbean coast lodge bordered by primitive rain forests. The Hawaii site is Kalani Honua, a luxurious oceanside retreat center near black sand beaches and Volcanoes National Park. The northwest U.S. site is a hot springs resort in Oregon's Cascades Mountains or near Mt. Shasta, CA.

Each retreat is led by Chris Luth, a teacher with a warm, life-centered approach. Chris is also the 1990 American Tai Chi Forms Champion and internationally recognized for his abilities and innovations in Push Hands (interactive tai chi) and tai chi Energetics.

All retreats include at least seven hours of daily instruction for all levels — beginner, intermediate and advanced. Areas of instruction include tai chi Energetics and Forms, applied tai chi philosophy, Push Hands, and chi gung (energy work). Retreatants share comfortable rooms and enjoy three daily gourmet vegetarian meals.

Address   P.O. Box 962, Solana Beach, CA 92075, USA

Phone   619/259-1396.

Season   February, late June & August.

Programs 6 to 8-day tai chi retreats.

Regions   Costa Rica, Hawaii, northwestern U.S.

Rates   8-day Costa Rica retreat $1,925 (including rain forest & river tours plus round trip air fare from southwestern U.S. cities). 6-day Hawaii & 6-day northwest U.S. retreats each $650.

Vipassana Meditation Centers   North America

The four major North American Vipassana Meditation Centers (VMCs) are Vipassana Meditation Center (Shelburne Falls, MA), Northwest Vipassana Center (Onalaska, WA), Southwest Vipassana Meditation Center (Kaufman, TX) and California Vipassana Center (North Fork, CA). The Massachusetts and Washington centers each conduct 14 to 16 meditation courses each year. Course schedules for the Texas and California centers (each conducting 4 or 5 courses each year) may be obtained from the Washington center.

Virtually all VMC meditation courses are 10 days long, and all are taught by instructors trained by S.N. Goenka — a Burmese native (now resident in India) who has taught meditation for over 25 years. Students are asked to adhere to the daily schedule. Each day begins with a 4 AM wake-up bell and ends with lights out at 9:30. During the day, group and individual sitting meditation periods span at least 10 hours. There is also a daily 1 1/4 hour evening videotape of S. N. Goenka meditation teachings.

VMC accommodations are generally quite simple. Meals are also simple — vegetarian breakfast and lunch plus an evening tea. New students may take fruit with their tea. All students observe silence except during teacher interviews and evening question and answer periods.

Address	For Eastern U.S. retreat schedules: Vipassana Meditation Center, P.O. Box 24, Shelburne Falls, MA 01370, USA For Western U.S. retreat schedules: Northwest Vipassana Center, P.O. Box 10261, Portland, OR 97210, USA
Phone	Massachusetts: 413/625-2160. Oregon: 503/227-1065 No visits without prior arrangement.
Season	Late February through late December.
Programs	Rigorous, 10-day guided Vipassana meditation retreats.
Regions	Northwestern Massachusetts, southwestern Washington, northeastern Texas, and central California.
Rates	Instruction, food & lodging are financed solely by donations from people who have completed at least one 10-day course.

8 Journeys

This chapter contains profiles of organizations that lead trips and tours with a significant spiritual or holistically healing orientation.

All journey profiles are arranged in alphabetical order within the regions ("Asia", "Europe," "North America" and "South America") that define geographical areas of trip specialization. Organizations that lead trips to more than one continent are profiled under the "Two or More Continents" category.

As it happens, all of the organizations profiled in this chapter are based in the United States. Consequently, the U.S. is the point of departure and return for all trips that include international airfare. Be that as it may, non-U.S. trip participants can usually arrange to pay for only the land portion of a journey, book their own flights, and join the group in the country that is the trip's initial destination.

Catalist Journeys	Two or More Continents

Catalist Journeys are advertised through "Catalist" — an international hybrid magazine/catalog for "rediscovering your personal magic." 1993's offerings were two, back-to-back Hawaiian rejuvenation weeks plus two, back-to-back tours in south Asia — one to Nepal and one to India. The back-to-back format created the option of a one or two week trip.

The Hawaiian retreats were at Akahi Farm and Silver Cloud Ranch, both on the island of Maui near white sand beaches and the dormant Haleakala volcano. Each included morning yoga and fitness classes, afternoon nature adventures, and evening programs — Hula, storytelling, bodywork sessions, talks on holistic medicine. Other options included massage, scuba diving, horseback riding, gourmet cooking classes, tarot and astrology readings.

The Nepal Sacred Cities tour included visits to sacred Hindu and Buddhist sites in the Himalayan cities of Kathmandu, Bhaktapur and Patan. It was followed by an India Ashram Tour with visits to sacred places such as the Taj Mahal, Rishikesh, and the Ganges River. Each day included cultural study, leisure activities, prayer and meditation.

Address   245 Fairview Ave., P.O. Box C.C., Boulder Creek, CA 95006, USA

Phone   408/338-7587.

Season   Summer (Hawaii) and fall (India/Nepal).

Programs   One week pilgrimages & rejuvenation retreats — each including spiritual/centering practices such as meditation & hatha yoga.

Regions   1993 Hawaii, Nepal & India tours — likely to be repeated.

Rates   India & Nepal double occupancy with most meals: each $1,350-1,400. Hawaii single occupancy with 3 daily vegetarian meals: $1,395-1,495. Prices do not include intercontinental airfare.

Deja Vu Tours   Two or More Continents

Deja Vu Tours each year conducts at least eight tours, each led by an experienced clairvoyant able to provide insights into special places and events. Each tour includes optional daily meditation sessions, ample leisure time, plus potentially healing encounters and/or explorations of sacred places. In the San Francisco Bay area, Deja Vu previews each tour through low cost evening workshops and daylong field trips.

Annual tours include a 10-day Hawaii retreat for working women, an India/Nepal trip that includes a 12-day beginner's trek in the Everest region, a 3-week trip to some part of the United States, one or two 10-day sea cruise/dolphins swimming expeditions in the Bahamas, plus two 2-week explorations of the world of Philippine faith healers — those that employ laying-on-of-hands and the "psychic surgeons."

New since World War II, Philippine psychic surgeons are trance mediums who act as conduits for healing spirits said to originate from an energy vortex near a mountain village. Without use of any instrument other than a hand, these healers effect physical and spiritual healing by reaching into the body and drawing out diseased parts or materializations of negative energy.

Address   2210 Harold Way, Berkeley, CA 94704, USA

Phone   510/644-1600.   Fax 510/644-1686.

Season   Year-round.

Programs   7 to 21-day spiritual adventures to sacred and magic sites.

Regions   Philippines, Nepal, India, the Holyland, Egypt, British Isles, Europe, the Bahamas, North America, Brazil, Peru & Hawaii.

Rates   Sample rates: 10-day Bahamas $1,500-2,200; 2-week Philippines $2,950-3,395; 3-week Nepal $4,295-4,995; 3-week Brazil 3,990-4,690. All costs (except low rate Bahamas option from Miami) include round trip transportation from San Francisco.

Discovery Passages   Two or More Continents

For over 15 years, Discovery Passages has conducted tours led or co-led by David Brandstein, professor of folklore, anthropology, and Native American studies at The New School For Social research. Annual passages include explorations of Central America's Mayan and Carib cultures plus the Hopi, Navajo and Pueblo cultures of the American southwest. New in 1993 were special trips to Nepal/Tibet and the Pine Ridge (South Dakota) Reservation of the Oglala Lakota (Sioux) people.

Accommodations are generally at national, state or private campsites with Discovery Passages providing all equipment except sleeping bags. Most meals are prepared in an outdoor, chuckwagon style with an emphasis on local cuisine. Land travel is usually by van, though some trips include river or sea excursions. The focus is on cultural and environmental awareness, but some trips include optional group activities such as visits with Native families, participation in Native ceremonies, guided yoga or meditation. There is also time for individual or group leisure activities.

Address   330 East 80th Street, New York, NY 10021, USA

Phone   212/628-4658.

Season   February through early September, plus December.

Programs 6 to 16-day journeys that explore the "spirit of place" through living simply on the land among Native peoples.

Regions   Western US (California, Arizona, Utah, Colorado, New Mexico & South Dakota), Central America, the Caribbean, Nepal & Tibet.

Rates   Sample 1993 rates: 12-day Pine Ridge, SD 1,650; 12 & 14-day US Southwest $1,600 each; 14-day Belize/Guatamala $1,999. Prices include airfare from New York (participants from other cities deduct air cost), land transportation, first and last night hotel accommodations, tents or tipis, most meals, & special events.

Eagle Connection   Two or More Continents

The Eagle Connection is an international network of individuals and organizations working for personal, communal and global transformation through cross-cultural and spiritual exploration. It is also a sponsor of trips to New Zealand, Bali/Lombok, and the Himalayas. Trip co-sponsors have included the Kalani Honua and Shenoa Retreat Centers, Omega Institute, New York Open Center, and the Institute of Transpersonal Psychology.

All trips are led by the Eagle Connection's co-directors — husband and wife John Broomfield and Jo Imlay. Inveterate campers who find spiritual inspiration in wilderness, John and Jo have traveled widely and lived for extended periods in India.

John is a native New Zealander, long-time student of shamanism, ethno-historian, and author. His latest book explores cross-cultural and inter-species learning. John is also past president of the California Institute of Integral Studies and past director of the University of Michigan's Center for South and Southeast Asian Studies.

Jo is an artist, teacher, and award-winning journalist who has focused her spiritual search on the integration of Buddhist, Hindu and shamanic understandings with the practice of contemplative Christianity.

Address   457 Scenic Road, Fairfax, CA 94930, USA

Phone   415/457-4513.   Email <eagle@igc.apc.org>

Season   Generally late winter, late summer & fall.

Programs 15 to 24-day journeys to places of great natural beauty and ancient spiritual traditions.

Regions   New Zealand, Bali & Lombok, the Indian Himalayas.

Rates   2-week Bali/Lombok trip $1,850. 3+ week New Zealand & Himalayan trips $2,700-2,800. Rates do not include international airfare.

Harmony Tours   Two Or More Continents

Harmony Tours each year conducts several trips ranging from 7 to 14 days in length. The 1993 schedule included a 14-day Bali trip and a 12-day Peru trip. The Bali trip was led by an American hypnotherapist and ordained Spiritualist minister. The Peru trip was led by a Quechua Indian, an American psychotherapist, and a spiritual messenger in the Incan tradition.

Each trip is designed to immerse travelers in the spirit of the people and the land. The Bali trip included morning meditations; visits to sacred lakes and temples; instruction in Balinese dance and sacred offerings; meetings with healers and mask makers; beach, jungle and volcano explorations. The Peru trip included visits to ancient Inca villages and sacred sites; a boat trip on Lake Titicaca; meditations, Machu Pichu sunrise rituals and four Medicine Wheel ceremonies.

Address   6 Angus Lane, Ashville, NC 28805, USA

Phone   704/299-0396.

Season   March through October.

Programs Spiritually oriented cultural tours.

Regions   Bali, Belize, Guatamala, Peru, New Mexico & Wyoming.

Rates   1993 rates: Bali trip $2,490 from Los Angeles & $2,790 from U.S. East Coast; Peru trip $2,350 from Miami. Trips include round trip airfare, all lodging & breakfasts, some lunches & dinners.

Noetic Sciences Travel Program   Two or More Continents

The Noetic Sciences Institute each year sponsors about a half dozen "Journeys to Awareness — of Self and Other." 1993 trips were as follows:

- 18 days "Exploring Healing, Spirituality and the World of the Maya" at Chiapas, Mexico. This trip included visits to Mayan ruins; talks with shamans; plus body/soul healing workshops with Joan and Myrin Borysenko.
- 17-day "Exploring Other Realities" trip to Brazil. This study tour included experiences with shamans, spiritual healers and trance mediums.
- 15-day "Remembering Who We Are" pilgrimage through Egypt, traveling by boat along the Nile, visiting temples, connecting with village people.
- 13-day "Land of the Totem" exploration of British Columbia, where the Cedar and Salmon Native people live at one with the Earth.
- 10-day "America the Ancient" tour of the American Southwest, a land of painted desert and mesas, Navajao and Pueblo cultures, and Anasazi ruins.
- 10-day "Experience of Wahi Pana" (sacred place) on Hawaii, sleeping by the ocean and exploring rain forests, waterfalls and volcanos.

Address P.O. Box 909, Sausalito, CA 94966, USA

Phone 415/461-7854 or 415/331-5650. Fax 415/331-5673.

Season Year-round.

Programs 10 to 18-day "journeys to awareness — of self and other."

Regions Recent trip destinations: Brazil, Egypt, the Himalayas, Mexico, southwest North America, British Columbia and Hawaii.

Rates 1993 rates: Brazil $4,045 from L.A. or $3,870 from Miami; Egypt $3,428 from New York; Hawaii $1,750 from the U.S. West Coast; British Columbia $2,775 from Vancouver; U.S. Southwest $2,295 from Albuquerque; Mexico $3,335 (airfare not included).

Power Places Tours & Conferences   Two or More Continents

For over 15 years, Power Places has been leading tours and conducting conferences at some of the world's most magnificent and spiritually powerful places. In 1993, the company hosted 11 tours and 3 annual conferences. A new and potentially fourth annual conference was held in early 1994. All programs are selected (and often led, co-led or facilitated) by Power Places owner Toby Weiss, a multi-lingual expert in transformative travel and holder of a Ph.D in the History of Consciousness.

Tours are led by guides chosen for their sensitivity to the essential spirituality of the region. For example, the 1993 Ireland tour was co-led by Tom McPherson and Kevin Ryerson. Known for his pragmatic wit and insight, Tom is an Elizabethan era Irishman who is channeled by Kevin.

Noted Egyptologist John Anthony West led two 1993 tours focusing on sacred science in ancient Egypt. And a trip to Tibet (plus Nepal) was led by the first two Westerners to live in Tibet since the Chinese takeover.

There are four annual conferences — one on channeling, one on sexuality and spirituality (new in 1994), one on healing, and one on Earth. The channeling conference features many of the world's best known channelers. Other conferences focus on the year's particular conference topic. For example, speakers at 1993's England-based "Crop Circles & Stonehenge" Earth conference included several crop circle experts. All conferences include workshops, rituals, ceremonies, music, dance, and community building.

Address   285 Boat Canyon Drive, Laguna Beach, CA 92651, USA

Phone   714/497-5138 or 800/234-8687.Fax 714/494-7448.

Season   Year-round.

Programs   1 to 3-week conferences & tours at sacred & mystical sites.

Regions   Bali, Egypt, Continental Europe, British Isles, New Mexico, Amazon/Brazil, India, Tibet/Nepal.

Rates   Tours: 2-week Peru $2,699 from Miami; 2-week Egypt $2,999 from New York; 2-week Amazon/Brazil $3,499 from Miami; 3-week Tibet/ Nepal $4,994 from California. Conferences: 1-week England $1,999 from New York; 1-week New Mexico $1,199 (airfare not included); 1-week Egypt $1,999 from New York; 11-day Peru $2,199 from Miami; 1-week Bali $2,499 from California.

Purple Mountain   Two Or More Continents

Purple Mountain Tours leads several trips each year to Europe and the eastern Mediterranean region. Regular journeys include a pilgrimage to Egypt and Mt. Sinai; a France "Grail-Quest" journey along the route of the Black Madonna; a mystical journey to the ancient God and Goddess centers of Greece and Turkey; and an Earth mysteries initiation journey to the British Isles. Each journey includes rituals and attunements to align with the power of these sacred places.

All tours are led by Helene Shik — a scholar, metaphysical teacher, psychic healer and spiritual midwife. At her combination home and healing center in southern Vermont, Helene also hosts mystery school and healers training programs. The 1993 school was co-facilitated by Dorothy Tod — a dowser, astrologer and independent film maker. The 1993 training programs were co-led by Helene, a chiropractor/holistic health doctor, and an expert in body centered emotional repatterning.

Address   R.D. 2, Box 1314, Putney, VT 05346, USA

Phone   802/387-4753 (also accepts fax). Call before visiting.

Season   February through October.

Programs Journeys of exploration into ancient sacred and metaphysical traditions. Also Vermont mystery school & healers trainings.

Regions   2-week trips to France, the British Isles, Greece/Turkey, and Egypt/ Mt. Sinai. Purple Mountain Healing Center in Vermont, USA.

Rates   1993 trip rates (with round trip airfare from New York): France $3,055 (or $2,411 without airfare); Egypt/Mt. Sinai $3,220 (or $2,470 without airfare); Greece/Turkey $3,300 (or $2,640 without airfare). Healing Center: 10-day mystery school $600, 2-week healers training $800, both programs together $1,300.

Rim Institute Pilgrimages   Two or More Continents

Arizona's Rim Institute each year sponsors several pilgrimages led by experts in sacred places and ancient cultures. Trips scheduled for 1994 were as follows:

- 16-day journey to the ancient sacred sites and crop circle regions of Great Britain. Led by Gestalt therapist Robert Mosby, assisted by experts on geomancy and England's sacred places.
- 14-day exploration of Maya culture on Mexico's Yucatan Peninsula. Led by author/ethnobotanist/explorer/philosopher Terence McKenna.
- 8-day visit with the Huichol Indians of Nayarit, Mexico. Led by shamanic counselor/photographer/visionary arts and healing expert Larain Boyll.

Address   Summer: HCR Box 162-D, Payson, AZ 85541, USA
Winter: 4302 N. 32nd St., Phoenix, AZ 85018, USA

Phone   602/263-0551 (summer). 602/478-4727 (winter).

Season   Winter and summer.

Programs 8 to 16-day journeys to sacred sites and mysterious places.

Regions   Mexico and Great Britain in 1994.

Rates   Sample rates: land cost for 6-day Mexico pilgrimage $1,050; land cost for 15-day Great Britain trip $3,500. Cost includes hotel lodgings, most meals, land transport, tuition and entrance fees.

Visions Travel   Two or More Continents

Visions Travel claims to be the only full service, bonded travel agency specializing in deluxe metaphysical tours to all areas of our planet. Each tour is led by a well known author or teacher plus a guide familiar with the region. The purpose is to bring together people in the spirit of the New Age for an interactive experience with the energies of sacred sites.

Recent trips included a 3 week exploration of India and states of consciousness led by Mystery Schools scholar and teacher Dr. Jean Houston; a 2 week U.S. Southwestern tour of Native American sacred sites led by Canada's Tanis Helliwell; and a 10-day Earth healing gathering of planetary lightworkers at Ayers Rock, Australia.

Directed by Abbas Nadim and Noah Linda Gale, Visions Travel provides an escort for each group to insure that all promised services are provided. The agency also insures that all rituals and ceremonies are conducted in private. For example, Visions Travel arranged exclusive private entry to the King's Chamber in the Great Pyramid of Giza for the 11:11 planetary activation.

Address   9841 Airport Blvd., Suite 520, Los Angeles, CA 90045, USA

Phone   310/568-0138 or 800/888-5509. Fax 310/568-0246.

Season   Year-round.

Programs 7 to 21-day metaphysical adventure tours to wild & sacred places.

Regions   U.S. Rocky Mountains & Southwest, Mexico, Peru, Australia, Bali, India, Israel, England, the Bahamas.

Rates   7-day Bahamas $1,644 on boat from Ft. Lauderdale, 12-day Bali $2,200 from Los Angeles, 14-day American Southwest $2,871 ground transport from Albuquerque to Phoenix, 10-day Australia $2,992 from Los Angeles, annual 21-day India $3,500 from Los Angeles.

Well Within   Two Or More Continents

Well Within enhances it's tours to mysterious, sacred and healing places with on-trip experiential workshops, pre and post-trip home study courses. Many trips include anywhere from 15 to 30 contact hours for nurses in attendance. Trips scheduled from fall 1993 to fall 1994 included:

- 17-day tour of Scottish sacred sites and healing centers. Workshops on homeopathic medicine, Bach Flower Remedies, meditation, yoga, alternative healing therapies, Celtic & pre-Celtic mythology & legends.
- 17-day trip to England & Wales. Workshops: same as on Scottish trip with Goddess workshop replacing meditation workshop.
- 17-day tour of Ireland with workshops on shiatsu, aikido, painting, homeopathy, Celtic myth and legend.
- 16-day trip to Greece. Workshops: introduction to homeopathy; women as healers; mythology, psychology & health.
- 15 days touring hot springs and spas of Switzerland and Germany with workshops on hydrotherapy, homeopathic medicine, lymphatic/acupressure facial massage, and spa therapy in the European health care system.

- 8-day trip to the Hawaiian island of Kauai with workshops including "Living Your Vision" and "Hawaiian Myths and Legends."

Address   2517 El Camino del Norte #1, Encinitas, CA 92024, USA

Phone   619/632-1646.   Fax 619/632-0709.

Season   Year-round.

Programs 8 to 17-day trips to healing places with workshops conducted on site and en route.

Regions   Bali, Egypt, Greece, British Isles, Switzerland, Germany, Mexico, Hawaii.

Rates   15 to 17-day trips range from $1,700 to $1,00. The Hawaii trip is $695-720. All trips include lodging, some meals, entrance fees, ground transportation, and (in some cases) continuing education for attending nurses.

Danu Enterprises — Asia

Danu Enterprises specializes in tours of Indonesia and Bali. Danu's Bali arts tours usually spend at least 14 nights in Ubud, Bali's cultural center, plus several days at beachside villages. All Bali arts tours include seminars on local customs and culture, village festivals, language instruction, visits to Hindu and Buddhist temples, music and dance performances, visits to the Elephant Cave, plus leisure time.

Danu's "Healing Arts" tours include meetings with traditional healers; trance purification ceremonies; Balinese music and dance performances; herbal medicine instruction; massages by Balinese healers; daily morning Iyengar yoga sessions and evening discussion sessions. And Danu's "Experiencing the Arts" tours include instruction in traditional dance, batik, water color, mask carving, or Gamelan orchestra with some of Bali's finest working artists.

Danu tours are organized and led by the husband/wife team of Made Surya and Judy Slattum, who live in Bali for half of each year. The son of a Bali Hindu priest, Made performs and teaches mask dance in California. Judy is author of the book "Masks of Bali: Spirits of an Ancient Drama" and has been leading Bali tours since 1979. On the "Healing Arts" tour, morning yoga and evening discussion groups are led by Roberta Bristol — a licensed massage therapist, yoga instructor and college professor of dance.

Address   313 McCormick Ave., Capitola, CA 95010, USA

Phone   408/476-0543 (also accepts fax).

Season   January through March, July through September.

Programs Four annual 16 to 21-day trips: 2 "Healing Arts" trips & 2 "Experiencing the Arts" trips.

Regions   Bali.

Rates $2,850-2,950 includes round trip airfare from San Francisco, Los Angeles or New York; shared accommodations; and daily breakfast.

Insight Travel   Asia

Insight Travel leads pilgrimages to archaeological sites, villages and temples important to Buddhist and Hindu culture in south central Asia. Each trip includes background lectures; opportunities to meet with Buddhist and Hindu teachers at pilgrimage destinations; daily group meditation; and free time for individual explorations.

Seven trips are scheduled for 1994: 21 days in India and Nepal, a 17 day trip to Dharamsala, 15 days in Ladakh, two monthlong expeditions to Tibet, and two trips (17 and 21 days) to Bhutan. Several of these trips include stays in Kathmandu, Nepal and 3-day treks — around Mount Kaila (axis-mundi of Buddhist cosmology) in the case of Tibet. The India/Nepal trip also includes visits to the Buddha's birth place and place of enlightenment.

Address   602 South High Street, Yellow Springs, OH 45387, USA

Phone   800/688-9851 or 513/767-1102.

Season   January through October.

Programs Pilgrimages to traditional Buddhist & Hindu sites.

Regions   Bhutan, India, Ladakh, Nepal & Tibet.

Rates   1994 trip land costs: India/Nepal $3,250, Dharamsala $2,850, Ladakh $2,600, Tibet/Mt. Kailas $5,950, Bhutan $4,850. Costs include air transport within Asia but do not include round trip airfare from North America.

Kathmandu Valley Tours   Asia

Kathmandu Valley Tours leads 21 to 23-day cultural and religious explorations (five in 1993) in and around Kathmandu, Nepal. Each trip includes tours of Tibetan monasteries in Boudhanath and Swayambhu; 2 nights in Kathmandu; visits to sacred Buddhist sites in the Banepa Valley; tours of the cities of Bhaktapur and Patan; and 2 days on the valley rim with a sunrise view of the Himalayas. And each trip coincides with major Hindu and Buddhist festivals, some of which may be joined by trip participants.

All trips are led by Cilla Brady, a former Kathmandu resident. Cilla's business partner is her husband Ananda, who she met in Kathmandu while both were studying goldsmithing under blood related jewelers. Cilla had felt "mysteriously drawn to the east" and found in Kathmandu that she had "a natural affinity with both the Nepali and Tibetan people." Each trip includes visits to the homes of Cilla's Tibetan and Nepali friends.

Address   P.O. Box 873, Bolinas, CA 94924, USA

Phone   415/868-0285.

Season   Mid-February through mid-November.

Programs   Participatory exploration of Buddhist & Hindu religious culture.

Regions   Kathmandu Valley, Nepal.

Rates $3,000 per 21 to 23-day tour, includes round trip airfare from 3 U.S. West Coast cities + possible overnight stopover in Bangkok.

Mindful Journeys   Asia

Mindful Journeys conducts Asia tours for individuals and groups. Late 1993 offerings included a mystic journey to Bhutan with a monastery stay during a traditional festival; a Buddhist journey through China, Tibet, Nepal and India with a stay at Tibet's Tsurphu Monastery; plus a trek around the base of Tibet's sacred Mt. Kailas. Other 1993/1994 expeditions included two Yangtze River voyages, a "Bengal Rivers" trip, an "India's Arts" trip, and a "Himachal Himalayan Holiday" with a visit to Dharamsala.

Address   1242 24th Street, Santa Monica, CA 90404, USA

Phone   310/828-5443.   Fax 310/829-9169.

Season   August through May.

Programs   7 to 45-day Asia adventure, culture and pilgrimage tours.

Regions   India, Nepal, Pakistan, Bhutan, Tibet, China, Indochina, Thailand, Bangladesh, Sri Lanka.

Rates   Trips rates of $1,495 to $5,110 include round trip airfare from U.S. West Coast + (usually) all meals & double occupancy lodging.

Sai Ram   Asia

For over 12 years, Dr. Wilma Bronkey has led pilgrimages to the presence of Sathya Sai Baba — a south Indian saint worshipped by millions as God incarnate. Dr. Bronkey also hosts regional Sai Baba retreats and directs a residential care facility for older people at her home in southwest Oregon.

Since he was a child, Sai Baba has regularly performed miraculous healings and object materializations — intended to prove his divinity and to help all people realize that they too are divine. Over the past 45 years, Sai Baba has inspired many books — on his life, his teachings, and their impact on the lives of his devotees. Sai Baba has also inspired the building of hundreds of clinics and schools, where human values are learned through study of the lives of saints from all religions.

The pilgrimage destination is Prasanthi Nilayam ("Abode of Great Peace"), the birth place and primary residence of Sai Baba. The ashram provides simple vegetarian meals and dorm facilities for men, women and families. All daily activities are entirely optional. These include early morning devotional worship, darshan (viewing of the saint) at 7 AM and 4 PM, bhajans (group chanting in praise of God) at 9 PM and 9 AM, and educational lectures at 8 and 10 AM for overseas devotees.

Address   Enchanted Acres, 1151 Summit Loop, Grants Pass, OR 97527, USA

Phone   503/479-9066.

Season   Summer (usually August) & winter (December/January).

Programs   Twice yearly, 2 to 4 week pilgrimages to the ashram of Sai Baba.

Regions   South India — Madras, Bangalore & Puttaparthi. Stops in Singapore & Hong Kong on way to & from U.S. West Coast.

Rates   3 week trip $1800-1950 with round trip airfare from West Coast U.S. cities such as San Francisco, Seattle & Portland.

Yoga in Bali   Asia

Yoga in Bali is a vacation and study tour in a land where art is so much a part of the culture as to be a way of life. Each tour group spends five nights by the ocean at Candi Dasa's ashram for orientation to Bali's food, language and culture. The group then spends one or two weeks in Ubud, Bali's cultural center. Ubud accommodations are Balinese bungalows set among tropical gardens, a swimming pool, and an open-air yoga pavilion.

Each trip includes daily yoga classes with trip leader Ann Barros, a Certified Yoga Instructor who has studied in India with B.K.S. Iyengar. Ann also has a strong dance background plus interests in art, music, Yoga and Hindu guidance. She has led Yoga in Bali tours each year since 1985.

Address   Ann Barros, 1540 Merrill Street, Santa Cruz, CA 95062, USA

Phone   408/475-8738.

Season   February & August.

Programs   2 & 3-week yoga vacation/study tours.

Regions   Bali.

Rates $2,500-2,700 including airfare from California. Does not include lunch or dinner during stay in Ubud.

Ana Tours   Europe

Ana Tours conducts two annual tours of Asia Minor, the cradle of the ancient religion of the Great Mother. The tour guide and lecturer is Dr. Resit Ergener, author of "Anatolia, Land of the Mother Goddess." Dr. Ergener is also a professional tour guide and a professor at Bosporus University in Istanbul, where each tour starts and ends.

Tour highlights include Catalhoyuk, the prehistoric temple city dedicated to the Goddess; the Tomb of Mevlana, founder of the mystical Sufi sect; a visit to an active goddess shrine in Ephesus, center of the religion of the Great Artemis; exploration of the site of Troy; and Istanbul's Great Mother at Aya Sofia, a monumental church dedicated by Byzantine Christians to Saint Sophia — Goddess of Holy Wisdom. Tours also include opportunities for swimming in the Gulf of Antalya, a Turkish bath and a hot springs stop.

Address   315 Crestview Drive, Santa Clara, CA 95050, USA

Phone   408/246-7646 (also accepts fax).

Season   Spring through late summer.

Programs   "On The Trail of the Great Goddess" 10 & 13-day tours open to all but often including only women. Private tours can be arranged.

Regions   Turkey.

Rates   Group rate land package of $1,710-1,990 includes double occupancy in 4 star hotels, porter service, all fees & meals (vegetarian options), restaurant tips, taxes & all transportation in Turkey.

Spirit of Medugorje   Europe

On June 25, 1981, in the small mountain village of Medugorje, Herzegovina, an apparition identifying Herself as Blessed Virgin Mary, Queen of Peace appeared and spoke to six children. She has continued to appear to these young people, now in their 20s, with the message that "God exists. He is the fullness of life, and to enjoy this fullness and obtain peace, you must return to God" through prayer, fasting and penance.

Since 1981, millions of pilgrims have come to Medugorje. Some villagers and pilgrims notice rays of light when Mary appears daily to the original visionaries. Most people feel a deeply peaceful, healing presence. And there have been many spiritual healings among returning pilgrims, some of which also experience emotional, psychological or even physical healings.

Halted for a time by the civil war in the former country of Yugoslavia, the Center For Peace is again leading pilgrimages to Medugorje. Pilgrims stay as guests with local families who provide breakfast and dinner. They also meet with the visionaries and Father Jozo, a parish priest recognized by the Queen of Peace as "a living saint." "Come to Medugorje. Our Lady will protect you," is the message of Father Jozo, who relates that peace will come to the country through the prayers of brave pilgrims.

Address   Center For Peace, P.O. Box 1425, Concord, MA 01742, USA

Phone   508/371-1235.   Fax 508/369-4472.

Season   Year-round, with special trips for June anniversary of first appearance and early December Feast of Immaculate Conception.

Programs 9-day pilgrimages to site of ongoing Marian apparitions.

Regions   A small village in a primitive mountainous region of Herzegovina, one of the nations liberated by the Yugoslavian civil war.

Rates   Pilgrimage $1,199-1,399. Includes food, lodging, ground transportation and round trip airfare from Boston or New York.

Creative Energy Options   North America

Creative Energy Options (CEO) ran three, 8-day inner/outer adventures in 1994: a Mexico trip including exploration of Oaxaca's ancient pyramids, a New Year's festival, Pacific coast sun and beaches; and two U.S. southwest trips including white water rafting, Native American medicine teachers, sweat lodge and pottery. All trips are led by CEO directors Herb Kaufman and Sylvia Lafair (both amateur potters) plus a psychotherapist/southwest native who gives workshops on "Geomancy: the Healing Power of Place."

CEO also hosts weekend holistic healing retreats at its 50 acre Pocono Mountains retreat center, 1 1/2 hours from Philadelphia or New York City. Popular, repeat include "Bridges to Remembering" with Pat Rodegast and Emmanuel, "Lighten Up" (addressing chronic weight problems), and "Healing Paths" (for those with chronic or life threatening illnesses).

Address   909 Sumneytown Pike, Ste. 105, Spring House, PA 19477, USA

Phone   215/643-4420.   Fax 215/643-7031.

Season   Year-round.

Programs Inner/outer adventure vacations plus weekend healing retreats.

Regions   Southern Mexico, New Mexico/Arizona, and Pennsylvania Poconos.

Rates   1994 8-day trips: Mexico $2,175; New Mexico $1,850. All trips include double occupancy lodging, all meals on trail & 2 daily meals in town. Weekend retreat $225-325.

Omega Journeys   North America

Omega Journeys sponsors trips that harmonize outer journey with inner exploration. Each trip is led by experienced guides and is limited to no more than 20 participants. The following 1992 trips were repeated in 1993:

- 1-week "Wilderness Rite of Passage for Women" involving 2 days of Southwestern mountain country backpacking, campwork, singing, drumming, and sacred teachings from Buddhist and Native American traditions.
- 10-day "Questing for a Vision" including 2 days of preparation through dreamwork, meditation, drumming, dance and sweat lodge followed by 3 days and nights alone in the Utah Canyonlands.
- 1-week "Catskills Wilderness Encounter" including backpacking, animal tracking, campcraft skills, chanting & sweat lodge ritual.

Other recent journeys have included "Bali: Land of Spirit"; rafting with Cree Indians on the Great Whale River in northern Quebec; tracking animals, rock writings and thousand-year-old footprints in the New Mexico desert.

Address   Omega Institute, RD 2, Box 377, Rhinebeck, NY 12572, USA

Phone   914/266-4444 or 800/944-1001.

Season   April through October.

Programs   Adventure travel trips combining inner & outer exploration.

Regions   Mountain & high desert areas of southern California, southern Utah & northwestern New Mexico; Quebec's James Bay and Magpie River regions; the Florida Keys.

Rates   5 to 10-day North American trips $415-850 including meals, lodging & ground transportation. 14-day Bali trip $2,950 including round trip airfare from Los Angeles.

Magical Journey to Peru   South America

Magical Journey leads four annual transformative journeys to Peru — to visit and explore the ancient Andean city of Cusco, the Sacred Valley of the Incas, the medicinal hot springs of Aguas Calientes, the Amazon jungle, and the ruins of Machu Pichu — once the Inca's great City of Light. Transformative journey participants spend two days on a Quechua farm below Machu Pichu Peak and usually have the option of a two-day Inca Trail trek.

Transformative journeys are led by Carol Cumes and Romulo Lizarraga, co-authors of a book on the traditions and spirituality of the Quechua people — descendants of the Incas. Additional, Peruvian wilderness treks are led by Carol's husband David, an M.D. interested in the psychological effects of the wilderness experience. All trips include meditations at sacred sites plus participation in shamanic healing ceremonies.

Address   Carol Cumes, 4147 Marina Drive, Santa Barbara, CA 93110, USA

Phone   805/682-6920.   Fax 805/682-8440.

Season   Spring and fall.

Programs   16-day transformative journeys & wilderness treks.

Regions   Peru.

Rates $3,250 with round trip airfare from Los Angeles, or $2,450 for land costs only. Rates include all transportation within Peru, entrance fees, trail meals, Quechua farm & Amazon lodge stays.

9 Wilderness Programs

This chapter contains profiles of organizations that run programs (e.g. vision quests) in which the wilderness experience is a major component. The profiles are arranged in alphabetical order under "Two or More Continents" and "North America." The first three organizations offer wilderness experience programs in both North America and on other continents.

Great Round — Two or More Continents

The Great Round leads 10-day vision quests in California, Nevada and southern Australia. Each quest incorporates shamanic traditions to encourage in participants a more expanded and confident sense of self. Programs range in size from 4 to 14 participants plus 2 to 5 staff members. And all are led by trained psychologists Sedonia Cahill and Barton Stone. Sedonia is a counselor and co-author of "The Ceremonial Circle." Barton is a sculptor, dreamwork teacher and long time Zen practitioner.

U.S. quest programs begin an hour north of San Francisco with a day of orientation, instruction and ceremony in a private home. On day 2, staff and questers car pool to the desert. Base camp is established on Sunday, and each quester finds a quest spot on Monday. Tuesday through Thursday is solo time (fasting optional) ending with an all night vigil. Friday and Saturday is a time for telling one's story, celebrating and beginning the integration process. Final Sunday — hot springs stop on the way home.

Southern Australia quests scheduled for September and October, 1994 include one in the Grampians departing from Balharring, Victoria plus one in the Flinders Range leaving from Stirling, South Australia.

Address   P.O. Box 1772, Sebastopol, CA 95473, USA

Phone   707/829-6681.   Fax 707/829-6691.

Season   Late March through October.

Programs 10-day vision quest programs.

Regions   California & Nevada desert: low desert in spring, high desert in summer. Also Southern Australia mountains.

Rates   U.S. quest — $500, including transportation & all meals (ample & delicious vegetarian food). Australian quest — about $900.

Sacred Passage   Two or More Continents

Sacred Passage conducts guided wilderness "Sacred Passage" experiences designed to help participants realize the oneness of their inner nature and the outer world. Most "Sacred Passages" are 11 days long, with seven days (six nights) of solo wilderness time. Pre-trip training covers camping and safety skills, discovering one's natural totem, healing movement, awareness skills, meditation, recognizing the Sacred View, and opening the heart. Participants bring their own camping equipment and food.

All "Sacred Passages" are guided by John Milton, a full time teacher of deep ecology, meditation and tai chi with over 19 years of wilderness retreat leadership experience. Drawing on his current and prior work as a professor of environmental studies, John has also written numerous books and articles on ecology and inner development.

Sacred Passage also conducts hybrid "Sacred Passage"/pilgrimage trips plus weekend tai chi, chi gung, meditation and/or awareness trainings.

Address   Drawer CZ, Bisbee, AZ 85603, USA

Phone   602/432-7353.

Season   Year-round.

Programs 8 & 11-day Sacred Passage wilderness programs, 21 to 23-day hybrid Sacred Passage/pilgrimage programs, weekend intensives.

Regions   "Sacred Passages" conducted in Mexico's Baja California peninsula; Arizona's Chiricahua Mountains; Colorado's San Juan & Sangre de Cristo Mountains; and West Virginia's Appalachian Mountains. Hybrid "Sacred Passage"/pilgrimage trips to Nepal & Mexico. Weekend intensives in Arizona, Florida & Massachusetts.

Rates   "Sacred Passage": 8-day $580; 11-day $680. 2 & 3-day intensive $188-270 (food & lodging arranged by each participant).

Wild Retreats   Two Or More Continents

Wild Retreats conducts wilderness retreats at a roadless site on Fall Lake, MN. On the site are several cabins with wood stoves, outhouses, cold water wells, a large tipi for indoor gatherings, a firepit for outdoor gatherings, a sweat lodge, many tent sites, and a lakeside cedar sauna. Though Ely, MN is only 8 miles away, one can travel north from the camp through 100 miles of lake and forest wilderness before crossing a road.

In 1993, there were five Fall Lake retreats: a women-only retreat, two mixed gender retreats, and two men-only retreats. Some retreats offer the option of a 3-day solo fasting quest. All retreats are organized (and some co-led) by Joe Laur, Executive Director of the New Warrior Network.

Wild Retreats allow time for fishing, canoeing, swimming and forest hikes. They also ground each participant in a strong sense of community through various cooperative and small group activities — camp building and food preparation; morning workshops on waking to the wildness of soul and nature; drumming, dance and dreamwork; campfire council meetings, poetry and storytelling. Night skies sometimes glow with the Northern Lights.

Joe Laur also co-leads an annual men's Africa trip, which includes 5 days at Kenya'a Masai Mara Nature Reserve during the great wildebeest migration plus a 7-day Rift Valley trek with Samburu/Maasai warriors and elders.

Address   8426 N. Regent Road, Fox Point, WI 53217, USA

Phone   414/352-5053. 800/766-9199 (Tamu Safaris) for Africa trip.

Season   June through October plus 1 winter event.

Programs 5 to 8-day men only, women only, and mixed gender wilderness retreats. 16-day men's cross-cultural trip to Africa.

Regions   Most retreats in far northeast Minnesota. One in Kenya, Africa.

Rates   8-day retreat — sliding scale $375-575. Kenya trip $4,985 including roundtrip airfare from New York City.

Animas Valley Institute   North America

Animas Valley Institute (AVI) is situated at an altitude of 7,300 feet on 5 acres near the San Juan National Forest. The main house is a passive solar structure of rammed-earth and adobe. The property also contains a large yurt, campsites, sweat lodge, medicine wheel, and permaculture garden. It is here that most AVI programs begin and end.

The Institute offers many vision quest programs including ones for men, women, physicians, adolescents plus an annual 16-day "Returning to Earth Institute" — a rite of passage for current and potential (self-identified) leaders. Most questers fast during their time alone in the wilderness. AVI also runs non-quest programs such as a 7-day "Desert Mystery Journey" for people with wilderness ritual experience, and a 5-day wilderness "Quest for the Creative" ending with a 1-day "performance event" back in Durango.

The Institute's founding director is Bill Plotkin, a psychologist who has led quests and trained guides since 1980. AVI's two other senior guides are Steve and Jessica Zeller. Steve is an addictions counselor and creator of a wilderness program for people recovering from addictions. Jessica is a psychotherapist originally trained as an actress and dancer.

Address   54 Ute Pass Trail, Durango, CO 81301, USA

Phone   303/259-0585 (phone & fax) or 259-5656. Call before visiting.

Season   Mid-April through mid-October.

Programs   Vision quest & other wilderness programs (most 10 or 11-days long); vision quest guide training program; workshops on first-aid, ceremonial drum & rattle making, and sustainable living.

Regions   Spring & fall: slickrock canyon country of southeast Utah. Summer: San Juan Mountains & desert peaks of southern Colorado, the Rocky Mountains of western Montana.

Rates   16-day Returning to earth Institute $2,500; 11-day vision quest $850; 10-day vision quest for adults $795, for adolescents $450; 7-day Desert Mysteries Journey $475; 5-day Quest for the Creative $425; 6-day vision quest $359; 1-day Rattle-Making Workshop $75.

Breaking Through Adventures   North America

Breaking Through Adventures leads about a dozen wilderness trips each year. Each trip includes backpacking, rock climbing, mountaineering and/or white water rafting. Each also includes centering/attuning experiences such as solo vision quest, wilderness navigation, stalking, drumming, chanting, meditation, yoga and tai chi. Most trips are open to both men and women. A few are restricted to men only or women only.

All trips are led by a staff of therapists and wilderness skills experts directed by Rick Medrick, a pioneer in the field of transformative outdoor learning. His 32-day "Summer Outdoor Leadership Intensive" draws on the full gamut of Breaking Through Adventures' physical and centering disciplines. Rick also directs Arkansas River Tours, the Whitewater Training School, Centered Climber and Centered Skier workshops.

Address   P.O. Box 20281, Denver, CO 80220, USA

Phone   303/333-7831 or 800/331-7238.

Season   Late April through October.

Programs   2 to 32-day wilderness adventures designed to expose & transform self-limiting behaviors & beliefs.

Regions   Southern Colorado's Sangre De Cristo and San Juan Mountains, plus southeastern Utah's Canyonlands.

Rates   Typical rates: weekend equinox celebration $275, 6 to 8-day "Quests" $550-625, other 7 to 10-day Breaking Through Adventures $650-725, 32-day "Outdoor Leadership Intensive" $1,850. Meals included. BYO tent, sleeping bag & trail snacks.

Circles of Air and Stone   North America

Circles of Air and Stone conducts vision quest programs as ceremonial gateways to spiritual transformation. Each program is an 11-day experience in the traditional 3-step vision quest format — four days of preparation, four days of solo fasting in the wilderness, and three days of re-entry. The 1993 schedule included four programs in New Mexico, two in Vermont, one in New Hampshire, and one in Georgia. Each is limited to six people.

All programs are led by Sparrow Hart, a man who has logged thousands of hours alone in U.S. and Mexican wilderness areas. Sparrow has apprenticed with native and non-native "medicine teachers" including Stephen Foster and Meredith Little, whose School of Lost Borders (Box 55, Big Pine, CA 93513) trains and certifies vision quest teachers. Foster and Little recognize Sparrow Hawk as "perhaps the best who has ever enrolled in the program."

Address   P.O. Box 48, Putney, VT 05346, USA

Phone   802/387-6624.

Season   April through November.

Programs   11-day vision quest programs.

Regions   New Mexico, Vermont, New Hampshire and Georgia wilderness areas.

Rates $400-600 per program.

Earth Rise Foundation   North America

Each summer and fall since 1980, Earth Rise Foundation has run at least two "Touch The Earth" wilderness quests. The annual men's trip includes a 3-day solo vision quest. The leader is Earth Rise founder Joseph Jastrab — a psychotherapist, former chief instructor of the North American Wilderness Survival School, and author of "Sacred Manhood — Sacred Earth."

The annual women's quest is a gathering of women in nature that includes an optional 3-day solo vision quest. The leaders of the 1993 quest were Lynn Margileth and Catherine Cantrell. Lynn is a professional NYC artist and Medicine Wheel student with 14 years of group facilitator experience. Catherine is an all-season wilderness trip leader.

Address   70 Mountain Rest Road, New Paltz, NY 12561, USA

Phone   914/255-2782.

Season   Summer, fall and winter.

Programs   10-day men only, women only & mixed gender wilderness quests. Also 5-day winter quests. Fasting optional in solo portions.

Regions   Adirondack Mountain Wilderness near Keene, NY.

Rates   10-day quest $825. 5-day quest $450.

Earth Rites   North America

Since 1979, Earth Rites has guided nine-day wilderness rites of passage in the high desert wilderness of southeastern Utah. There were five such trips in 1993 — three in April/May and two in September/October. One annual trip is for women only. All trips are backpacking journeys that include group ritual, music and dance; 3 days of solitary fasting ending with an all night vigil; and story sharing to celebrate new beginnings.

Each trip is led by two experienced guides from a staff of five, including Earth Rites founders Leav Bolender and Ron Pevny. Leav is an artist, social worker in private practice, and certified Emergency Medical Technician. Ron is an educational consultant and 15 year vision quest veteran. Other senior guides include a graduate of the School of Lost Borders, a feminist therapist, and a therapist/expert canoeist.

Address   1550 South Pearl Street, #204, Denver, CO 80210, USA

Phone   303/733-7465 or 303/444-0373.

Season   Early spring & early fall.

Programs 9-day wilderness rites of passage.

Regions   Southern Colorado, Utah Canyonlands and northern Ontario.

Rates $650 per program. Participants in Colorado and Utah quests carpool from Denver or Durango, CO.

Four Seasons Healing   North America

Four Seasons Healing facilitates wilderness experiences designed to empower men and women with greater vision and purpose. Programs include "Breakthrough Weekends" and five-day vision quest trips, each with 24 hours of solo fasting in remote areas of the Green Mountains. Weekend programs are held at a 20 acre private campground on the Vermont side of the Connecticut River a short drive from Hanover, NH. The grounds include a campfire circle, a sweatlodge, and a creekside swimming hole.

Quest and weekend leaders are B. Israel Helfand, Ari Kopolow, Cathie Helfand and Eve Greenberg. Israel is a certified marriage and family therapist. Ari is a psychiatrist. Both Israel and Ari have been trained in vision quest leadership by Animas Institute and are involved at a national level in the men's movement. Cathie is a psychotherapist with vision quest training from the School of Lost Borders. Eve is a pschychodramatist-in-training specializing in women's issues.

Address   RR 1, Box 399, Norwich, VT 05055, USA

Phone   802/649-5104.

Season   Year-round.

Programs Men-only, women-only and mixed gender Breakthrough Weekend & 5 to 7-day vision quest programs.

Regions   Vermont's Green Mountains & Connecticut River valley.

Rates   Breakthrough weekend $250. Vision quest program $340-475.

Holos Institute   North America

Among other things, the Holos Institute conducts "Quest For Wholeness" and "Medicine Time" trips. Each of the 3 annual "Quest" programs is a 7-day trip on which each of 5 to 8 participants spends 4 days fasting, alone. Each program includes four weekly pre-trip meetings and a 1-day post-trip meeting. There are also 3 annual "Medicine Time" trips — each a 1-day guided group wilderness excursion with time alone for healing in nature.

The Institute's Director is Alan Levin, a licensed Marriage, Family and Child Counselor. Alan has over twenty years of experience in teaching a wide range of approaches to personal change and transformation. Those approaches include meditation, yoga, shamanism, and western psychotherapy.

Address   5515 Taft Avenue, Oakland, CA 94618, USA

Phone   510/287-8816 or 415/750-0478.

Season   Spring, summer and fall.

Programs 7-day "Quest for Wholeness" & 1-day "Medicine Time" programs.

Regions   Southern California desert for "Quests." San Francisco Bay area wilderness sites for "Medicine Times."

Rates   "Quest for Wholeness" $400 — includes 4 pre-trip meetings & a 1-day post-trip meeting. "Medicine Time" $50.

Inside/Outside   North America

Inside/Outside leads women's wilderness retreats in the pristine Trinity Alps of northern California. For participants in or near the San Francisco Bay area, each trip is introduced at a pre-trip healing circle. Trips include backpacking, massage, meditation, breathwork, singing, dance and ritual. Each trip also includes 1 to 3 days in solitude for each woman. Occasional weekend campouts include sweat lodge, meditation and group work.

Trip leaders are Debra Chamberlin-Taylor and Linda Weisenberg, who have worked in partnership for over 15 years. Debra is a licensed Marriage and

Family Therapist specializing in relationship and women's issues. Linda works as a teacher in the interface of psychology and spirituality to uncover the essential self. Weekend sweats are guided by Annie Prutzman, a naturalist, ritualist and long time student of the medicine way.

Address   20 Sheridan Court, Mill Valley, CA 94941, USA

Phone   415/669-1807 or 415/388-5726.

Season   May through October.

Programs 9 & 7-day women's wilderness backpack/quests. Also weekend women's sweat lodge campouts.

Regions   Northern California mountains.

Rates   9-day $475. 7-day $400. Weekend $175. Rates include meals.

Men in the Wilderness   North America

Men in the Wilderness runs summer wilderness canoe and camping trips in the Temagami wilderness — 4 1/2 million acres laced by lakes and rivers with over 2,000 miles of maintained portage trails. Trips are designed to sharpen wilderness skills, foster an experience of community, and allow men to ground themselves in their emotions. In 1993 there was a flat water lake trip and a white water river trip, each limited to 12 men.

Trip leaders are Mike Madden, Dan Torres and Jody Grosse. Mike is a counselor/therapist experienced with adapting the community spirit of Native American ritual to wilderness exploration. Dan is an expert white water canoeist and occupational/physical therapist. Jody is a canoeist, kayak instructor and experienced leader of men's groups.

Address   Michael Madden, Box 261, Wallingford, PA 19086, USA

Phone   215/891-0182.

Season   July & August.

Programs Canoe trips for men and men's emotional healing.

Regions   Temagami wilderness region of northern Ontario, Canada.

Rates $695 includes 1-week tuition, food, tent space and round-trip float plane fare from Temagami village to Langskib island.

Men's Council Project   North America

The Men's Council Project (MCP) is dedicated primarily to empowering men. This is done through "Spirit Camp," "Men's Passages" and "Leadership Training" programs. "Spirit Camp" is a weekend of creative self-expression and co-created ritual to explore deep masculine potentials. "Leadership Trainings" are a three part initiation process, each part of which can be taken separately as a "Men's Passage" weekend. Those parts focus, respectively, on connecting to the deep masculine; exploring body and soul relationships; and establishing the kingdom of the self within.

All programs are conducted in a wilderness environment and include meals plus cabin space or tent sites. Empowerment tools include drumming, storytelling, sweat lodge, wilderness solo fasting time, calling for ancestral blessings, guided personal and group ritual process, plus acknowledging personal boundaries and creating a sacred space.

MCP programs are led by Tom Daly, Jeff Duvall and Keith Fairmont. Tom is a teacher, essayist, and nationally recognized men's work elder. His Ph.D thesis explored the importance of sacred ceremony in men's initiations in both ancient and contemporary cultures. Jeff's experience includes massage therapy, guiding solo quests, wilderness and environmental education. Keith guides sweat lodge ceremonies and is an expert drum maker.

Address   P.O. Box 17341, Boulder, CO 80301, USA

Phone   303/444-7741.

Season   Year-round.

Programs Men's ritual weekend gatherings & weeklong leadership trainings.

Regions   Colorado & elsewhere in the USA at invitation of men's groups.

Rates   Weekends: "Spirit Camp" $95-150; "Men's Passages" $175-250. Weeklong "Leadership Training" $650-950.

Mind-Body River Adventures   North America

Mind-Body River Adventures runs river raft trips designed to create a relaxed, intuitive relationship among the participants and also between the participants and their environment — the desert sandstone canyons of the U.S. Southwest. All trips include yoga sessions. Some also include massage, meditation, tai chi, biokinetics, and/or drawing and painting.

Most trips are four to five days including one layover day. On non-layover days, participants practice a mind-body discipline for up to 2 hours in the morning; float down the river for 7 to 14 miles during mid-day; then spend 1 to 2 hours in group activity, hiking, meditation or rest. Evening is a time for group sharing. Meals are vegetarian unless otherwise requested.

In 1993, there were five scheduled trips led by a total of eight guides and facilitators — river guides, psychotherapists, massage therapists and yoga teachers. Most trips are in May and September, when days are warm, nights are cool, and insects few. Mind-Body River Adventures also runs trips for private groups.

Address   P.O. Box 863, Hotchkiss, CO 81419, USA

Phone   303/921-3455.

Season   Spring & early fall.

Programs 2 to 5-day river raft trips focusing on ecology plus various creative & mind-body disciplines (e.g. painting, yoga & tai chi).

Regions   Portions of the Colorado, Dolores and Green Rivers in southwestern Colorado & Utah.

Rates   Weekend trip $215. 4 & 5-day trips $360-600.

Northwaters Wilderness Programs   North America

20 year old Northwaters Wilderness Programs operates two camps, Langskib and Northwaters, in the Temagami wilderness area of northern Ontario. For much of each summer, both camps are used for youth programs. They also are used as sites and base camps for adult workshops and canoe expeditions.

Most adult programs integrate adventure with Native American ritual and, in some cases, interpersonal training. Typical programs are as follows:

- 6-day "Father and Son Canoe Trip": training in cooperation, communication and trust; Native American philosophy and ritual; father and son canoeing and fishing in the Temagami wilderness. Offered twice each summer.

- 7-day "Vision Quest": applies mythology, metaphor and dream tracking to shamanistic teachings, sweat lodge and vision quest rituals. Based at the Langskib Island camp and offered once each summer.

- 7-day "Dumoine River Canoe Trip": dream sharing and interpretation during a white water trip from northern Quebec's Laurentian Highlands to the low-lying Ottawa River Valley. Offered once in both 1991 and 1993.

- 9-day "Woman's White Water Canoe Trip": sweat lodge, overnight vision quest, daily discussion and ritual during the course of a Temagami wilderness flat and white water journey. Offered once each summer.

- 11-day "Temagami Experience": supportive feedback, group meetings, outdoor initiatives and Native American rituals — sweat lodge, long dance and a 40-hour solo vision quest. Held once a summer on Langskib Island to strengthen leadership skills, deepen personal and spiritual growth.

Northwaters programs are run by a highly qualified staff of experts in canoeing, wilderness survival, Native American rituals, Jungian psychology, leadership and team-building.

Address   Sep-June: P.O. Box 477, St. Peters, PA 19470, USA
            July-Aug: Bear Island, Temagami, Ontario POH ICO, CANADA

Phone   Sep-June: 215/469-4662 or 518/962-4869.

Season   July through September.

Programs   Canoe trips & wilderness island camps integrating adventure with personal & spiritual growth opportunities.

Regions   Canadian wilderness areas — the Temagami region of northern Ontario and the Dumoine River area of northwestern Quebec.

Rates   Representative rates: 1-week "Vision Quest" & "Dumoine River Canoe Trip" $950 each, 10-day "Temagami Experience" $1,250.

Pilgrim Warrior Training   North America

Pilgrim Warrior Training is a physically and emotionally intense women's empowerment program honoring each woman's sacred relationship with Spirit and Earth as expressed through ritual, music, dance and meditation. Activities include psychodrama, high and low ropes courses, communication skills, 1-day vision quest, shield-making and goal setting.

Each training is conducted in a primitive forest setting where women camp or sleep dorm style in a cabin. A typical day begins at 7 AM with a sacred circle meeting. Programs run from 9 AM to 9:30 PM with two hour breaks for meals. Except in the case of special dietary needs, meals are vegetarian. The tasks of maintaining and nurturing community are shared by all.

Pilgrim Warrior Training was founded in 1985 as the vision quest of Sandra Boston de Sylvia, a licensed communication skills instructor, social change activist, feminist therapist, and parent of three sons. The Massachusetts trainings are co-facilitated by Alisa Starkweather, an intuitive healer, body worker, herbalist and ritual artist. Other PWT graduates assist at other training locations.

Address   Full Moon Rising, 15 Abbott Street, Greenfield, MA 01301, USA

Phone   413/774-5952.

Season   April through September.

Programs   5 annual, 8-day women's empowerment trainings (4 limited to 10 women & the Prince Edward Island training limited to 5 women).

Regions   Western Massachusetts (2 trainings), Virginia, Ohio & Prince Edward Island.

Rates   Determined by each woman in discussion with the group in order to cover program costs. Individual pledges range $350-1,500. Time payments & barter are possible.

Rites of Passage   North America

Rites of Passage runs vision quest programs for adults in any stage of life transition. All programs begin with a series of pre-trip meetings in the northern San Francisco Bay area during the month before trip departure. Questers living outside the area receive the meetings' contents by mail and phone. The one week trip includes a three day solo quest of fasting (or light meals) alone in the wilderness. Two weeks after the quest, the group meets again for a reunion — deepening integration by sharing stories.

Founded in 1977 by Steven Foster and Meredith Little, Rites of Passage is now directed by Michael Bodkin — a licensed family therapist with 10+ years of vision quest guide experience. Michael is assisted in leading and co-leading quests by a staff of at least six other experienced guides — most in the care giving professions. In 1993, Rites of Passage conducted a men's vision quest plus spring, summer, fall and New Year's vision quests.

Address   P.O. Box 148, Sonoma, CA 95476, USA

Phone   707/537-1927.

Season   Year-round.

Programs 7-day vision quest programs plus "Fathers & Sons" weekends.

Regions   Southern California desert — high desert (often over 8,000 feet) in summer & low desert (often under 2,500 feet) in winter.

Rates   Vision quest program $450 (not including food en route or potluck food in the field). Weekend program $125.

Vision Quest Wilderness Passage   North America

Vision Quest Wilderness Passage usually operates one 7-day vision quest program each month from spring through fall. Quest sites are remote desert and mountain regions such as Joshua Tree National Monument, Mt. Shasta, and the White Mountains of southeastern California. A day long preparation meeting is held in the southern San Francisco Bay area one week prior to each trip. On the trip, each participant spends 3 days in the wilderness alone and without food (unless unable to fast for medical reasons).

All trips are led by two licensed psychotherapists — Brian Winkler and Chayim Barton. Brian has more than 15 years of wilderness experience, including vision quest leadership training at the School of Lost Borders. Chayim contributes expertise in dreamwork, meditation and Jungian psychology. Both are also available to lead ad hoc quests for couples, families, groups or businesses.

Address   Brian Winkler, 139 Forest View Road, Woodside, CA 94062, USA

Phone   415/851-1715 or 408/479-1564.

Season   April through October.

Programs 7-day vision quest programs.

Regions   California desert & mountain regions.

Rates $510 includes pre-trip meeting, handbook, sweat lodge & 2 meals.

Wilderness Rites of Passage   North America

Each year, Wilderness Rites of Passage leads two public weeklong trips plus trips included in the curriculum of Naropa Institute (Boulder, CO). All trips are to southeast Utah and western Colorado. Each is designed to foster personal and spiritual growth and give meaning to life transitions -past as well as current. The number of participants is limited to eight, who depart and return as a group from the Denver area. Out-of-state participants are briefed by phone and mail in lieu of the pre-trip meeting.

Wilderness Rites' leaders are John Davis and Dianne Eichenour. John is a professor of psychology and a teacher in the Ridhwan School of spiritual work. He has guided wilderness quests since 1983 and is certified in this work by the School of Lost Borders. Diane has led quests since 1989. Her other interests include art, poetry, story telling and nursing.

Address   Lykins Gulch Farm, 3743 Nelson Road, Longmont, CO 80503, USA

Phone   303/449-5579.

Season   May through July.

Programs One-week wilderness programs with 3-day solo fast.

Regions   Utah Canyonlands (late spring) & western Colorado (summer).

Rates   Tuition & pre-trip preparation materials $400. Participants share food costs & carpooling expenses.

Wilderness Transitions   North America

"A simple, yet extraordinary experience" is one participant's summary of a Wilderness Transitions vision quest. Each quest includes three or four days of solitude (fasting optional) in a California mountain or desert area, chosen shortly before departure on the basis of weather forecasts. The 8-day program is preceded by four evening meetings in the northern San Francisco Bay area. Out-of-area participants are prepared through phone calls, letters and written materials — including a 64-page handbook.

Wilderness Transitions conducts five or six trips each year led by Marilyn Riley and Betty Warren. Marilyn is a life transition counselor who was one of the original (1979) staff with Rites of Passage. Betty is a naturalist, student of meditation, and experienced wilderness guide. Trips do not require prior backpacking experience. All are designed to create a profound group experience as well as a time of individual self-discovery.

Address   70 Rodeo Ave., Sausalito, CA 94965, USA

Phone   415/331-5380 or 415/332-9558.

Season   Year-round.

Programs 8-day vision quest programs, each with preparation & reunion.

Regions   Central & southern California mountain & desert wilderness areas east of the Sierra Nevada range.

Rates   Each trip $475, including pre-trip meetings & materials, some equipment, vegetarian base camp meals & snacks. Does not include carpool transportation & meals en route.

Wild Places   North America

Wild Places conducts workshops utilizing therapeutic experience in nature. It also runs two annual nine-day vision quest programs, each consisting of a three-day preparation period, a four-day solo fasting quest, and two days to assimilate the quest experience.

All quest programs are conducted in northern New England wilderness areas by Hannah Lermann and James Wright. Hannah is a naturalist and expressive arts practitioner. James is a psychotherapist. Hannah and James have both trained with the School of Lost Borders.

Address   9 Smith Street Court, Rockport, MA 01966, USA

Phone   508/546-2000.

Season   Summer, spring and fall.

Programs 9-day vision quest programs. Also nature-based, therapeutic workshops.

Regions   Northern New England (e.g. Cape Ann, MA; the Maine coast; & the New Hampshire White Mountains).

Rates   9-day vision quest program $350-450.

Supplementary Information

Here is some additional material that may be of some interest to certain readers. It includes the listing criteria governing the selection and placement of most organizations in this book; a list of other, somewhat related directories; and a short profile of this book's author.

Listing Criteria

All of the organizations profiled in this directory have four common characteristics:

- a commitment to enhancing well being in a context broader than the physical body alone
- provision of programs/services/activities emphasizing experiential learning/healing
- a total immersion environment with accommodations plus meals (generally vegetarian) or cooking facilities
- English language offerings open to people of all races, cultures, religions and nations

In addition, every organization profiled in this book had to meet the criteria of one of the book's four profile chapters.

SINGLE SITE VACATIONS & RETREATS (chapter 6) and MULTIPLE SITE VACATIONS & RETREATS (chapter 7) both include organizations that a) host programs at fixed physical locations and b) offer either at least 3 weekend programs each year or at least one annual program of at least 5 days in length.

A host organization is listed in chapter 6 if it conducts programs at either a single site (including a shipboard site) or a few sites in a local area (e.g. a region within a state or province). But if the organization runs programs at sites distant from one another (e.g. in different states, provinces or countries), it is listed in chapter 7.

JOURNEYS (chapter 8) profiles organizations that each year conduct at least two trips, each at least one week long. Most trip rates include round trip long distance airfare. All include regional ground transportation, accommodations, most meals, and fees for any special cultural or spiritual events.

Some organizations offer both trip and fixed site programs. If such a provider hosts at least two trips each year, all of its programs are described in a single listing in chapter 8. But if it conducts only one trip each year, all of its offerings are described in a single listing in chapter 6 or 7.

Organizations profiled under WILDERNESS PROGRAMS (chapter 9) run programs with a heavy emphasis on the transformative potential of wilderness experience. To qualify for listing in this category, a service provider must each year offer at least two scheduled programs, each of at least five days in length.

Most organizations profiled in chapter 9 specialize in vision quest programs. But not all quest operators are listed in this category. Organizations that run quests primarily from a site supporting other programs are listed in chapter 6.

Other Directories

Here is a list of 12 other directories that provide additional information on specific types of day facilities, getaways, vacations, adventures or retreats with a spiritual, holistic or physical therapy orientation. These directories are listed in order of publication, beginning with the most recent:

- Specialty Travel Index is published twice each year in magazine format by Alpine Hansen Publishers. Each issue includes more than 500 advertiser-paid profiles of tours, expeditions and charters addressing virtually all travel interests.

- Directory of Intentional Communities. Second (1994) edition published by Communities Magazine. Profiles more than 400 North American and 50+ overseas intentional communities of all types. It also contains more than 200 resource listings.

- Healthy Escapes by Bernard Burt. Second edition published in 1993 by Fodors. Profiles 240 fitness and beauty resorts (plus 17 luxury fitness cruises) in the U.S., Canada, Mexico and the Caribbean.

- 1992-1993 Holistic Health Directory was published by New Age Journal. It identifies natural and holistic practitioners listed by U.S. state under 27 categories of alternative medicine.

- Hot Springs and Hot Pools of the Southwest by Jayson Loam and Marjorie Gersh. Published in 1992 by Aqua Thermal Access. Profiles over 220 rustic and resort hot springs facilities in 7 southwestern U.S. states plus Baja, Mexico.

- Hot Springs and Pools of the Northwest by Jayson Loam and Marjorie Gersh. Published in 1992 by Aqua Thermal Access. Profiles over 220 rustic and resort hot springs facilities in 6 northwestern U.S. states plus 2 western Canadian provinces.

- A Guide to Monastic Guest Houses by Robert J. Regalbuto. Published in 1992 by Morehouse Publishing. Profiles 80 monasteries in Canada and 33 U.S. states that allow visitors on an overnight or short stay basis.

- Sanctuaries: the West Coast & Southwest: a Guide to Lodging in Monasteries, Abbeys and Retreats of the United States by Marcia Kelly. Published in 1992 by Bell Tower. Profiles 90+ places, in British Columbia and 6 western U.S. states, that accommodate individual retreatants.

- Sanctuaries: a Guide to Lodgings in Monasteries, Abbeys and Retreats of the United States: the Northeast by Jack and Marcia Kelly. Published in 1991 by Bell Tower. Profiles 90+ places in 9 eastern U.S. states that accommodate individual retreatants.

- Spas: The International Spa Guide by Joseph Bain and Eli Dror. Published in 1990 by Bain Dror International Travel, Inc. Profiles over 300 fitness and beauty spas in the U.S. and 35 other countries around the world.

- Healing Centers and Retreats by Martine Rudee and Jonathan Blease. Published in 1989 by John Muir Publications. Profiles roughly 220 U.S. and Canadian holistic healing centers, clinics and retreats (about 1/3rd residential).

- Buddhist America: Centers, Retreats, Practices by Don Morreale. Out of print (published in 1988) but available at public libraries. Profiles Buddhist practice, teaching and meditation centers (mostly non-residential).

About The Author

John Benson is both the author and the publisher of this book. He lives in Portland, Oregon and is an active member of the Northwest Association of Book Publishers.

John is a native of Illinois. He has also lived in New England, New York City and Virginia. His travels have included visits with a number of the organizations profiled in this book.

Throughout most of his life, John has read widely on the subjects of spiritual practice and human potential. He has also enjoyed the benefits of hatha yoga, meditation, prayer and selfless service.

John has explored many religions but is most comfortable turning for spiritual guidance to "divine intuition" — otherwise known as "the still, small voice," the Holy Spirit, the Higher Self, or the Inner Light.

He believes that peace in the world, in society, in one's community and in one's family begins with peace within oneself. He hopes this book will be of help to others following or embarking upon a path to inner peace.

Ordering Information

Buyers in the book business should call the publisher at (503) 297-7321.

All other buyers have 2 options for payment on cost of book plus shipping:

1. Call toll free (800) 879-4214 from anywhere in North America and charge to VISA, Master Card or American Express. Calls accepted 9 a.m. to 11 p.m. (U.S. Eastern Standard Time).

2. Send a check: in U.S. dollars drawn on a U.S. bank; or in an "accepted foreign currency" drawn on a foreign bank in an amount (based on current exchange rates) equal to the U.S. dollar cost of book(s) plus shipping.

"Accepted foreign currencies" — Canada, the U.K., Australia, France, Italy, Germany, Switzerland, the Netherlands, Denmark, Sweden, and Japan. Payment from other countries accepted only as a foreign bank draft in U.S. dollars.

Payment by check must be accompanied by the following order form, a photocopy of it, or a letter containing equivalent information.

ORDER FORM

For 1 to 3 Books . . . . U.S. $ 14.95 each

SHIPPING COST:	USA	CANADA	ELSEWHERE
First book	$ 3.50	$ 4.00	$ 3.00
Each additional book	$ 0.35	$ 1.00	$ 1.00

SHIPPING TIME:

4 to 7 day delivery for U.S. (UPS) and Canadian (Air Mail) orders.

4 to 6 week delivery for shipments (surface mail) elsewhere.

ORDER:

No. of Books _____	Book Cost _____	Shipping Cost_____	Total Payment _____

NAME _____

STREET ADDRESS _____

TOWN/CITY _____

STATE/PROVINCE_____

POSTAL CODE_____ COUNTRY _____

Make checks payable to New Millennium Publishing and mail to:

New Millennium Publishing, P.O. Box 3065, Portland, OR 97208, USA